READING THERAPY

READING THERAPY

edited by

Jean M. Clarke

and

Eileen Bostle

LA

The Library Association
London

Published by
Library Association Publishing Ltd
7 Ridgmount Street
London WC1E 7AE

First published 1988

British Library Cataloguing in Publication Data
Reading therapy.
1. Medicine. Bibliotherapy
I. Clarke, Jean M. II. Bostle, Eileen,
615.8′516

ISBN 0-85365-637-1

Typeset in 10/11 pt Linotron Palatino
by Input Typesetting Ltd, London SW19 8DR
Printed and made in Great Britain by
Redwood Burn Ltd, Trowbridge, Wiltshire.

In memory of Wylva Partington

Contents

The Contributors

Gerard Benson. Poet. Paronomasia Press, 116A, Englefield Road, London N1 3LQ

Eileen Bostle, ALA. Librarian, General (Patients') Library, Northwick Park Hospital, Harrow.

Jean M. Clarke, MBE ALA. Formerly District Librarian, St. Thomas' Hospital, West Lambeth Health Authority.

Sara D. Coomaraswamy, BSc(Hons) MA MSc ABPS MBPS. District Top Grade Clinical Psychologist, East Hertfordshire Health Authority.

Heather George, BSc Dip. Clin. Psych. Senior Clinical Psychologist, St. Mary's Hospital.

Clare Gillies, Cert. in Soc. Sci., DASS, Adv. Cert. in Casework. Principal Lecturer, Department of Social Studies, Oxford Polytechnic.

Mary Howie, BSc(Social Science), Dip. Lib. Dip Soc.Wk, CQSW, Formerly a Librarian and lately Social Worker, Professorial Geriatric Unit, City Hospital, Edinburgh.

Stephen Hunt. MSc. Senior Clinical Psychologist, Petersfield Family Centre, Huntingdon.

Margaret R. Marshall, FLA. Freelance Consultant: Handicapped Children and Books. 6A Harmer Green Lane, Digswell, Welwyn, Herts.

D. R. Morris-Jones, L1B. Senior Probation Officer, North Wales Probation Service.

Andrew Quarry, BA(Psychology) MSc(Clinical Psychology). Unit Psychologist, Tone Vale Hospital.

Jocelyn Rodin, MPhil SRN ONC. Project Officer, National Association for the Welfare of Children in Hospital.

Pauline Shelley, BA Dip. Soc. Work, Dip. Lib., ALA. Librarian, National Association for the Welfare of Children in Hospital.

M. Skelton-Robinson, BSc PhD Dip. Psychol. Principal Clinical Psychologist, Great Yarmouth and Waveney Health Authority.

Jan Wanless, MAOT SROT. Community Occupational Therapist, The Eye Hospital, Swansea. (Formerly Occupational Therapist, Derby City Community Mental Health Team).

Note

For convenience and ease of reading some authors have used 'he, 'him' etc. where both sexes are meant; certainly no discrimination is intended.

An appreciation of Wylva Partington

The death of Wylva Partington in February, 1984, was a sad blow to her friends and fellow librarians. Members of the Medical, Health and Welfare Librarians Group (MHWLG) of the Library Association wanted to mark her achievements in some way and so the editors offered to produce a book on reading therapy, a subject dear to Wylva's heart. The royalties from this book will be used to help young librarians attend courses and meetings, including those on reading therapy.

Wylva was Librarian at the Queen Elizabeth II Hospital (QE2), Welwyn Garden City at the time of her retirement in 1982 and her role there is mentioned in several of the tributes from friends and colleagues which follow; her career prior to that is outlined in a profile at the time of her becoming Chairman of the Group.[1]

Someone who had a lasting influence on Wylva, and who first introduced her to the therapy of reading, was the late Margaret Secchi, formerly Librarian of the Southern Hospital, Dartford; Wylva acknowledged her debt in an obituary of Mrs Secchi, published in 1974.[2]

Wylva's deep love and knowledge of books and her interest in reading therapy were a major part of her life and work at QE2 and this led her to start an informal Bibliotherapy Sub Group within the MHWLG.

The obituaries published after Wylva's death give a background for all those who did not know her; [3,4] the short contributions from eight colleagues and friends which follow paint a fuller picture of a librarian who offered so much to the patients she met.

Mona Going, first Chairman of the Hospital Libraries and Handicapped Readers Group and former Hospital and Welfare Librarian for Kent County Library, knew Wylva early in her hospital library days, writes:

> The inspiration of Wylva's interest in the value of reading to patients came, like mine, through the work of an unqualified librarian. Hers was through Mrs Peg Secchi of the Southern Hospital, while mine came through Mrs Dorothy Hutton at King's College Hospital and Mrs Mary Harrison at the Kent and Sussex Hospital. All three,

though very different characters, were well-read women who recognized the importance of providing books to patients. Wylva worked under Dr Henderson and Mrs Secchi at the Southern where patients were in hospital for long periods and library provision, art and music appreciation were all part of the rehabilitation programme. Needless to say, Wylva's attractive personality and interest in reading contributed to the work there and later, after she qualified, in her final job at QE2 in Hertfordshire, where she built up a full service. After her retirement she came twice to spend the day with me and to discuss her chapter in *Hospital libraries and work with the disabled in the community* and her interest was as keen as ever. We reminisced especially about her old days at the Southern – where now a main road has replaced it! Over the years many librarians will agree that Wylva brightened our Conferences with her unfailing enthusiasm for the aims of the Group.

Joy Lewis, one of the founder members of the Group and its first Hon Treasurer and later Chairman, and until recently Senior Lecturer at the School of Librarianship and Information Studies, Polytechnic of North London, writes:

My first contact with Wylva (then Mrs Coombs) was through a slightly critical response in the March 1962 *LAR*[5] to an article I had written. Her letter demonstrated her long experience of hospital library work and the importance she attached to developing and responding to patients' reading interests. Wylva had learnt a basic lesson when, in 1946, the Medical Superintendent and the Chief Librarian of the hospital where she worked emphasized that 'time should be spent chatting to the patients, discovering their interests and encouraging them to read'. Her own practice as a hospital librarian followed: 'I started a readers' interest file, in which notes were kept of all patients' reading according to a definite plan or following up particular interests.' She later expanded on this theme,[6] and an accompanying article by that 'Chief Librarian', Margaret Secchi,[7] showed *her* wide and deep knowledge of books.

Wylva soon became a valued colleague and a personal friend and she was one of the former hospital library colleagues who kept me informed of developments when I entered teaching. We often met, wrote or talked on the 'phone late into the night. Her interest in students and young librarians was obvious, she enthusiastically accepted PNL students for visits or practical work placements, giving generously of her time and experience. Those undertaking bibliotherapy projects always received support and advice.

Reading therapy became of great interest and appeal to Wylva. She conveyed her enthusiasm to a colleague, Sara Coomaraswamy, a clinical psychologist who, at a Group meeting held at QE2 in October, 1974, presented an informed and sensitive paper on 'The therapeutic aspects of a library service to hospital patients'.[8] Wylva and Sara worked in liaison in this area until her retirement in 1982 and their joint interest continued until her death.

Jean Clarke, another founder member and first Hon Secretary of the Group and later Chairman, formerly District Librarian, West Lambeth Health Authority, based at St. Thomas' Hospital, writes:

Whenever Wylva and I travelled together by train, perhaps to a one day meeting, we would talk non-stop to our destination; matters of professional interest were discussed first then inevitably we would get on to the subject of books. Wylva had a catholic taste in reading and our discussions would range from the established classics to the latest detective novel. We would compare our reading since we last met or corresponded and Wylva introduced me to many authors whose works have given me much pleasure, for example E. H. Young's *Miss Mole* and *The Curate's Wife*, Antonia White's novels and Pat Barr's writings on the Far East.

I remember at one weekend conference in Bristol being suddenly and inexplicably depressed by the concrete jungle in the centre of the city and this feeling of depression lasted well into the evening until, after dinner, Wylva, (the late) Frank Gardner and I met in the bar and talked books for the rest of the evening; the enjoyment generated by our sharing of favourite authors lifted my depression.

Wylva's love of reading, her wide knowledge of books and her genuine interest in people were admirable qualities for her work with hospital patients and her enthusiasm for her work kindled a spark in many students and librarians. It seemed a natural progression for Wylva to start an informal group for those interested in reading therapy and the first meeting in April, 1981, was a milestone along an ever widening road.

David Matthews, at one time Librarian of the Northern Branch of the National Library for the Blind, also an Hon Secretary and Wylva's successor as Chairman of the Group, now Principal Lecturer at the College of Librarianship Wales, writes:

Wylva's letters were marvellously herself: spontaneous, hastily handwritten, amusing, sharply observed. I have seventy-five of them dating from 1967 till 1983 and they could inspire a chapter, at least. My paragraph of tribute will be limited to just two of Wylva's concerns. First I must record her exceptional kindness to students attached to her library for fieldwork. This often extended beyond the merely professional commitment to hospitality in her own home and concern for them as people. The other concern was her growing fear in recent years that the 'cause' of patients librarianship was going by default. She was worried that the shift in emphasis in health care librarianship towards NHS staff libraries, important and overdue though that was, could be at the expense of patients' library services. Limited resources make choices inevitable but when asked what the priorities were in her co-sited library service to patients and staff she would answer: 'The priorities tend to be horizontal rather than vertical. The priority is what has to be done next, whether that is a medical literature search or the eagerly awaited ward round with the trolley.' 'Bibliotherapy' entered our correspondence in 1980 and her hopes of deepening and developing services to patients now rest in her successors. This book is a continuation of her vision. I often stayed with Wylva and Robin at their delightful home in Blackmore End and it was a particular joy that they were able at last to visit us beside the sea in what was to be, alas, her last summer. Characteristically they had taken in the bookshops of Hay-on-Wye on their return journey through Wales.

Antonia Bunch, Director of the Scottish Science Library, National Library of Scotland, who was at one time Librarian of the Scottish Hospital Centre and involved in hospital library affairs both north and south of the Border, writes:

I first met Wylva Partington in October 1965. I had just recently been appointed Librarian of the new Scottish Hospital Centre with a brief to start a library from scratch. A visit to the south to find out what was happening there seemed a must and it was Keith Morton of the King's Fund Centre who said 'of course you are going to see Wylva Partington'. I had to confess that, at that time, I did not know of the exciting events at QE2 and so Keith arranged a visit. As a result I acquired not only a colleague whose dedication and professionalism I was to admire increasingly over succeeding years, but also a close personal friend, for we shared much in common. Not only did Wylva put an immense amount of enthusiasm and commitment in running her two libraries at QE2, thus proving that it *is* possible to be both a good patients' librarian and medical librarian, she also gave unstintingly of her time to innumerable committees. She was thus one of a small but exciting group of people furthering the cause of libraries in hospitals in the 1960s and 1970s. Wylva and Robin were both very fond of the Scottish hills. At the time of her death they were planning to spend some time with me in my cottage in the Lammermuirs. I shall always deeply regret that that holiday was not to be.

Phyllis Noaks, former Hospitals Librarian for the London Borough of Greenwich, who was at one time Chairman of the Group, also of the IFLA Section and is still actively involved in the international field, writes:

When I started working as a hospital librarian in 1965 I was privileged to have the help and advice of several librarians already working in the field, one of whom was Wylva Partington. In the years that followed I came to appreciate and envy Wylva's dedication to her work – and to value her friendship. During the 1970s we worked together on the committee of the former Hospital Libraries and Handicapped Readers Group, when Wylva began to formalize her ideas and plans for a reading therapy group, and I could see how much time and effort she gave to this project, and the results can be seen today.

After her retirement, in addition to her work for the reading therapy group, Wylva also became Secretary of the Standing Committee of the IFLA Section for Libraries Serving Disadvantaged Persons. She brought to this international work all her enthusiasm and experience and contributed greatly to the work of the Section in the brief time allowed her. Her death deprived us of a colleague and friend always ready to give generously of herself, both professionally and personally.

Doreen Noble, at one time Group Librarian to S.W. Middlesex Hospital Management Committee, in charge of fourteen hospitals, a Group committee member for a number of years and now a Senior Lecturer in the Department of Library and Information Studies, Manchester Polytechnic, writes:

Wylva Partington will always be remembered by countless students from both Newcastle and Manchester Library Schools for her enthusiasm for the job, her good relationships with hospital staff and her concern for the patients.

For many students it was their first visit to a hospital but her carefully planned tour, in cooperation with other staff and which always included a visit to the children's ward, did much to reassure them and to show them the wide variety of the work involved.

The appreciation of the library services expressed by medical, nursing, paramedical and teaching staff was a revelation to them. While accepting the Queen Elizabeth II Hospital had been a new hospital without inhibiting traditions and entrenched departmental positions, they appreciated the high regard in which the library was held came from Wylva's dedication to her work and her genuine interest in both staff and patients.

Her interests were not confined to the Queen Elizabeth II Hospital and her work for the Group and at Conferences enabled her to interest students in all aspects of hospital librarianship. She had a rare gift for combining enthusiasm with a hard-headed grasp of the practicalities of the job. She did not ignore the problems but she did not allow them to defeat her, and her discussions with the students were always lively, well-informed and down to earth.

They paid her a rare compliment, not once did a student say they had been 'bored' by their day with Wylva at QE2 – quite the contrary!

Lorna Paulin, a former LA President and County Librarian of Hertfordshire County Library, of which the hospital library at QE2 is a part, writes:

> When the Queen Elizabeth II Hospital in Welwyn Garden City was built in the early 1960s its greatest stroke of good fortune in setting up its medical and general library service was the appointment of Wylva Partington as the Hospital Librarian. She already had what was then very rare, considerable hospital library experience, as well as wide experience in the public library field.
>
> By her temperament, character and personal interests, Wylva seemed born to be a hospital librarian. Her compassionate, deeply human approach to her work combined with competence and practical good sense. Only the highest standards of work were acceptable to her, and however much her feelings may have become involved in the service to patients she was devoid of sentimentality. As County Librarian of Hertfordshire I was able to observe Wylva's remarkable professional and personal skills in action. It was always a real pleasure to be with her, and I have never known anyone more universally liked and appreciated. The medical and auxiliary staff at the Hospital treated her with respect and adulation, rather to her amusement; the patients loved her.
>
> The way Wylva did every job that came her way, with tact, charm and ability, was unique. No wonder she was in demand, locally, nationally and internationally, to work for the development of hospital librarianship. To this cause she generously devoted an immense amount of time and energy – perhaps too much for her own good. There could hardly be a more appropriate person than Wylva Partington for the dedication of a book on reading therapy. It is sad that it has to be dedicated to her memory rather than to her, alive and still active among us.

The contributors to this book come from a variety of professions and demonstrate the ever widening interest in, and use of, reading therapy; this interest was expanded by Wylva Partington, to whom this book is dedicated.

Jean M. Clarke

References

1 'Profile: Mrs Wylva W. Partington A.L.A.', *The Book Trolley*, 2,(9), March 1970, 10.

2 Obituary – Margaret Secchi, *Health and Welfare Libraries Quarterly*, 1,(4), December 1974, 96.

3 Obituary – Wylva Partington, *Library Association Record*, 86,(4), April 1984, 188.
4 Obituary – Wylva Partington, *Health Libraries Review*, 1,(2), 122–3.
5 Correspondence, Mrs W. Coombs, *Library Association Record*, 64,(3), March 1962, 103.
6 Partington, W. W., 'The Southern Hospital Library: reminiscences of an assistant', *The Book Trolley*, 2,(11), September 1970, 7–10.
7 Secchi, M., 'Zelo zelatus sum . . .: reminiscences of a Hospital Librarian', *The Book Trolley*, 2,(11), September 1970, 3–7.
8 Coomaraswamy, S., 'The therapeutic aspects of a library service to hospital patients', *Health and Welfare Libraries Quarterly*, 2,(2,3 and 4), December 1975, 29–32.

1 Reading therapy – an outline of its growth in the UK

Jean M. Clarke

There is much current interest in reading therapy in the UK not only among librarians but also among people from other professions. How has this interest grown and what is meant by reading therapy? Before attempting to answer these questions let us first look at practice in the USA and the definitions used there.

Bibliotherapy, the term by which reading therapy is known in the USA, has been used to a far greater extent in that country than in the UK and there is a wealth of literature on the subject. Eleanor Brown's book on bibliotherapy devoted a chapter to definitions,[1] as did Rhea Rubin in her book *Using bibliotherapy: a guide to theory and practice*;[2] both these writers quote perhaps the best known definition of bibliotherapy, that from *Webster's Third New International Dictionary (1961)*:

> 'The use of selected reading materials as therapeutic adjuvants in medicine and psychiatry, also: guidance in the solution of personal problems through directed reading.'

In an article published in 1979,[3] Rubin extends the definition to:

> 'A program of activity based on the interactive processes of media and the people who experience it. Print or non-print material, either imaginative or informational, is experienced and discussed with the aid of a facilitator.'

Both the books on bibliotherapy mentioned above are worth reading for their contents, as well as the chapters on definitions. Other significant publications on USA practice include *Bibliotherapy sourcebook*,[4] the whole issue of October 1962 and articles in Fall 1979 and Spring 1982 issues of *Library Trends*;[5,6,7] *Bibliotherapy: an overview*,[8] edited by Clara Lack.

In the UK Mary Howie, formerly a librarian, now a social worker, has one definition of reading therapy in the chapter which follows (page 16); in another article she explains the background and aims of reading therapy.[9] Perhaps a wider definition is: 'The therapeutic use of books and other materials with individuals or with groups of people.'

In England and Scotland in the nineteenth century books were used to help in the treatment of patients in hospitals, particularly those in mental hospitals; one of the most often quoted examples is that of 'The Retreat' at York. Those hospitals which had libraries or small collections of books generally left the distribution of the material to the chaplain.

The history of hospital libraries in England and in particular the early days has been described by Ronald Sturt,[10] who gives examples of the early use of books for therapeutic purposes. Antonia Bunch has painted a similar picture in Scotland.[11]

After the First World War and particularly in the 1930s, public libraries showed interest in hospital libraries; the Library Association issued various policy statements and papers were given at five of the annual conferences. Despite all this interest, however, there was no real concerted effort to promote reading therapy, which seemed to be left to individuals. The main concern was with the setting up of hospital libraries.

In May, 1930, the British Empire Red Cross Conference was held at St. James's Palace, and one of the speakers was Charles Hagberg-Wright, Librarian of the London Library. The conference expressed approval of the principle of reading as a part of curative medicine in hospitals.[12]

The following month, at a conference of the Royal Institute of Public Health held at Portsmouth, Sir Bruce Bruce-Porter spoke on 'The need for libraries in hospitals as part of the scheme for curative medicine'.[13] Sir Bruce expressed his considered opinion that good literature of all types was more essential than most of the drugs commonly prescribed. He was to speak on similar lines at the LA Conference the following year.

In November, 1930, a meeting was convened at the Public Health Congress, to discuss the development of libraries in institutions. Speakers, including doctors, a nurse and a hospital administrator, emphasized the great therapeutic value of reading and the necessity of a supply of clean and up-to-date books distributed by a librarian with some psychological training. A summary of the meeting was included in the *Lancet*.[14]

In 1931 W. J. Bishop, at that time Assistant Librarian at the Royal College of Physicians, produced a three part bibliography in three issues of the *Library Association Record* entitled 'Hospital libraries and bibliotherapy: a bibliography'.[15] The bibliography is somewhat disappointing to those who are looking for evidence of early examples of bibliotherapy in the UK. The articles cited are arranged under seven headings: General works; bibliotherapy; organization and administration; book selection; lists of books for the sick; war hospital libraries; libraries in mental hospitals; libraries in sanatoria. Virtually all the articles are American or German, including those in Part 2, on bibliotherapy; one or two which are British are rather misleading, such as the entry 'Reading in bed' from the *Lancet* of 1908,[16] this short article deals with the problems of eye strain or setting light to the curtains(!) rather than with the therapeutic aspect of reading.

During the 1930s and 1940s the need for hospital libraries was discussed and some were set up but reading therapy made little or no progress in the UK; this was in great contrast to the USA where, according to *We call it bibliotherapy*,[17] a number of articles were published from the 1920s onwards. The other major step forward in the USA in 1939 was the setting up of a Bibliotherapy Committee in the Hospital Division of the American Library Association.

In 1939, a well-known British librarian, L. Stanley Jast, wrote a book, *The library and the community*.[18] Jast believed there should be a new profession, that of physician-librarian, whose prescriptions would be authors and titles.

In 1945 Sir Drummond Shiels, a physician, gave an address on 'The therapeutic value of reading' which was reprinted in *The Book Trolley*.[19] Although of a fairly general nature it conveys the speaker's 'conviction of the importance of reading from the point of view of healing . . .'.

Librarians and doctors in Scotland were also working towards providing better libraries in hospitals after the Second World War and Antonia Bunch describes this in her book on hospital libraries in Scotland.[20] In 1948 the *Lancet* published an article in which the therapeutic value of reading was discussed.[21]

Joyce Coates, in the *Library Association Record*,[22] demonstrated how far the UK was still behind the USA in bibliotherapy in 1950. Miss Coates was librarian at Netherne Hospital, near Coulsdon, Surrey, at that time a large psychiatric hospital with over 2,000 patients and its library had been in existence only since December 1948 and in her words 'the possibilities of bibliotherapy have yet to be fully explored'.

The Library Association published a pamphlet in 1951,[23] in which Kathleen Allsop, formerly a librarian on the staff of Lancashire County Library, described her work at Lancaster Moor Hospital from 1947 to 1949. She wrote of the activities of the library which were of a therapeutic nature and could only be very loosely described as reading therapy.

In 1952 William Bishop whose 1931 bibliography on hospital libraries and bibliotherapy has already been mentioned,[24] made a further comment on that field of librarianship.[25] He felt there had been confusion between libraries for patients and technical libraries for medical students and staff and regarded work in medical libraries as one of the most highly specialized departments of librarianship and did not wish public libraries to enter this field. Although members of the Medical Section were willing to let public libraries serve the patients there were certain aspects of bibliotherapy in his view which were more in the province of the medical librarian than of the general librarian. It was not made clear how medical librarians, who by their own choice did not wish to serve patients, would be able to carry out any bibliotherapy with patients they never saw.

No great advances were made in the reading therapy field in the 1950s and according to a report published in 1959,[26] the number of hospitals in one area of London alone that were without adequate library facilities was not encouraging.

An article on the activities organized and carried out by the librarian of a large mental hospital appeared in the *Library Association Record* in 1961.[27] Lorna Aldrich was at one time Librarian at Saxondale Hospital where the library was a branch of Nottinghamshire County Library. After describing the setting up and running of the library service she went on to describe the special activities she organized; these activities, known as recreational activities, to distinguish them from those organized by the Occupational Therapy Department, included play reading, music appreciation, discussions and lectures. The Librarian was helped in her work by the Medical Superintendent 'whose great interest and intense belief in the value of the library is a constant source of inspiration'.[28]

In 1962 the Hospital Libraries and Handicapped Readers Group of the Library Association officially came into being and in 1963 the first of its annual weekend study conferences was held in Nottingham. Duncan Leys, an Honorary Consultant Physician at Farnborough Hospital in Kent, gave a paper entitled 'Literature in healing'.[29] His paper was of a general nature but Dr Leys did express his view on the word 'bibliotherapy' in quite strong terms: 'Another (English) psychiatrist has, I find, actually been using the term *bibliotherapy* to describe what he thinks are, or can be, the effects of books on sick people, and this title I would, if I were you, reject with contempt. A form of therapeutic alcoholism.'

Dr Leys also contributed to a book on hospital libraries.[30] His chapter, entitled 'The place of literature in healing' was also reproduced in the *Bibliotherapy sourcebook*,[31] under Part IV, 'Foreign perspectives'; the chapter deals in a very generalized way with the place of literature in healing.

The following year's weekend conference found David Boorer, a Registered Mental Nurse turned librarian, speaking on the 'Librarian at large: mental library services'.[32] This interesting paper had much sensible advice for the would-be librarian in a mental hospital, (or psychiatric hospitals as they are known today), but he barely touches on bibliotherapy or reading therapy – 'What Americans call bibliotherapy, but which I prefer to call guided reading is another field hardly touched on in this country'.

At Southampton, in 1965, a number of papers were given at the weekend conference and later published under the collective title of *Reading and Health*. Jennifer Andrewes, Librarian at Fulbourn Hospital, Cambridge, a large psychiatric hospital, gave a paper entitled 'Bibliotherapy'.[33] In agreeing to undertake a project on bibliotherapy the author first thought about a controlled experiment but gave up the idea after talking to a clinical psychologist. She next tried to find articles written on bibliotherapy in the UK but those she found were at a very elementary level. She then goes on to describe her cooperation with several occupational therapists working with groups of disturbed girls in an Intensive Nursing Unit, young long-stay patients in a chronic ward and in an admission unit. The work described in the paper is inconclusive and rather low key.

In 1970 at the Group conference in Bristol, several papers were given on bibliotherapy, including one by Ronald Sturt. Among other comments in the subsequent discussion, David Boorer said that he was unconvinced that similar results to those claimed for bibliotherapy could not equally well be achieved by almost any concentration of attention on the patient.

So far this chapter has, in the main, been concerned with the reactions of librarians and physicians to possibilities of reading therapy. Members of other professions had been looking at the possibilities, for instance in the field of social work, where literature is used to help students understand themselves and their clients. In 1975 the Library Association published a pamphlet entitled *Literature and the social worker* edited by Clare Morris.[34] In a foreword Elizabeth Irvine, who herself had used literature to help her and her students to understand human nature wrote, 'Many social workers are making increasing use of creative literature to humanise the knowledge derived from the behavioural sciences'.[35] Clare Morris, in her introduction, writing about helping students overcome problems in study, said 'We find that complicated concepts, in psychology and sociology for example, are often more meaningfully and more movingly illustrated by fiction than by textbooks'.[36] The reading list is divided into seventeen headings and subheadings, beginning with Childhood and Puberty, Adolescence, Family interaction, Courtship and marriage, etc.

Clare Morris, later to become Clare Gillies, has maintained her interest in this field; she was one of the speakers at the first 'Reading therapy' meeting held at the Library Association in April, 1981, a report of which appeared soon after,[37] and is also a contributor to this book.

David Millard, of the Probation Service, in an article published in 1977, 'Literature and the therapeutic imagination',[38] reinforces the views of Clare Morris. He also believes literature needs to be an integral part of social work. Margaret Valk, a retired Social Work Education Adviser, who has written on the use of poetry as therapy, commented on David Millard's article two years later.[39]

A general practitioner, writing in his college journal on 'Some books for the general practitioner',[40] lists books, with brief annotations, under similar headings to those used by Clare Morris. In the brief paragraphs before the titles are listed the author, Dr Tomson, 'At our peril do we ignore the sensitivity of writers and the store of knowledge of human nature contained in our literature'.

Throughout the 1960s and 1970s librarians working with patients had been using books to help patients and their relatives to come to terms with illness by using accounts by other sufferers: the publication *Reflections: a subject guide to works of fiction, biography and autobiography*, edited by Roy Tabor,[41] brought such books to the attention of a wider audience. This annotated bibliography, a third edition of which is being compiled, is intended for two main audiences. Firstly, for health care practitioners – doctors, nurses and others who care for patients, to help them to understand more about their patients than can be found in a medical or nursing textbook. Secondly, the books can be recommended to patients and relatives to show how others have coped with illness and disability.

Wylva Partington had long been interested in reading therapy and in the 1970s she and Sara Coomaraswamy, then Senior Clinical Psychologist at Queen Elizabeth II Hospital, collaborated with each other until Mrs Partington's retirement in 1982. A meeting of the Hospital Libraries and Handicapped Readers Group of the Library Association was held at the hospital at which Mrs Coomaraswamy spoke and her paper was later published.[42] (It was also reprinted in the *Bibliotherapy source book*).[43] She said 'Literature can be used to sensitise patients to human situations, to deepen their understanding and enrich their contacts with other people'. Mrs Coomaraswamy later contributed a chapter to the third edition of *Hospital libraries and work with the disabled in the community* called 'Bibliotherapy and the psychological needs of patients'.[44] The chapter included sections on the principles underlying bibliotherapy as a service, planning therapeutic reading to match the needs and experience of patients, and expanding the frontiers of bibliotherapy.

Another comment on the use of bibliotherapy came in 1975 when John Lickorish of the Institute of Family Psychiatry published a paper on 'The therapeutic use of literature'.[45] The author questioned the technique of 'recommended reading' but finished his paper in the following way 'Perhaps it is too much to expect the client to gain any direct benefit from the reading of literature. Perhaps it is the therapist himself who must enter the world's storehouse of literature and bring out the treasure to enrich the life of his client.'

Occupational therapists have, over the years, used prose, poetry and drama to help their clients in a variety of situations. In 1967 M. Krall described the illustrating of myths and legends in an article which was published in *Occupational Therapy;*[46] in the same journal in 1977 Irene Affleck described the use of poetry in a unit for the treatment of alcoholism.[47] Poetry as a form of therapy is also the subject of an article by J. K. W. Morrice, published in the *British Journal of Medical Psychology*.[48]

A successful poetry group run by occupational therapy staff and volunteers is described by Margaret Valk in a 1985 article.[49] A small group of elderly, chronically-ill patients in a geriatric hospital meet regularly to listen to poetry on a topic and then try to write their own poems. The idea for the group came from Margaret Valk, herself a volunteer, as she has retired as a Social Work Education Adviser but still retains a great interest in poetry therapy. The poems written by the patients were published by the Friends of the Hospital.[50]

The therapeutic use of archives has been developed in Wales with the appointment of a Bibliotherapist by Dyfed County

Libraries jointly with Dyfed Social Services. Since 1982 the Bibliotherapist and the Archivist have developed a programme of archive therapy in the Carmarthenshire Record Office. The programme, which is described in an article by Susan Beckley,[51] aims to help the elderly, the mentally ill and young offenders.

What of children and reading therapy? A number of individuals, including librarians, as well as organizations, have compiled lists of books aimed at helping children in a variety of situations; one such is 'Stories about some family problems' by Margaret Good in *The School Librarian*.[52] Subjects covered include adoption, foster-homes, orphans, step-parents, etc. An American librarian, when speaking to a branch of the School Library Association, posed the question in the title of her talk 'Bibliotherapy: what is it and will it be an influence on British children's literature?'[53] The author defined bibliotherapy and went on to ask 'does bibliotherapy work?' and to talk of criticisms of it in America. One point she made is that 'In the USA too many children's book publishers have been jumping on the bibliotherapy bandwagon and as a result have published titles with little literary merit, which seem to have been constructed solely for the purpose of being listed under a particular problem in a bibliotherapy book list'. The point of quoting this American librarian is to highlight that criticism and to suggest a similar situation may be created in the UK – some may say it is already happening.

Various organizations and groups have produced booklists dealing with particular problems: for instance: *We don't all live with Mum and Dad* from One Parent Families;[54] *Count me in: books for and about disabled children*, published by the Library Association Youth Libraries Group.[55] Another publication about handicapped children is that compiled by Grace Hallworth, a professional storyteller, entitled *My mind is not in a wheel chair: books and the handicapped child*.[56] Other organizations producing booklists include the British Agencies for Adoption and Fostering, the National Association for the Welfare of Children in Hospital, ILEA Learning Resources Branch and a veritable flood of booklists stemming from International Year of Disabled People in 1981.

Margaret Marshall, in her book *Libraries and the handicapped child*,[57] mentions bibliotherapy briefly and includes a reading list on the subject. It could be argued that the use of books with children with different handicaps and in different situations is all part of reading therapy.

Interest in literature as a means by which members of several different professions have come to a greater understanding of human nature, and by so doing be better able to help their clients, has continued over the past decade. Following on from Millard[58] and Morris[59] an article in the *Nursing Mirror* 'A novel approach' by Maureen Swanwick,[60] describes how general literature, including novels, is used to teach student nurses how to broaden their experience and to help them to understand their patients' needs. Teachers of psychology use both novels and non-fiction to illustrate various aspects of psychology as David Rose and John Radford illustrated in their article 'The use of literature in teaching psychology'.[61] Social work education is the subject of another article by Margaret Valk,[62] in which she tries to show, through illustration and example, how literary works can be useful tools in the hands of the social work educator. Psychiatrists, too, are interested in the use of creative literature in the study of psychiatry. Correspondents, writing to the *Bulletin of the Royal College of Psychiatrists*, suggest various authors and titles. Two correspondents went so far as to suggest the College sanction a specific list of about twenty titles (given in an Appendix) and an additional *optional* paper to be taken at the time of the Final Membership examination. A specimen examination paper is also included.[63] The correspondence continued until it was closed by the Editor in March, 1987.[64,65]

A number of different therapists have been engaged in what has become known as 'Reminiscence therapy' – the use of books, photographs, slides and all kinds of materials, to stimulate the memory of elderly people. *Recall*,[66] a series of tape/slides and booklets, produced by the DHSS and Help the Aged, was designed to encourage elderly people to discuss events in their past; these programmes seemed to start a reminiscence bandwagon which is still gaining momentum and much useful material has come, and is still coming, on the market specially produced for use with elderly people. Whether reminiscence therapy has a true place in reading therapy could be debated: certainly the reading of the many books produced has had a therapeutic effect on some elderly people. An article by Glenys Jones describes the use of the *Recall* programme in a large psychiatric hospital,[67] and Mel Wright, writing in *Community Care*,[68] describes the use of other similar material.

While interest in reading therapy by members of other professions was growing, so too, was the interest of librarians, through the initial work of Wylva Partington. One of the first steps on the road to the setting up of a Reading Therapy Subgroup was a Bibliotherapy Workshop, held as part of the

MHWLG Annual Weekend Study Conference at Guildford in July, 1980. The Workshop, in which about thirty people took part, was led by Wylva Partington and generated so much interest that it was agreed that a one-day meeting on bibliotherapy should be held in the Spring of 1981. Workshop participants felt, however, that the word 'bibliotherapy' should be avoided in the course title. In April, 1981, a successful one-day meeting 'The therapy of reading' was jointly organized by the Library Association and the MHWLG, a report of which appeared in the *Library Association Record*.[69]

A number of people interested in the subject got in touch with Wylva Partington and another meeting was held at St John's Hospital, near Aylesbury, in October 1982.[70] At that meeting it was suggested a Reading Therapy Information Exchange should be set up and this came into being early in 1983; the Exchange scheme consisted of letters and comments circulating among members on topics relating to therapeutic reading. Later in 1983 a meeting was held at Rotherham District General Hospital.[71] Of the forty-five people attending, nearly half were non-librarians and included occupational therapists, social workers, psychologists and representatives of voluntary organizations.

Wylva Partington, who had started arranging a meeting which was to take place in Manchester in March, 1984, sadly died in February of that year. Eileen Bostle, Librarian of the General (Patients) Library at Northwick Park Hospital, Harrow, took on the task of completing the arrangements for the meeting, which was attended by fifty-five people. A report of this meeting and of a subsequent one in Leicester that autumn appeared in *Health Libraries Review*:[72] the Leicester meeting was dedicated to the memory of Wylva Partington.

At the meeting in Manchester, Eileen Bostle and six others volunteered to form a Steering Committee working towards the formation of a Sub-Group within the MHWLG; it was agreed to call it the Reading Therapy Sub-group as the term 'Bibliotherapy' was generally disliked by almost everyone present.

1985 saw two further meetings arranged, in Southampton and Edinburgh, reported in *Health Libraries Review*.[73,74] 1985 also saw the start of the *Reading Therapy Sub-group Newsletter*, published two/three times a year, for which a small subscription is charged to cover production and postage costs. At the time of writing there are over two hundred and fifty members of the Sub-group from countries as wide apart as Poland, Sweden, Australia and New Zealand.

Greenwich was the venue for a meeting in October, 1986, where once again the speakers were drawn from several different professions.[75] The most recent meeting was in Cambridge in May, 1987 and further meetings are planned. Space does not permit comment on the individual speakers and their papers at these meetings, which have taken place every year since 1981, particularly as each meeting has been reported upon fairly fully, as indicated.

What then of the future? As has been clearly illustrated earlier, by a number of people from different professions, the use of books and other artefacts is clearly capable of influencing people in trouble and distress, whether they turn to them independently for solace or instruction or whether they are assisted by a person whom we might agree to call a 'bibliotherapist'. The largest problems seem to me to be, first, the subjective nature of the reading process and the difficulty of *predicting* a certain outcome. In other words books don't operate on the mind as drugs operate on the body, much though we might wish to make such a claim. Secondly, therapy programmes tend to be experimental and pragmatic and may 'work' or not because of the chance response of striking a chord. (This second point is carrying the first point a little further.) The use of literature in the training of health professionals is perhaps less contentious. The need for training begs the question of what qualities are required. Two areas of *knowledge* are essential: selection of *materials* appropriate to the patient's (or client's) needs and *empathy* with the client/patient. Psychology appears to be one kind of desirable expertise but a personality capable of enlisting the client's cooperation, and flexible enough to learn continuously from experience is probably of pre-eminent importance. That is why the practitioners or would-be practitioners of the art (or science) of bibliotherapy may come from any of the caring professions – or perhaps from collaboration between a number of them. These views are certainly held by David Matthews, Principal Lecturer at the College of Librarianship Wales, who, for many years has had an interest in reading therapy.

The Reading Therapy Sub-group appears to have become the focal point for a large number of people: what should its role be and what problems should it be tackling? Perhaps it should be posing such questions as what is the role of the librarian? What qualities and qualifications are required by the Reading Therapist? (Reading therapy lags far behind Art Therapy, Music Therapy and Horticultural Therapy, which are all recognized within the National Health Service.) What training is needed? The Sub-group would seem well placed to coordinate training, as the knowledge and training of people from several professions would be needed for such courses to succeed.

Whatever the future holds it is fair to assume that books will continue to be used in ever widening situations to help people of all ages.

The author acknowledges the help of Eileen Bostle, M. Joy Lewis, and in particular, David Matthews, in the preparation of this chapter.

References

1 Brown, E. F., *Bibliotherapy and its widening applications*, Metuchen, N.J., The Scarecrow Press, 1975.
2 Rubin, R. J., *Using bibliotherapy: a guide to theory and practice*, Oryx Press, London, Mansell, 1978.
3 Rubin, R. J., 'Uses of bibliotherapy in response to the 1970's', *Library Trends*, Fall, 1979, 239–52.
4 Rubin, R. J. (ed.), *Bibliotherapy sourcebook*, Oryx Press, London, Mansell, 1978.
5 *Library Trends*, 11(2), October, 1962.
6 Rubin, R. J., *op.cit.*, (3).
7 Elser, H., 'Bibliotherapy in practice', *Library Trends*, Spring, 1982, 647–59.
8 Lack, C. (ed.), *Bibliotherapy: an overview*, Chicago, American Library Association, 1981.
9 Howie, M., 'Reading therapy', *Interim: newsletter of the Association of Scottish Health Service Librarians*, 15, August 1985, 10–14.
10 Sturt, R., 'Hospital libraries in England and Wales to 1960', *Hospital libraries and work with the disabled in the community*, 3rd ed. compiled and edited by Mona E. Going and Jean M. Clarke, London, The Library Association, 1982, 27–59.
11 Bunch, A. J., *Hospital and medical libraries in Scotland: an historical and sociological study*, Glasgow, Scottish Library Association, 1975.
12 *Lancet*, 1930, i, 1357.
13 Bruce-Porter, *Sir* B., 'The need for libraries in hospitals as part of the scheme for curative medicine', *Journal of State Medicine*, 38, 1930, 710–15.
14 *Lancet*, 1930, ii, 1195.
15 Bishop, W. J., 'Hospital libraries and bibliotherapy: a bibliography', Three parts, *Library Association Record*, 1931, 198–200, 231–2, 274–5.
16 'Reading in bed', *Lancet*, 1908, ii, 1089.
17 Dolan, R. et al., *We call it bibliotherapy*, Washington, D.C., Veterans Administration, 1967.

18 Jast, L. S., *The library and the community*, London, T. Nelson, 1939, 189.
19 Shiels, *Sir* D., 'The therapeutic value of reading', *The Book Trolley*, 1, Autumn 1945, 67–70.
20 Bunch, A. J., *op.cit.*
21 *Lancet*, 255, ii, 1948, 577.
22 Coates, J. L., 'Books and mental health', *Library Association Record*, 52,(1), January 1950, 8–10.
23 Allsop, K. M., *A mental hospital library*, London, The London Association, 1951, (LA pamphlet no. 6).
24 Bishop, W. J., *op. cit.*
25 Bishop, W. J., 'The Medical Section and its work' in *Library Association Conference, Papers and discussion, Bournemouth*, Library Association, 1952, 14.
26 King Edward's Hospital Fund for London, *Hospital library services: a pilot survey*, London, King Edward's Hospital Fund for London, 1959.
27 Aldrich, L., 'Saxondale: a mental hospital library', *Library Association Record*, (7), July 1961, 248–53.
28 *Ibid.*, 253.
29 Leys, D., 'Literature in healing', *Library Association Record*, April 1964, 161–4.
30 Leys, D., 'The place of literature in healing', *Hospital libraries and work with the disabled*, edited by Mona E. Going, London, The Library Association, 1963, 44–50 (also in the 2nd ed. 1973, 184–191).
31 *Ibid.* in Rubin, R. J., (ed.), *op. cit.* (4), 327–32.
32 Boorer, D., 'Librarian at large: mental hospital library services', *Hospital library services surveyed*, Papers given at the Hospital Libraries and Handicapped Readers Group Conference . . . Sorby Hall, University of Sheffield July 1964, London, The Library Association, 1965, 33–54.
33 Andrewes, J., 'Bibliotherapy', *Reading and health*, Papers given at the Hospital Libraries and Handicapped Readers Group Conference . . ., University of Southampton, July 1965, London, Hospital Libraries and Handicapped Readers Group, The Library Association, 1967, 42–51.
34 Morris, C. (ed.), *Literature and the social worker: a reading list for practitioners, teachers, students and voluntary workers*, London, The Library Association, 1975.
35 *Ibid.*, 5.
36 *Ibid.*, 7.
37 Leary, G., Report on a one day meeting at the Library Association, April 1981, *Library Association Record*, 85,(5), May 1981, 228.
38 Millard, D. A., 'Literature and the therapeutic imagination', *British Journal of Social Work*, 7,(2), Summer 1977, 173–84.
39 Valk, M., 'The therapeutic imagination: a comment', *British Journal of Social Work*, 9,(1), Spring 1979, 87–91.

40 Tomson, P. R. V., 'Some books for the general practitioner', *Journal of the Royal College of General Practitioners*, 26, 1976, 588–90.
41 Tabor, R. B. (ed.), *Reflections: a subject guide to works of fiction, biography and autobiography on medical and related topics*, 2nd ed., Southampton, Wessex Regional Library and Information Service, 1983.
42 Coomaraswamy, S., 'Therapeutic aspects of a library service to hospital patients', *Health and Welfare Libraries Quarterly*, 2,(2–4), June–December, 1975, 29–32.
43 *Ibid*. reprinted in Rubin, R. J. (ed.), *op.cit*. (4), 333–7.
44 Coomaraswamy, S., 'Bibliotherapy and the psychological needs of patients', *Hospital libraries and work with the disabled in the community*, edited by M. E. Going and J. M. Clarke, 3rd ed., London, The Library Association, 1982, 229–34.
45 Lickorish, J., 'The therapeutic use of literature', *Psychotherapy: theory, research and practice*, 12,(1), Spring 1975, 105–9.
46 Krall, M., 'Illustrating myths and legends as a group activity', *Occupational Therapy*, 30,(2), February 1967, 20–30.
47 Affleck, I., 'Poetry as medium in a Unit for the Treatment of Alcoholism', *Occupational Therapy*, XI, 1977, 277.
48 Morrice, J. K. W., 'Poetry as therapy', *British Journal of Medical Psychology*, 56, 1983, 367–70.
49 Valk, M., 'Reflections on the life of a group in a geriatric hospital', *Issues in Social Work Education*, 5,(1), Summer 1985, 13–23.
50 Redhills Poetry Group, *Poetry from Redhills Hospital, Exeter*, Exeter, League of Friends of Redhills Hospital, 1980.
51 Beckley, S., 'Archive therapy in Carmarthenshire', *Journal of the Society of Archivists*, 7,(4), October 1983, 245–6.
52 Good, M., 'Stories about some family problems: a select list', *School Librarian*, 26,(3), September 1978, 218–24.
53 Butcher, P. S., 'Bibliotherapy: what is it and will it be an influence on British children's literature?', *School Librarian*, 28, (I), March 1980, 11–13.
54 *We don't all live with Mum and Dad . . .*, London, One Parent Families, 1981.
55 Smyth, M. (comp.), *Count me in: books for and about disabled children*, Towcester, Youth Libraries Group of The Library Association, 1981, (Pamphlet no. 23).
56 Hallworth, G., *My mind is not in a wheelchair: books and the handicapped*, Hertford, Hertfordshire County Library, 1982.
57 Marshall, M. R., *Libraries and the handicapped child*, London, Andre Deutsch, 1981.
58 Millard, D. A., *op. cit.*
59 Morris, C. (ed.), *op. cit.*
60 Swanwick, M., 'A novel approach', *Nursing Mirror*, July 8, 1981, 38–9.
61 Rose, D. and Radford, J., 'The use of literature in teaching

psychology', *Bulletin of the British Psychological Society*, 34, 1981, 453–5.
62 Valk, M., 'Imaginative literature and social work education: an extended comment on Barker', *Issues in Social Work Education*, Summer 1983, 17–26.
63 Letters, *Bulletin of the Royal College of Psychiatrists*, 9,(2), February 1985, 38–9.
64 Letters, *Bulletin of the Royal College of Psychiatrists*, 10,(10), October 1986, 284.
65 Letters, *Bulletin of the Royal College of Psychiatrists*, 11,(3), March 1987, 99–101.
66 *Recall*, Available from Help the Aged Education Department, 316 St. Pauls Road, London, N1.
67 Jones, G., 'The use of Recall to re-inforce the here and now', *New Age*, Issue 25, Spring 1984, 12–13.
68 Wright, M., 'Using the past to help the present', *Community Care*, October 18, 1984, 20–2.
69 Leary, G., *op.cit.*
70 Brown, H., 'Reading therapy', *MHWLG Newsletter*, 19, March 1983, 45–7.
71 Cooper, L., 'Reading therapy', *MHWLG Newsletter*, 22, December 1983, 39–42.
72 Shapland, P., 'Reading therapy 1984: a report of two meetings', *Health Libraries Review*, 2,(2), June 1985, 85–7.
73 Wallis, J. P., Report, 'The therapy of reading . . .', *Health Libraries Review*, 2,(4), December 1985, 207–9.
74 Spencer, B., Report on 'Reading Therapy Study Day', *Health Libraries Review*, 3,(2), June 1986, 126–8.
75 Smith, D., 'Report on One Day Reading Therapy meeting', *Health Libraries Review*, 4,(2), June 1987, 97–8.

2 Reading therapy and the social worker

Mary Howie

A book

He ate and drank the precious words,
His spirit grew robust;
He knew no more that he was poor,
Nor that his frame was dust.

He danced along the dingy days,
And this bequest of wings
Was but a book – what liberty
A loosened spirit brings.

Emily Dickinson

Reading therapy (RT) simply means the therapeutic use of literature. American workers prefer the term 'bibliotherapy' or more recently 'biblio/poetry therapy'. More extensive definitions have been provided by various professional workers including educational and clinical psychologists, teachers, psychiatrists and social workers, which serve to highlight reading therapy's multidisciplinary origins and applications. For our purposes RT can be defined as the use of literature and/or audio/visual materials, by a trained worker, to facilitate a therapeutic activity, usually guided discussion, which promotes personal growth for the participant(s). In this chapter the theory and practice of reading therapy will be discussed in general followed by a look at social work applications, and a detailed description of a reading therapy group for elderly depressed patients. Research findings regarding the effectiveness of RT conclude the chapter.

Reading therapy – philosophical perspective and theoretical roots

Although the term 'therapy' comes from the Greek 'to cure', RT does not claim to 'cure' but to enlighten, and promote insight. In this way power is released within the individual to become more 'self-actualized', to use Maslow's[1] concept. In orientation it is related to the humanistic view of therapy together with the other art therapies e.g. psychodrama, music, dance etc. which focus on facilitating personal growth through difficult and enriching life experiences. It rejects preoccupation with mental illness common to Freudian and behaviourist psychologies and attachment to the medical model. This positive orientation has attracted many workers including psychologist Daniel Sweeney. In an article from the *Bibliotherapy sourcebook*[2] entitled 'Bibliotherapy and the elderly' he stated, 'the essential difference between RT and the other therapies as I have seen them employed is that RT addresses itself directly and consistently to healthy, progressive aspects of a person's character'.

Despite the fact that RT is allied to humanistic psychology it draws on both Freudian and behaviourist psychology. The process of RT closely corresponds to the phases of Freudian psychotherapy as outlined by Caroline Shrodes in a doctoral dissertation in 1949 entitled *Bibliotherapy: a theoretical and clinical experimental study.*[3] In this seminal work she laid much of the current theoretical groundwork, and identified the three stages in the process of RT as identification and projection, abreaction and catharsis, and insight and integration. Identification and projection mean a real or imagined affiliation of oneself with another person, institution, symbol etc. and in the case of RT, with a character and his/her situation in a story. Abreaction and catharsis literally mean a 'purging of the emotions', and involves an uncensored and spontaneous release of feelings expressed either verbally or non-verbally. Insight and integration is achieved when one gains emotional awareness of one's own motivations and experiences in the story characters, and applies the new self knowledge to problem solving. *The particular power within literature and other art forms is that it can lower defenses thereby increasing psychological accessibility so that this therapeutic process can take place.* Those who have participated in counselling, therapy or group discussion are aware of the various degrees of risk and fear that can be felt. The ability to relax and feel safe helps to reduce resistance and release creative energies for personal growth. Michael Shiryon,[4] a psychologist, illustrates how a story allows a person both distance and involvement at the same time from the Biblical description of how Nathan the prophet used a story to confront King David about the Bathsheba affair. Direct confrontation would have produced the natural reaction of raised defenses and denial. To enable him to take a second look at his actions, Nathan told David the story about the rich man who took away the poor man's only sheep. This enabled David to react with full emotional outrage at the moral wrong. All that was left for Nathan to do was to make the connection by saying 'You are this man'. Obviously within the modern day situation the therapist/facilitator would be working towards enabling the participants to make these kinds of connections themselves, but this story does demonstrate how the psychological distance of a story allows involvement through projection, identification, emotional reaction and vicarious experiencing of the situation described. RT also draws on the principle developed by learning theorists; that human beings learn by imitation. Jean and John Pardeck in their recent book entitled *Young people with problems: a guide to bibliotherapy*[5] point out that fictional characters can be useful as models for positive adaptive behaviour, particularly for children who lack positive role models. They also state that 'there is agreement among virtually all the studies that the reading of a book *must* be accompanied, and/or followed by, discussion and/or counselling'. These activities together with other projective techniques are regarded as an integral part of the RT process. With this in mind we will now look briefly at RT in practice including the main types of RT used, the role of the therapist/facilitator, the therapeutic techniques involved and the selection of materials.

Reading therapy in practice

From the literature on RT the two main types of RT which can be identified are Clinical and Developmental RT. The main features of these are shown in Figure 1. Clara Lack, a librarian and director of bibliotherapy training at St Elizabeth's Hospital in Washington DC, defines Clinical RT as 'a mode of intervention in aiding persons severely troubled with emotional or behavioural problems' and Developmental RT as 'the personalisation of literature for the purpose of meeting normal ongoing life tasks'.[6]

Clients and setting

Generally speaking Clinical RT tends to be based in institutional settings whereas Developmental RT is based in the community. Rubin[7] sees the trend for the 1980s as a move from the institutional to the community setting, particularly with the growing move towards de-institutionalization. By 'community' she means:

> small local institutions, such as halfway houses, addiction centers, outpatient services, nursing homes and group homes (which) are obvious locations for bibliotherapy programs which have been developed in the larger institutions . . . the National Council on the

	Clinical	Developmental
Client	Person with an emotional or behavioural problem.	'Normal' person – possibly in a crisis situation (e.g. adolescence, retirement).
Setting	Institutional e.g. psychiatric hospital, drug addiction centre, child guidance centre.	Community: day centres, schools, libraries.
Therapist or Facilitator	Nurse, doctor, psychologist, social worker, librarian, OT.	Teacher, librarian, social worker, community worker, adult education worker.
Format	Individual or group. Voluntary or involuntary.	Individual or group. Voluntary or involuntary.
Technique	Discussion and/or counselling using literature and other projective materials and techniques as vehicles for communication.	Discussion using literature and other projective materials and techniques e.g. psychodrama, creative writing, art work.
Materials	Imaginative and/or informational literature and other projective materials.	Imaginative and/or informational literature and other projective materials.
Goals	Insight → attitudinal and behavioural change. Improved quality of life.	Informational – Insight. Solution of normal developmental problems of adjustment and growth. Improved quality of life.

Fig. 2.1 Types of reading therapy

Aging Inc. has an exemplary reading and discussion program to foster the self esteem and personal potential of participants which it offers to senior residences and centers and nursing homes.

In California two examples of community-based RT programmes are in Santa Clara and San Raphael public libraries. The former programme was begun in the Agnews State Hospital in 1973, but was transferred to the public library when the hospital closed down. Librarians run RT groups in both these settings as well as in local nursing homes. RT is increasingly used in the educational setting in the USA, by teachers and librarians to help meet developmental needs or solve adjustment problems, whilst psychologists, social workers etc. working in child guidance and other treatment centres also use RT to help those whose normal developmental needs and problems have become more acute producing mental ill-health.

Turning to Britain where RT has only begun to develop in recent years there are numerous examples of RT in its various forms. Leicestershire Libraries in cooperation with Age Concern run six library clubs for the elderly. The development since 1981 of these clubs, including one for Asian elderly and housebound people, is described in an article by Stephen Hoy.[8] There is considerable national interest at present in the recording and use of oral and community history and reminiscence work has played an important part in these clubs. The value of reminiscence to elderly people is well established,[9] and this has been a beneficial spin-off from such projects where reminiscence therapy was not in itself the primary aim. Examples of institutionally-based RT groups have also been written up. Margaret Valk,[10] a social worker, ran a poetry group in Redhills Geriatric Hospital and an anthology of poetry produced by this group of long-term patients has been published.[11] Eileen Bostle,[12] a librarian, describes a Poetry and Music activity in her article which was carried out as part of a rehabilitation project at St John's Hospital near Aylesbury. More recently, a new project based on creative writing, poetry and reading therapy has been having good results at Fairfields Hospital, Stotfold, providing chronic mentally ill patients with a means of expression and the confidence to express their views.[13] These are just a few random examples, and it is indicative of the growing interest in RT that a Reading Therapy Group has now been formed in Britain under the auspices of the Library Association Medical, Health and Welfare Libraries Group. The varied membership including librarians, psychologists, social workers, occupational therapists, teachers etc. demonstrates the variety of settings and ways in which RT is practised. Conferences and a newsletter provide a useful forum for the exchange of information and views on RT and the proceedings of these conferences will, I am sure, provide a rich source of examples of the ways in which RT is currently employed with both individuals and groups. Other books on the theory and practice of RT include the companion volume to the *Bibliotherapy sourcebook* entitled *Using Bibliotherapy: a guide to theory and practice,*[14] and a discussion of RT in rehabilitation, educational and mental health settings by Zaccaria *et al.*[15]

The therapist

We have now established that RT can be viewed as a tool both in the clinical setting for dealing with severe to minor emotional and adjustment problems, or in the community setting to help meet the developmental needs of 'normal' individuals. The field of practice is very wide therefore, and its usefulness extends to those not necessarily trained as counsellors and therapists, such as teachers and librarians. In the treatment approach as outlined by Pardeck *et al.*[16] the therapist/facilitator is required to a) assess client readiness, b) select appropriate literature and other materials, and c) facilitate the RT process by using projective techniques usually based on guided discussion, where readers are encouraged to analyse, respond, evaluate and relate to the literature. With regard to client readiness social workers are all aware of the importance of timing in their work, and librarians know the value of 'the right book at the right time'. Timing is very important in the RT process and the therapist, therefore, has to have a good knowledge of the client(s) and the problem(s) as inappropriate timing may impede the process. In clinical work with an individual, an adequate working relationship must be established based on trust, there should be agreement on the presenting problem and some preliminary exploration of the problem carried out. The role of the therapist is evidently crucial. As Pardeck points out 'although it is possible for a client to experience projection through reading a book on his or her own, normally the three stages of the RT process . . . especially catharsis and insight . . . occur only as a result of interaction between the client and therapist'. The need for the combination of skills required by the therapist is evident, and frequently librarians and other workers have voiced their concern that their lack of training in therapy may 'damage' a person, particularly in the clinical setting. Certainly the literature on RT tends to emphasize the need for training in therapeutic techniques. Arthur Lerner, founder of the Poetry Therapy Institute in California has pointed out the lure of the field to 'well intentioned individuals who have little or no training'.[17] Regarding the use of poetry he states that unless one understands 'the dynamics of individual behaviour and group process poetry would be just another reading experience'.[18] Obviously the degree of training in therapeutic techniques required will vary according to the type of RT practised. Workers including educators and librarians have been using literature for many years as an aid in their 'helping' role though they may have been unaware of the RT approach. For those using RT in the clinical setting without prior formal training in therapeutic techniques e.g. librarians, relevant professional support and supervision will be required. In connection with this a textbook on RT published this year and co-authored by Arleen Hynes and Mary Hynes-Berry[19] may help to fill the gap until training in RT becomes available. The text is based primarily on the elements of the bibliotherapy training course developed by Arleen Hynes and Dr Kenneth Gorelick at St Elizabeth's Hospital, Washington DC.

Some final but important points regarding the personal qualities and skills required of the therapist are worth mentioning. Elser,[20] a retired medical librarian with 15 years' experience in the field, highlights two essential personal qualities. Firstly, 'you must value people as individuals and as human beings with the result that you feel strongly motivated to help them', and secondly a therapist needs the ability to communicate and to read non-verbal clues which are another aspect of communication skills.

Barbara Allen,[21] a librarian at the San Raphael public library who has trained in RT at St Elizabeth's Hospital, Washington DC, states that some of the skills of the therapist should include 'fostering group interaction (which) requires awareness and use of group process' and an understanding of the 'importance of building confidence by being sincere and honest so that there is an atmosphere of trust and acceptance'. Taking on a group implies responsibility and commitment without which there can be no building up of trust. I wholeheartedly endorse these views, and would say that the relationship between therapist and client(s) is such an important factor in the success of RT that without these personal qualities and skills the most extensive knowledge of theory and materials is rendered ineffective.

Selection of materials

This implies a good knowledge of literature, but it is a truism that even librarians do not have to know everything, or be aware of each new book that has been published. Their skill lies in knowing how to find out, and where to look for particular information.

Books are available now on virtually any problem, but it is essential that they contain believable characters and situations and offer realistic hope for clients. Questions to be asked are: does it address whatever goal I have in mind, and do I like it enough myself to be enthusiastic in presenting it to others? Literature should not offend – at least not too much! During her training, Barbara Allen[21] found that short modern poetry with simple language and concrete images was the most useful with chronically mentally disabled patients. She also came to the conclusion that 'a key to choice of literature . . . (is) providing room for a group to move around in comfortably'. Elser,[22] working with a group of similar patients whose attention span was short, chose brief poems e.g. Robert Frost's 'The road not taken' (20 lines) and 'I'm nobody who are you' (4 lines) by Emily Dickinson. Hynes[23] in her work found that chronic and older patients and disturbed children could relate better to concrete subjects than to abstract ones, and that amplification by touch, sight, sound and smell for example, could strengthen the impact of the basic concept. She also used psychodrama, music, recorded material etc.

Dr Mary Jalongo,[24] Associate Professor of Elementary Education at Indiana University, in her article on 'Using crisis-orientated books with young children' suggests basic guidelines for selection including clarity of style, interesting characters, suitable illustrations, relationship to the child's experiential background, freedom from stereotypes, brevity. She also makes the important point that care must be taken not to impose personal values on children that may be in direct conflict with those of their parents and their community.

There is a wealth of information on this topic of selecting books, and many booklists, but I would just like to mention one or two books which have particularly caught my attention.

Books to help children cope with separation and loss by Joanne E. Bernstein.[25] Following a useful introduction on separation and loss and the way in which books can be used, there is an annotated bibliography with headings like 'Learning to face separation,' 'Coping with tragic loss,' 'Who will take care of me?,' etc.

Cushla and her books by Dorothy Butler.[26] I was introduced to this book by Grace Hallworth, who is a professional storyteller with disabled children. It is the story of the significant part played by books in the early cognitive development of a severely handicapped child. Books became Cushla's chief means of learning as well as her chief source of enjoyment in her initial painful and restricted years. The conclusion regarding the contribution of books to Cushla's quality of life was that, 'It seems clear that access to such a wealth of words and pictures, in a setting of consistent love and support, has contributed enormously to her cognitive development in general and her language in particular'. Included are lists of books which Cushla found helpful at the different stages in her development as well as some of the illustrations which so caught her attention. The picture of 'My brother Sean' crying his heart out, with whom Cushla readily identified and always kissed solicitously at each reading, is a good example.

My mind is not in a wheelchair by Grace Hallworth.[27] Subtitled 'Books and the handicapped child', this has 115 titles arranged under headings, e.g. Asthma, Blindness, Down's Syndrome, etc. A classified index mentions the reading age and there is also an author index. It is a useful booklet for those who wish to gain some insight into the problems of children with handicaps.

Windows to our children by Dr Violet Oaklander.[28] Maureen Thom introduced me to this delightful book, a large part of which consists of children speaking about themselves. The section on the use of books, writing and poetry as projective techniques will be of particular interest.

Bruce's story by Maureen Thom and Celia McLiver.[29] Bruce is a spaniel sort of dog who enjoys telling his life story. As his story unfolds, it becomes apparent that Bruce has a lot in common with children in care. This illustrated book is accompanied by worksheets encouraging children to share their story with Bruce, and will be a useful tool for those who are working with children.

Maisie comes to Morningside by Aileen Paterson.[30] Maisie is a Highland kitten from a single parent family. She comes to Edinburgh to stay with Granny while her father, a famous explorer, goes off to the jungle. There are numerous possibilities for identification with Maisie, as she comes through the excitement of leaving home, the pain of separation from those she loves and her familiar surroundings, and the eventual settling in period where the Morningside Library Children's Story Hour provides a turning point for the better! The book is beautifully illustrated.

The Velveteen Rabbit by Margery Williams.[31] First published in 1922, this is a simple story of a toy rabbit who learns that becoming *real* is a long and painful process, and involves being loved.

Reading therapy in social work

The use of literature in training

The relevance of creative literature in the training of 'helping' professionals is increasingly being acknowledged. One of the first booklets I came across on this topic was *Literature and the Social Worker: a reading list for practitioners, teachers, students and voluntary workers*, edited by social work teacher Clare Morris[32] and published by the Library Association in 1975.

Freud said of creative writers, 'they are apt to know a whole host of things between heaven and earth of which our philosophy has not yet let us dream. In their knowledge of the mind they are far in advance of us everyday people, for they draw upon sources which we have not yet opened up for science.' Creative literature, therefore, can serve to humanize the knowledge derived from the behavioural sciences, and help workers extend their empathic understanding of clients. There is not space to dwell on this aspect of the use of literature, but for those who are interested other articles are available on this topic.[33,34,35]

The use of literature in social work practice

For the social worker in particular RT has much to offer as a helping tool with a wide range of client groups both in individual casework and group work.[36] The Pardecks' recent book *Young people with problems: a guide to bibliotherapy*[37] is perhaps the most significant contribution to the field by a social worker to date. John Pardeck and his wife Jean, a reading specialist, have produced this book primarily for psychologists, psychiatrists, social workers and other helping professionals to provide them with available information on the theory and practice of RT and its application for those working with young people with problems. Some problem areas identified include alcohol and drug abuse, divorce and separation of parents, physical handicaps, emotional and behavioural problems etc. Nearly 300 children's books are annotated illustrating all of these problem areas. Another recent publication, already mentioned, from two social workers Maureen Thom and Celia McLiver entitled *Bruce's story*[38] will provide, I am sure, a useful tool for those working with younger children. At a recent RT conference Maureen Thom also delivered an excellent paper[39] on how books can be used to help children cope with separation and loss, drawing on her experience both as a case worker and as coordinator of the BAAF in Scotland. She passed on an interesting anecdote revealing a little of the value of 'Bruce'. Correspondence had been established between a small boy and Bruce. One day the boy refused to write to Bruce and spoke very harshly about him. A little later he told his social worker that he was not angry with Bruce at all, but with his mother who had not visited him as she had promised.

Since my own experience of the RT approach has been with elderly people, we will now look at a particular practice example of an activity/support group for elderly depressed patients attending a psychiatric day hospital. 'The Wednesday Group', as it was known, has previously been written up in some detail,[40] but I will outline the principles underlying the RT group and follow this with an account of the first two meetings.

The Wednesday Group

The psychiatric day hospital took approximately 36 patients per day. Following a staff discussion, it was agreed that the proposal for an activity/support group run on RT lines for some of the functionally ill patients would be useful to help bridge the gap between attendance at the PDH and full discharge. By 'functionally ill' I mean patients who are experiencing 'problems in living', many with long-standing neurotic or personality disturbances i.e. conditions labelled as the schizophrenias, manic/depressive psychoses, the neuroses and affective illnesses like severe depression. Depressive illness, to quote Moyes,[41] is 'the disease of old age'. He states that 'in the majority of affective illness in people over 60, a traumatic event such as the death of a relative, a major physical illness, or separation from children, has occurred within the preceding few months'.

The group would be a 'closed' one, to be held initially for a period of 12 weeks and run by two social workers and a staff nurse. One social worker had group work skills, the staff nurse had a detailed knowledge of each patient, and I had a librarianship background to bring to the group. The 10 members were carefully chosen by the staff and only one dropped out as a result of her frailty. All members were diagnosed as having a depressive illness.

Following a 'warm-up' game, I reiterated the purpose of the group which was twofold. Firstly, to encourage sharing of life experiences past and present so that members would hopefully find the group both helpful and supportive; and secondly, to use an activity, e.g. poetry, reading, writing, to stimulate and focus discussions so that sessions would be both interesting and enjoyable.

For the first meeting I proposed that we write a collaborative poem based on childhood memories. A simple poem in free verse by Vernon Scannell entitled 'Autobiographical note' was read out. It reads as follows:

Beeston, the place, near Nottingham:
We lived there for three years or so.
Each Saturday at two-o'clock
We queued up for the matinée,
All the kids for streets around
With snotty noses, giant caps,
Cut down coats and heavy boots,
The natural enemies of cops
And schoolteachers. Profane and hoarse
We scrambled, yelled and fought until
The Picture Palace opened up
And we, like Hamelin children, forced
Our bony way into the hall.
That much is easy to recall;
Also the reek of chewing-gum,
Gob-stoppers and liquorice,
But of the flickering myths themselves
Not much remains. The hero was
A milky wide-brimmed hat, a shape
Astride the arched white stallion;
The villain's horse and hat were black.
Disbelief did not exist
And laundered virtue always won
With quicker gun and harder fist,
And all of us applauded it.
Yet I remember moments when
In solitude I'd find myself

Brooding on the sooty man,
The bristling villain, who could move
Imagination in a way
The well-shaved hero never could,
And even warm the nervous heart
With something oddly close to love.

Each member was then encouraged to think back to their youth – the smells, sounds, people, places etc. that had stuck in their memories. Bearing in mind that the average age was around 73, it was pointed out that there should be no lack of material as there was between 6–700 years of experience between them! Beautifully rhyming sonnets were not required. Much encouragement and practical help was needed since some patients were anxious, others shaky and some had forgotten their spectacles. Each 'poem' was then read out by the group member or staff member if the patient could not manage to do this. The group listened, clapped, laughed and enjoyed these contributions, and a title 'Memories of yesteryear' was chosen from the suggestions made.

There followed the second, more informal, part of the meeting when we had tea. This encouraged a sharing of problems between group members and with staff. Mr 'J' relaxed so much that he sang a Gaelic song learnt on his father's knee to the warm approval of the group. This led to the group looking at some childhood photographs one member had brought along, and a recollection of street songs.

First impressions from the group were that everyone had participated in some way, which was unusual for a first meeting, and that the mood of the group was optimistic, which was significant bearing in mind that the membership was composed of people who were usually depressed and withdrawn types of individuals.

For the second meeting a typed copy of the collaborative poem was given to each person and there was obvious pleasure in seeing their poem in print and a sense of achievement gained both as individuals and as a group. The theme of childhood memories continued. Miss 'W', who lived opposite a smithy as a child, spontaneously gave a full rendering of 'The Blacksmith', her voice quavering at the description of the blacksmith's sorrow over his dead wife. This was quite an achievement for a very nervous and quiet little lady, and received the warm approval of the group. Photographs had been brought along, some almost 150 years old. Two books used during this session were *The singing street*[42] and *The golden city*[43] by James Ritchie on Edinburgh street games and rhymes. Subsequent themes chosen by the group were on wartime, housing, modern technology, death, loneliness etc. Materials used included poems, novels, wartime memorabilia, newspapers, photographs, postcards, songs with guitar accompaniment, pictures – brought to the group by both staff and patients. Some examples are: the song 'The streets of London' by Ralph McTell;[44] *The view in winter* by Ronald Blythe;[45] *My Oedipus complex* by Frank O'Connor;[46] *Scars upon my heart – women's poetry of the 1st World War* selected by Catherine Reilly;[47] Joyce Grenfell excerpts;[48] and *Edinburgh 1929–79: 50 years of change* published by Edinburgh City Libraries.[49]

Two case studies (fictional names)

(1) Miss King was brought up in a very religious family and lived alone with no surviving relatives. She was therefore socially isolated. She tended to be manic-depressive, and was rather theatrical in her behaviour. At the end of one meeting she announced that she would be 90 on her birthday the following week, but followed this by saying she wanted no presents, in fact she simply wanted 'to go'. It was decided to pick up on this theme and thankfully Miss King turned up at the group the following week.

A chapter from Ronald Blythe's *A view in winter*[50] was read out entitled 'It can't go on – the clergyman's widow – aged 92'. Its usefulness lies in the fact that it acknowledges that many elderly people approach their death in an almost matter of fact type of way which may be difficult for others, particularly younger people, to accept. Miss King chose to kneel beside the reader throughout, and all the group listened carefully. A high emotional level developed and there opened up a real sharing of feelings about death and preparation for death – a very important task for the elderly person.

(2) Miss Paterson, a small hunchbacked lady, also lived alone, had very low self-esteem, and was depressed. A reading was given from *My Oedipus complex* by Frank O'Connor:[51] a witty chapter describing a five-year-old boy's rivalry with his father for his mother's affection. This stimulated the sharing of very personal accounts of early family relationships. Miss Paterson spoke about her parents' poor marriage relationship which was on the point of breaking up when her mother became pregnant. Both parents wanted a boy so when a girl was born she later felt unwanted. She also felt she was the only reason that her

parents stayed together. The group were very sympathetic and supportive. The significance of this was that this isolated lady with a long history of depression and hospital treatment had been enabled to share those feelings which burdened her, with a group of people whom she trusted and from whom she received support.

The group started in May 1981, and became self-sufficient in spring 1982 when staff were no longer needing to be involved, except to introduce new members. The group was still meeting in spring 1984. Many of the members have no other significant social contacts during the week and for them the Wednesday Group had become an important support. Other groups run on RT lines have also developed for long-term patients since this first group was set up.

Usefulness of the RT approach for the Wednesday Group

(1) The RT approach encouraged participation, lessened tension and a positive mood was engendered e.g. the collaborative poem gave both individuals and the group a sense of achievement and cohesion, and also served to facilitate the initial sharing of personal biographical information.

(2) The psychological distance afforded using RT aided the sharing of feelings and thoughts, and enabled the leaders to pick up on moods and themes emerging in the group.

(3) Despite covering such themes as death and loneliness, the group experienced many moments of joy and fun when otherwise withdrawn and depressed members were enabled to recite poetry, sing songs, share jokes and benefit from the support and appreciation of others.

(4) Finally the importance of reminiscing and life review as adaptive tasks of old age is well-established.[52] They provide an opportunity to relive happy times, times of achievement as well as painful ones too. This can improve a person's self-esteem and help resolve feelings about past events.

How effective is reading therapy?

As it has been my purpose to demonstrate the positive uses of RT, little has been said about any possible negative effects. Zaccaria *et al.* optimistically state that 'not a single study found bibliotherapy to be ineffective. . . . No-one has attacked the use of bibliotherapy on theoretical or ethical grounds either.'[53] They do however acknowledge that RT is not a panacea, that it cannot be used mechanically or indiscriminately, and that the technique is subject to certain limitations:

(1) Some people tend to rationalize or intellectualize their problems when reading about them.
(2) Reading imaginative literature may aggravate attempts to help the individual by raising his defenses.
(3) There is a tendency to believe that merely reading a piece of literature will resolve the problem.
(4) Insight gained through reading may be confused with the actual working through and coping behaviour required before the problem is solved.
(5) In some cases, fears and anxieties are reinforced by reading about mental health problems and the reader may actually acquire more symptoms.

They conclude that RT does not replace other techniques, that it is an adjunct to other types of helping relationships and that it cannot be used with all persons, in all settings and for all purposes.

The tested effectiveness of RT was the focus of a study carried out in 1980 by Schrank to provide an overview of all the findings and to look at implications for future research and practice.[54] The Pardecks in their recent book summarized these findings. RT was found to be effective in the following areas: assertiveness, attitude change, behavioural change, self development, and as a therapeutic technique. RT was not found to be effective for academic achievement, marital relations, reducing fear or changing self-concept.

Regarding implications for social work practice, the Pardecks state that RT focuses on the same strategies used by most persons in the helping professions including social workers. In social work, however, we are interested not only in psychotherapeutic intervention but in mobilizing community resources, i.e. affecting environmental systems. RT obviously has its greatest usefulness in its impact on the individual personality, but is a limited tool for changing environmental systems. The Pardecks suggest, however, that this can be partially overcome by using RT with families and other small group systems.

Schrank's conclusions on the effectiveness of RT were threefold:

(1) RT complements traditional patterns of counselling and psychotherapy with both individuals and groups.

(2) RT is useful to school counsellors and teachers as part of developmental programmes for students to help them gain an understanding of self and environment, find solutions to problems, and broaden interests and attitudes.

(3) RT requires further research as these outcome studies must stand the test of replications. There is also a need to develop an instrument to measure more accurately effects of RT, and a need to substantiate how, why and when it works.

Conclusion

Drawing upon my own limited experience of RT and the wider experience of others I do feel that RT should be viewed as an effective therapeutic tool which can be utilized by virtually all helping practitioners including social workers. In social work terms RT can be described as a third object technique providing an indirect, non-threatening approach which encourages minimal psychological defensiveness and maximal accessibility. The individual is respected as he determines the degree of identification, involvement and expression of feelings engendered. The appeal of the RT approach to my own working philosophy as a social worker is well expressed by Zaccaria *et al.*[55] when they say that RT is more than just a technique:

> It is an expression of a conception of man that envisions the individual as a unique and purposive being who strives for better mental health and personal adjustment. Bibliotherapy is an expression of a philosophy and an adjunctive type of helping relationship in which the practitioner attempts to help the student (or client) to maximize self-development through the media of didactic and imaginative literature.

Perhaps the final thought should be left to Cushla.[56] In summing up how books contributed to Cushla's development and quality of life, Dorothy Butler says that 'perhaps it was the characters themselves who helped Cushla as they went with her into the dark and lonely places that only she knew'.

So, in conclusion, we will leave the last word to the simplicity of a child who experientially knew the value of books. Recorded on 18 August 1975 when Cushla was just 3 years 8 months old, they tell us all we need to know. They were spoken as she settled herself on the sofa, her rag doll in her arms and the usual pile of books at her side: 'Now I can read to Looby Lou 'cause she's tired and sad and she needs a cuddle, and a bottle and a book.'

References

1 Maslow, A., 'The creative attitude' in Anderson, W. (ed.), *Therapy and the arts: tools of consciousness*, Harper and Row, 1977.
2 Sweeney, D., 'Bibliotherapy and the elderly' in Rubin, R. J. (ed.) *Bibliotherapy sourcebook*, Oryx Press: London, Mansell, 1978, 179–84.
3 Shrodes, C., *Bibliotherapy: a theoretical and clinical experimental study*, PhD dissertation, University of California, 1950.
4 Shiryon, M., 'Literatherapy: theory and applications', in Rubin, R. J. (ed.), *Bibliotherapy sourcebook*, *op.cit.*, 159–64.
5 Pardeck, J. A. and Pardeck, J. T., *Young people with problems: a guide to bibliotherapy*, Greenwood Press, 1984.
6 Lack, C. (ed.), *Bibliotherapy: an overview*, Chicago, American Library Association, 1981.
7 Rubin, R. J., 'Uses of bibliotherapy in response to the 1970's', *Library Trends*, Fall, 1979, 239–52.
8 Hoy, S., '"You're charging too little for the tea, me duck": library clubs for senior citizens in Leicestershire', *Health Libraries Review*, 1,(2), 1984, 99–104.
9 Butler, R. N., 'The life review: an interpretation of reminiscence in the aged', *Psychiatry*, 26, 1963, 65–76.
10 Valk, M., 'Reflections on the life of a group in a geriatric hospital', *Issues in Social Work Education*, 5,(1), Summer, 1985, 13–23.
11 Redhills Poetry Group, *Poetry from Redhills Hospital, Exeter*, League of Friends of Redhills Hospital, 1980.
12 Bostle, E., 'The listening club: a poetry and music activity', *Health Libraries Review*, 1,(4), 1984, 209–12.
13 Craft, R., *A report on a writing project at Fairfield Hospital, 5 March to 17 April 1985*, unpublished report.
14 Rubin, R. J., *Using bibliotherapy: a guide to theory and practice*, Oryx Press, London, Mansell, 1978.
15 Zaccaria, J. S., Moses, H. A. and Hollowell, J. S., *Bibliotherapy in rehabilitation, educational, and mental health settings: theory, research and practice*, Illinois, Stipes Pub. Co., 1978.
16 Pardeck, J. A. and Pardeck, J. T., 'An overview of the bibliotherapeutic treatment approach: implications for clinical social work practice', *Family Therapy*, XI, (3), 1984, 241–52.
17 Lerner, A., 'Editorial: a look at poetry therapy', *Art Psychotherapy: an International Journal*, 3,(1), 1976, i–ii.
18 Lippin, R. A., 'Poetry and poetry therapy: a conversation with Arthur Lerner', *The Arts in Psychotherapy*, 9, 1982, 167–74.
19 Hynes, A. M. and Hynes-Berry, M., *Bibliotherapy – the interactive process: a handbook*, Boulder, CO., 1986.
20 Elser, H., 'Bibliotherapy in practice', *Library Trends*, Spring, 1982, 647–59.
21 Allen, B., 'Bibliotherapy and the disabled', *Drexel Library Quarterly*, 16,(2), April 1981, 81–93.
22 Elser, H., *op.cit.*

23 Hynes, A., 'The goals of bibliotherapy', *The Arts in Psychotherapy*, 7,(1), 1980, 35–41.
24 Jalongo, M. R., 'Using crisis-oriented books with young children', *Young Children*, 38,(5), July 1983, 29–36.
25 Bernstein, J. E., *Books to help children cope with separation and loss*, Bowker & Co., 2nd ed., 1983.
26 Butler, D., *Cushla and her books*, London, Hodder and Stoughton, 1975.
27 Hallworth, G., *My mind is not in a wheelchair*, Hertfordshire Library Service, 1982.
28 Oaklander, V., *Windows to our children*, Real People Press, 1978.
29 Thom, M. and McLiver, C., *Bruce's story*, The Children's Society, 1986.
30 Paterson, A., *Maisie comes to Morningside*, Byway Books, 1984.
31 Williams, M., *The velveteen rabbit*, Carousel, 1976.
32 Morris, C. (ed.), *Literature and the social worker: a reading list for practitioners, teachers, students and voluntary workers*, London, The Library Association, 1975.
33 Millard, D. A., 'Literature and the therapeutic imagination', *British Journal of Social Work*, 7,(2), 1977, 173–84.
34 Miller, J., 'The use of autobiography in social work education', *British Journal of Social Work*, 11, 1981, 341–8.
35 Valk, M., 'The therapeutic imagination: a comment', *British Journal of Social Work*, 9,(1), 1979, 87–91.
36 Howie, M., 'Bibliotherapy in social work', *British Journal of Social Work*, 13, 1983, 287–319.
37 Pardeck, J. A. and Pardeck, J. T., *op.cit.*
38 Thom, M. and McLiver, C., *op.cit.*
39 Thom, M., 'How books can be used to help children cope with separation and loss', summary included in the 'Report on Reading Therapy Sub-Group study day at the Scottish Health Service Centre, 16 October 1985', *Health Libraries Review*, 3,(2), June 1986, 126–8.
40 Howie, M., *op.cit.*
41 Moyes, I., *The psychiatry of old age*, SK & F Publications, 1980.
42 Ritchie, J. T. R., *The singing street*, Edinburgh and London, Oliver and Boyd, 1964.
43 Ritchie, J. T. R., *The golden city*, Edinburgh and London, Oliver and Boyd, 1965.
44 McTell, R., Song *Streets of London*, London, Essex Music International, 1968.
45 Blythe, R., *The view of winter; reflections of old age*, Harmondsworth, Penguin Books, 1981.
46 O'Connor, F., *My Oedipus complex and other stories*, Harmondsworth, Penguin Books, 1963.
47 Reilly, C. (comp.), *Scars upon my heart – women's poetry and verse of the 1st World War*, London, Virago, 1981.
48 Grenfell, J., *Requests the pleasure*, London, Macmillan, 1976.

49 *Edinburgh 1929–79: 50 years of change*, Edinburgh City Libraries, 1979.
50 Blythe, R., *op.cit.*
51 O'Connor, F., *op.cit.*
52 Butler, R. N., *op.cit.*
53 Zaccaria, J. S. *et al.*, *op.cit.*
54 Schrank, F. A. and Engels, D. W., 'Bibliotherapy as a counselling adjunct: research findings', *The Personnel and Guidance Journal*, November 1981, 143–7.
55 Zaccaria, J. S. *et al.*, *op.cit.*
56 Butler, D., *op.cit.*

3 Reading and insight

Clare Gillies

Most people view the reading of novels as a pleasurable escape and, as such, a therapeutic activity. I suggest that selected novels can do more than aid escape, they can help each of us to develop a deeper understanding of ourselves and of others, and furthermore that this understanding is necessary for health and fulfilment.

Scholarly analyses of literature are concerned for the most part with style and characterization and few with the emotional impact that it has upon the reader. It may be said that to use literature for therapy is to debase it. I contend, however, that creative literature describes the vast number of influences on man's development as well as the complexity and diversity of his feelings and by doing so can illuminate and deepen the reader's knowledge of his inner world, that world that is often hidden from himself as well as from others. For the purpose of this paper I have called this knowledge insight. Everyone has flashes of insight, some more profound than others. In that it enriches human relationships, it is as rare and precious as musical or artistic talent. All great writers have it, certain professionals have to try to acquire it and to do so study sociology, psychology and philosophy. My theme is that the study of literature may serve the purpose as well and that everyone, in knowing themselves better would be more tolerant of their own failings and of others.

The term insight is ambiguous and complex and has its roots in religion, science and philosophy, but is most commonly used in psychology although here in a variety of ways reflecting the theoretical stance of the user.[1] In using the term I am referring to a quality of human understanding that sees below the surface, that understands the motives and feelings that may be at odds with expressed attitudes. It can perceive the nature of feelings that are complex, contradictory or fearful. Motives and emotions are often kept hidden in case their acknowledgement should offend others or disturb the pattern of established behaviour, or, most fearfully, change or even destroy important relationships. No one has complete insight and we all indulge in a degree of self deception; it is possible that we use a great deal of emotional energy keeping reality from ourselves and others. Thus many human contacts lack spontaneity and openness. The feelings that are most disturbing are those which differ from those considered by convention to be correct or praiseworthy.

To illustrate these ideas and at the same time look at the value of fiction it is useful to consider attitudes to disability. Most people feel sympathy or pity for another who suffers from mental or physical disability and see the relative or friend who cares for them as good and loving. It is easy to assume that the sick person is cared for through kindness and compassion. The carer who acts from a sense of duty and who is resentful will almost certainly feel guilty too. He may think these feelings are too bad to admit to himself and others and in denying them work even more painstakingly for the patient at the cost of his own health and lifestyle. A novel by Dick Francis, *Forfeit*,[2] not great literature but a decidedly good read, captures the complexity of such a relationship. Barbara Pym, writing with subtlety and compassion in *Excellent Women*,[3] captures the deceptive web that a mother and daughter have woven to fit in with a perceived view that the ageing parent needed the younger woman's presence. The television series *Steptoe and Son*, none the less moving because it made us laugh, showed how false were the glibly ascribed roles of needer and needed. If fiction is able to reflect for the reader his complicated and sometimes shameful feelings he feels less alone. He is, as it were, given permission to think and to feel those things that he has hitherto considered unacceptable.

The knowledge that most people can gain from personal experience is limited although we may believe, as Agatha Christie's Miss Marple does, that all life can be seen in a microcosm. For most of us, however, we can only guess at the feelings of someone whose environment and conditions are different from our own, so that a young white woman may sympathize with the plight of a woman, old, poor and black, but to perceive the world as she does requires creative imagination and the will to do so of a very high order. Literature can help us to make this imaginative leap. There are, for example, many textbooks about ageing and the plight of the elderly but none of these have the power to move the reader to tears or to inspire a passion to relieve the pain of the old mentally confused as does Paul Bailey's *At the Jerusalem*.[4] Should not this book and *Bruno's dream*,[5] *The poorhouse fair*,[6] as well as *The room upstairs*,[7] be compulsory reading for all aspiring geriatricians and social workers? All these books add to our understanding of the losses of old age in terms so persuasive that they cannot be dismissed as mere theory. Another novel that can take the reader into the lonely, frightening world of someone quite different from oneself is *Walter*[8] by David Cook. The emotional impact is searing and one is left wondering how anyone who writes as elegantly can share, and demand that the reader shares, the inner life of a mentally handicapped young man. Cook continues to take us into the different and difficult world of others in his most recent book *Missing persons*.[9] He is at his most convincing when he writes about the circular, enclosed world of frail people. Once one has been given such a powerful picture it is impossible to deny it.

To start to examine the ideas of novels inviting the reader into other peoples' inner lives and so increase the reader's understanding well beyond his own experience, is to produce longer and longer lists of fine books. *The secret diary of Adrian Mole*[10] is a great success, not only because it is amusing and well-written, but also because Sue Townsend captures the vulnerability of young people; the sadness of so much energy expended on worrying about those things that older people come to see as inconsequential. The anguish of adolescence is in the *Secret diary* and in sounding echoes of our own youth may increase our sensitivity to those still in the midst of these growing pains. *The bell jar* goes further along this line in its description of a young girl who did not come through adolescence undamaged psychologically and is particularly poignant in the light of the suicide of the author, Sylvia Plath.[11] Such novels as these are rich in comment about attitudes, emotions and relationships so that we can acquire deeper understanding as we take pleasure in them.

Novels can be used in a disciplined and structured way in the education and training of members of the caring professions. I discuss in the remainder of this paper ways of using literature in the training of social workers, but it could be used to equal effect with students of medicine. It is considered important that social workers should be sensitive, and one of the aims of training is therefore to promote sensitivity; literature is valuable as a means to this end. Sensitivity is distrusted by those who hold that the most urgent suffering is the poverty induced by capitalism, and that social workers should devote themselves to campaigning against such conditions. Sensitivity increases effectiveness, however, whatever method is used. It is essential that if the worker is to be able to respond effectively to the needs and attitudes of other people with whom he will be in contact in his job, whether the others are emotionally damaged clients, clients who are socially deprived or even landlords or city councillors.

One important effect of the use of literature is that it enables the student to integrate his theoretical teaching. Since literature describes the multifaceted nature of man and his environment, the student learns to see the conjunctive relevance of theories of psychology and sociology that in the classroom teaching may seem to be in conflict. It is true that he can learn to see this in his fieldwork, though the development of this integration can be limited by the quality of the field supervision and can, of course, be hampered also by the student's own involvement in the situation, by his need to be effective with the client, or even to justify in theoretical terms action that he has already taken. To some extent he is relieved of the stress of this kind of involvement in the study of literature.

An added value of the use of fiction is that it introduces or reinforces the idea that within such writing lies wisdom and knowledge about human experience. I hope, therefore, some students will read some of the recommended books again in the future, when their own development enables them to make better use of them. In other words, I hope that literature may become an inexhaustible source of insight with which to measure their understanding after the course has finished, and throughout their professional life.

A social worker has to learn to communicate effectively with a wide range of people. Much of the early learning is about the limitations of words in conveying ideas, and about the effect of role, authority and eloquence on getting an idea across. Often I use Gore Vidal's *The Messiah*[12] to provoke discussion on this, since it allows full exploration about the social, cultural and personal elements in effective communication, and feelings about manipulation are freed as well. Kobo Abe's *The face of another*[13] is, I think, a much more sensitive novel about human communication, but it is essentially despairing. It brings students to the realization of the triviality of most social contact, and for some, the lack of spiritual contact even in some relationships accepted as intimate. I use this for discussion only when I am reasonably sure that the group contains no one particularly sensitive in this area, or when I am confident that I can use the sadness creatively in the group, and the insight can be reinforced by the personal tutors.

Social workers often have to work with families or groups where one member is disliked or blamed by the others. They have to understand the nature of this scapegoating before attempting to remedy it. Malamud's *The fixer*[14] is an eloquent and moving account of a scapegoat. It illustrates the victimization of a Jew during the pogroms in Russia. The man is burdened not only with racial guilt, but also with problems stemming from an inability to maintain his marriage. In the picture of the guilt-laden man all the themes, sociological as well as psychological, are mirrored, and the inevitability of his self-selection made clear, as well as the historical and social reasons for his selection by others. The study of this book does more than illustrate the many facets of scapegoating as we use it in social work, it illuminates the nature of human co-existence, and individual performance in many different groups far beyond those studies on the course. It often leads to a more sensitive understanding of prejudice and fear.

Students of social work courses frequently fear that studying human development closely and looking for motivation in all behaviour will make them become mechanistic. As so much of the students' energy is given to disciplined intellectual learning that can seem to reduce man to a mass of theories, conflicting theories moreover, his emotional development has to be specifically addressed. In his struggle to understand, to develop the controlled emotional involvement so much talked about in social casework textbooks, the student can form the impression that he should have no emotional response to clients and fears that somehow his spontaneity and his ability for warm response have been taken from him. The use of Patrick White's *The solid mandala*[15] is an example of a way of freeing the student's emotions. This is a disturbing yet compassionate story of two brothers tied together; the student can rage about the waste, the sadness of the brothers' need for each other, and the crippling effect in both of the neurotic ways in which qualities such as goodness and wisdom are distributed between them by common consent and by the collusion of others. If the strength of feeling, albeit different feelings, is shared by most of the group, including the tutor, then the student comes to be more comfortable with his own strong feelings and, hopefully, more able to look at himself and at others, unafraid that he will be overwhelmed by his emotions. It is easier to release this emotional energy with fiction than with case discussions, not only because it seems 'safer', but also because the student is freed of the necessity to plan future work and clarify aims, and yet the need to integrate and take account of one's own emotional response is learnt. I suspect that many social workers feel powerless to help individuals within an unjust social system because they are afraid to share the feelings of sadness and frustration of the client in his personal relationships, and so their energy is spent in complaints against social inequalities, to the detriment of clients who need help immediately. When one releases the students' feelings about fictional characters, such as the brothers Waldo and Patrick in Patrick White's book, the discussion reveals such a range of strength and type that the students' fear that they will be moulded by their education into stereotyped social workers can also be dispelled.

In all my contacts with students I find myself recommending literature, so that sometimes I accuse myself of proselytizing. I wish to share with them the pleasure that I find in the richness and variety of literature, and I am saddened when, for example, a sincere, but slow-moving student struggles with a vast textbook and ends up knowing the sociological definition of labelling, but has achieved little understanding of what this means to people; such people as the boy in *Kes*,[16] the young man in *The loneliness of the long distance runner*,[17] as Doris Lessing's voice in *The golden notebook*.[18] If students have to prepare tutorial notes or write essays, I expect literature to be quoted as much as textbooks. Could one, for example, write a balanced and apposite comment on woman's role in society without having read Simone de Beauvoir, Violette Leduc or Doris Lessing?

I use literature, therefore, in teaching social work for the following reasons: firstly, it brings all theories together to a focus on human behaviour, and counteracts the tendency in social work education to segment and reduce man by opting for either the functionalist or interactionalist approach in explaining his behaviour. Secondly, literature is about the world outside, outside the student group, outside the course, but since the experience is echoed or extended the relevance of the immediate group learning is enhanced. Thirdly, literature is unarguably about people, and yet the theories apply there too. From a study of Solzhenitsyn's novels for example, one can achieve an understanding of the corrosive effects of institutionalization, that awakens concern for men and women in prison.[19,20,21] The fourth reason is the effect of literature on the students' use of words; this is so obvious that I only make the point because it is so important. The student, if he reads widely in selected literature, increases his vocabulary, learns how to express shades of meaning and writes grammatically.

The greatest benefit in the use of literature originates from the fact that there is no right or wrong way of interpreting it. The personal impact of any piece of work can be extended by discussion with others; the group discussion activates mutual learning and takes away from the teacher the responsibility and the status of seeming to have all the knowledge. Since much of the group's learning is concerned with the individual's acceptance and use of his own authority, this is invaluable; I could not as easily or as honestly move away from the position as the apex of the group if I were teaching theory didactically.

My final comment concerns my own teaching. I believe that the use of literature helps me to keep an approach to teaching about human behaviour which is fresh with the sense of discovery, for many of the same reasons that it is of value to students. Well-accepted theories can make a new impact through a novelist's presentation of individuals, relationships and societies. Moreover, I find a sense of personal achievement in bringing together the theories and the insights, and in helping others towards this discovery; I do not find the same satisfaction from reading textbooks, however fully illustrated with case histories, because in such books the links are made for me and the knowledge presented in such ways that it is lost more easily than knowledge acquired through a personal search. In reading fiction with students, I am able to share with them the search for increased insight, and so share with them too the doubts and the excitement that are involved in any exploration of human relationships.

References

1 Yelloly, M., 'Insight', in Jehu, D. *et al.*, *Behaviour modification in social casework*, Chichester, Wiley-Interscience, 1972.
2 Francis, D., *Forfeit*, London, Pan Books, 1970.
3 Pym, B., *Excellent women*, Harmondsworth, Penguin Books, 1980.
4 Bailey, P., *At the Jerusalem*, Harmondsworth, Penguin Books, 1982.
5 Murdock, I., *Bruno's dream*, Harmondsworth, Penguin Books, 1977.
6 Updike, J., *The poorhouse fair*, Harmondsworth, Penguin Books, 1980.
7 Dickens, M., *The room upstairs*, London, Heinemann, 1966.
8 Cook, D., *Walter*, Harmondsworth, Penguin Books, 1980.
9 Cook, D., *Missing persons*, Secker and Warburg, 1986.
10 Townsend, S., *The secret diary of Adrian Mole aged 13¾*, London, Methuen, 1985.

11 Plath, S., *The bell jar*, London, Faber, 1967.
12 Vidal, G., *The Messiah*, London, Heinemann, 1968.
13 Abe, K., *The face of another*, Harmondsworth, Penguin Books, 1972.
14 Malamud, B., *The fixer*, Harmondsworth, Penguin Books, 1969.
15 White, P., *The solid mandala*, Harmondsworth, Penguin Books, 1974.
16 Hines, B., *A kestrel for a knave*, Harmondsworth, Penguin Books, 1969.
17 Sillitoe, A., *The loneliness of the long distance runner*, London, Pan books, 1985.
18 Lessing, D., *The golden notebook*, London, Panther, 1973.
19 Solzhenitsyn, A., *Cancer ward*, Harmondsworth, Penguin Books, 1971.
20 Solzhenitsyn, A., *The first circle*, London, Fontana, 1983.
21 Solzhenitsyn, A., *One day in the life of Ivan Denisovich*, Harmondsworth, Penguin Books, 1970.

4 Two sides of the same story – issues in directed reading: a Probation perspective

D. R. Morris-Jones

'Misery acquaints a man with strange bedfellows.'

Shakespeare, *Tempest*, Act II Sc.II.

Although it was a shipwreck that prompted the above I find it a useful starting point for this chapter. Many recipients of the services of the Probation Department find themselves and their lives wrecked by offending behaviour and the purpose of any intervention whilst having to take account of clearing the immediate debris of recent behaviour must focus on the reasons or causes of such behaviour.

The Probation Service has in recent years been going through a process of rediscovery prompted by the need to clearly define objectives. The process of intervention with clients, however, remains an area of some confusion. There is beginning to emerge a body of research and opinion based on hard data which is pushing some areas in the direction of particular approaches. One such approach has its basis in a social skills approach which is an attempt to establish and then remedy the lack of particular skills held by an individual or group.

A very comprehensive account of the approach can be found in McGuire and Priestley's book *Offending behaviour*;[1] in that context they sum up as follows:

> The proposal that some forms of problematic behaviour may be explicable in terms of a lack or breakdown of social skills amongst those who exhibit them and further that the problem behaviour might be rectified were the individuals given help to bring their social skills onto an equal footing with others.

Another development would be the recognition that the effective handling of crime is not the prerogative of one agency but the responsibility of all of us. Whilst one agency may be charged with particular responsibilities the effective discharge of that responsibility can only occur if account is taken of all other resources available within the community.

Thus those in difficulties when directed to one particular agency may well find themselves assisted by a number of different people representing a wide range of disciplines.

Indeed tradition has linked a number of agencies or individuals together but innovation and fresh approaches have introduced some surprising alliances as well – or as the opening quotation suggests – created strange bedfellows.

One such relationship, when taken at face value seems puzzling, is the library service and the Probation Service and it is perhaps worth spending a little more time to develop the background to this.

The Probation Service in piecemeal fashion had been concerned about the lack of literacy skills amongst its charges. Certainly some research findings suggested that it was a critical problem for many and this was particularly demonstrated by informal research carried out within the penal establishments. In the 1981–3 period an attempt was certainly made under the sponsorship of the Adult Literacy and Basic Skills Unit and the direction of the Welsh Joint Education Council to give priority to this work in Wales and to provide some central themes for intervention and clearly this type of approach was also going on elsewhere.

The difficulties experienced by probation officers related to their clients inability to sustain interest in a 'teaching' relationship and the need therefore was to seek out other models which would hold their attention. This was thwarted on many occasions by lack of appropriate literature and some sterling work was done to counteract this by 'home-made' packages of very high standard.

At a local level in Dyfed at this time consultation developed with the library service in an attempt to organize access to any literature resources. The key to the direct reading programme however was what the response of individuals within the library was to this and the notions of bibliotherapy very much underpinned those developments.

Like any other agency the library was facing difficult economic decisions. George Cunningham,[2] for instance, commenting on the Annual Report on Public Libraries indicated the scale of the problem: 'If present trends continue there will be a relentless deterioration in the library service . . . what is the value of a magnificent collection if the staff are not there . . . to provide professional advice?'

Indeed it was that fundamental issue of the role of libraries and its staff that we had to address. If one accepts that the library is a service to the whole community and indeed has a responsibility to disadvantaged members of the community then we might have some common ground to start off with and fortunately that was the prevailing view at the time.

Thus on one hand there was the Probation Service wishing to develop strategies of intervention for its clients based initially on the premise that many lacked basic literacy skills. Some evidence existed to suggest that the lack of skills contributed in the causal chain of offending behaviour and thus it was right and proper to intervene. On the other hand was a library service, with vast resources of material, which was anxious to promote the idea that the library was not a moribund institution which simply sat reactive and passive to demands of those able to make demands but was a vibrant progressive force within a community, anxious to meet the needs of that community and perhaps pay special attention to the needs of those disadvantaged or disabled members of the community.

Once the ground rules were established the phase of an experimental interventionist strategy in the lives of the clients of both agencies could start. At its core was the recognition that books and other forms of art and literature could have an immense influence on people but any intervention had to be controlled and sustained. There also had to be a recognition not only of individual need but of different processes of intervention.

In a sense a compatible philosophy is to be found in the logotherapeutic approach and Joseph Fabry[3] sums up the sameness in reflecting on the crux of the approach: 'As long as we treat human beings as animals that can be trained, and machines that can be manipulated, we make them into animals and machines. If we make them aware of the resources of their human spirit we help them lift themselves into their true humanness.'

There in any event existed a growing expertise in the use of directed reading in group work situations and a developing recognition of its effectiveness with individuals. As a strategy for intervention it can form the basis for professional intervention but the dangers of a fragmented approach can only be remedied by a very close relationship developing between the appropriate agencies and a recognition of demarcation of skills. As a probation officer my skills lay in diagnosis; the librarian's skill lay in selecting appropriate material. Whilst they may sound rather simplistic statements they both have fundamental problems. A diagnosis needs to be formed in such a way that there is sufficient information contained within it to allow for judgements to be made as to the best way to intervene. The diagnosis needs to be shared with a professional from a different discipline and so issues such as trust, lack of jargon etc. are important. The selection of materials, whilst crucial to any developmental work, is probably the most difficult area. While lists and precis are available it may be unrealistic to expect a librarian to have both the time and skill to be able to select appropriate material and the process of selection needs to occupy a considerable amount of planning time. Some of the most dramatic accounts I have encountered occur because a particular passage or section has been selected for use which is so pertinent that it becomes the springboard for effective intervention. In terms of the actual practice Mary Howie,[4] in her excellent article, commented on the effectiveness of this method with children.

This is one area where a great deal of development is taking place particularly in relation to adoption and fostering. In terms of divorce experience however the child is uniquely placed. Very often the problems of divorce focus on the child in terms of disputes over actual custody or access and the intervention is geared to the parents with very little emphasis given to the child. An effective way to counteract this is to enlist the parents' help in introducing the child to selected reading material. The calming effect of a parent explaining separation can be a profound vehicle for positive communication in helping the child to come to terms with a new situation or removing feelings of guilt. The emphasis on some positive development can also be quite helpful as can be found for instance in the book *Two homes to live in* by Barbara Shook Hazen.[5]

One feature of this type of book is the link between the illustrations used and the written word. Where told as a story the cues that children pick up from pictures is very often more telling than words. One book I have used in this manner related to a young child whose mother had a drink problem and it was clear that the detail of illustration drove home the points very clearly.[6] Another series demonstrates this point and its aim is to provide a reassuring context for a child at a time of transition – such as entry into a new school.[7]

There is a tremendous potential in this area and a recent scan of available material suggests there has been something of a quiet revolution in the type of experimental books for young children. On a personal level I found it useful to use a book,[8] based on a family of rabbits who were moving, to explain to my then four-year-old son Matthew why we were moving house, in order to restore some calmness and reduce anxiety by seeing the positive and normal side of moving.

There may be a suggestion that we are over-protective to our children when problems occur and perhaps it reflects our own difficulties in finding a way to communicate with them without feeling embarrassed or guilty that is the real problem. The use of such books is an excellent vehicle for doing so but the lack of any coordination makes it very difficult for practice. It would surely be a very worthwhile task for someone to undertake a review of this work and with some guidelines publish a handbook so that at least the material becomes accessible, understandable and standardizes the selection process.

Some further developmental work in relation to children who are victims of sexual abuse demonstrates the extent to which the approach can overstep boundaries. A particular approach using arts therapy is worth considering and an excellent pioneering account can be found in an article by Connie E. Naitove.[9] Here the powerful nature of this process is aptly demonstrated and case studies reveal the true tenor of such therapeutic interventions at a time of crises for the very vulnerable.

Whilst not literature the basic philosophy can be demonstrated through the use by caseworkers of a geneogram in helping some adopted children and their families resolve problems and difficulties. A brief but comprehensive account of this process is described by Bob Finch and Penelope Jacques.[10] These approaches whilst having their philosophies in a different context, nevertheless demonstrate the capacity of forms of literature/art in very difficult and emotionally charged situations.

It would be outside my brief to dwell on a social skills type approach in group work but again I would merely emphasize that the use of selected material in this field certainly appears effective. As films, videos and computers become more and more available so the challenge relates not merely to coordinating material but must also take account of technological developments.

In establishing programmes for individual clients some reservations were expressed in relation to the seriousness of crimes committed in the sense of the appropriateness of intervention whilst other views focused on the literacy ability of clients and their lack of motivation.

In the pilot project at Cardigan initially most of those reservations were dealt with fairly quickly. The clients appeared to welcome a different approach and were interested and committed to it. Lack of reading ability was overcome by the use of talking books which proved effective particularly when the author him- or her- self spoke the words. The nature of the offence was a secondary factor because intervention is geared to a specific or task-related purpose leaving other aspects of supervision or oversight to be pursued as part of the overall strategy.

As an interventionist strategy it provided a mechanism to overcome blocks. Very often a position of stalemate is reached in a relationship and indeed the client may be unable to express or discuss experiences which are so painful in a normal setting.

Morrice,[11] talking specifically about the use of poetry with an individual puts it well and it holds true for other forms of literature: 'It may be that poetry reading and poetry making gave her a suitable language in which to talk to me and to herself. At one and the same time, I suspect, it gave her access to and expression of deep emotion while presenting a necessary space and distance.'

An example of this related to a young isolated client who avoided talking about his family. The problem was identified as involving the father and based on that information guidance was sought as to appropriate reading. As an illiterate the method also required some thought. The library suggested use of Freddie Trueman's own life story,[12] where a critical passage related to his own view of his father and the difficulties of that relationship. Using that in a cassette featuring Trueman himself the client was able to start talking about his own father through another's experience and indeed in terms of this relationship it fitted in with the theory of bibliotherapy as we understand it and as related so effectively and simply by Monroe's,[13] analysis of the process:

1. Read (or view or listen)
2. Identify with an element in the situation
3. Experience vicariously
4. Catharsis
5. Insight
6. Change in attitude or behaviour.

The cathartic process indeed demonstrated the power of this technique which when carefully controlled actually allowed a relationship to develop and remove blocks,[14] 'If problems are resolved, guilt removed, hope restored, alternatives opened, then actions are privileged to change and attitudes toward self and others are revised'.

In terms of linking in with issues directly related to offending behaviour there is much that can be done and a lot of lessons to be learnt from this type of approach.

A number of works focus on relationships and a variety of relationships are explored in terms of violence, aggression, jealousy and guilt. A mistake can be made in thinking of material in terms of unsuitability. In a sense when judgements are made about the nature of certain works the process of denying access begins. By making such judgements an insiduous form of censorship emerges instead of the fresh innovative and open approach so necessary. Indeed in one rather difficult situation some classic works – or key passages from them – were used to stimulate discussion. The case involved a young man who had been imprisoned for rape but was reconciled to his victim on release. The fear of physical violation remained and caused a steady deterioration in the relationship leaving them very tense and unable to communicate. The use of directed reading eventually led to a process which actually enabled the couple to re-start communicating. Their referral from another probation officer at a time when I was leaving the area actually demonstrated that the approach had gained credibility as a legitimate social work method of intervention. Both the strength and weakness of the approach lies within its apparent simplicity. Its strength because when two systems operate in understanding it is a relatively simple process to begin – its weakness is that the very notion of reading leads to an under-estimation of the very powerful forces that it can unleash. Its potential, which is where the directed reading process took us, showed at least how strange bedfellows could become close associates and indeed utilize their joint and respective skills in pursuit of the relief of the miserable condition of some of their charges which ultimately can only benefit the community at large.

A poem sums up for me the validity of the approach:

But what strange art, what magic
can dispose
The troubled mind to change its
native woes? . . .
This, books can do; – nor this alone,
they give
New views to life, and teach us
how to live,
They soothe the griev'd, the stubborn
they chastise.
Fools they admonish, and
confirm the wise.

(Lines from George Crabbe's poem 'The Library')

References

1 McGuire, J. and Priestley, P., *Offending behaviour skills and stratagems for going straight*, London, Batsford Academic, 1985, 80.
2 Cunningham, G., 'A testing time for libraries', *Sunday Times*, 2 March, 1986, 42.
3 Fabry, J., 'The frontiers of Logotherapy', *International Forum for Logotherapy*, 4,(1), 1981, 3–11.
4 Howie, M., 'Bibliotherapy in social work', *British Journal of Social Work*, 13, 1983, 287–319.
5 Hazen, B. S., *Two homes to live in – a child's eye view of divorce*, London, Human Sciences Press, 1978.
6 Kenny, K. and Krull, H., *Sometimes my Mum drinks too much*, Oxford, Blackwell Raintree, 1980.
7 'Sumiko', *My baby brother Ned* and *My school*, London, Picture Corgi, 1985.
8 Carruth, J., *Moving house*, London, Horizon, 1982.
9 Naitove, E. C., 'Arts therapy with sexually abused children', in *Handbook of clinical intervention in child sexual abuse*, Massachusetts, Lexington Books, 1982, 269–308.
10 Finch, B. and Jacques, P., 'Use of the Geneogram with adoptive families', *Adoption and Fostering*, 9,(3), 1985, 35–40.
11 Morrice, J. K. W., 'Poetry as therapy', *British Journal of Medical Psychology*, 56, 1983, 367–70.
12 Trueman, F., *The thoughts of Fred Trueman: every cricket maniac's anthology*, London, Macdonald and Janes, 1978.
13 Monroe, M. E., 'A bibliotherapeutic model for library service' in Rubin, R. J. (ed.), *Bibliotherapy sourcebook*, Oryx, London, Mansell, 1978, 257–67.
14 *Ibid.*

5 Directed reading in behavioural psychotherapy

Andrew Quarry

The use of reading as a therapeutic activity tends, in general, to reflect the philosophies, principles and objectives of the different therapies which employ it. The contribution of reading to the practice of behavioural psychotherapy is therefore best understood by first looking at the characteristics which make this style of therapy so distinctive and the kinds of problems for which it is used.

It is probably true to say that the majority of people who are referred for specific psychological treatment within the National Health Service will, in fact, receive some form of behavioural psychotherapy. Its practitioners will tend to be either psychologists or nurses who have had specialized training but, increasingly, its techniques are being used or adapted by other professionals such as psychiatrists or occupational therapists. There are a number of reasons for its growing popularity. Firstly, it is at least as effective as other therapies for most common psychological problems and could be considered the treatment of choice for some of the more crippling disorders such as severe obsessions. Secondly, its procedures often have a 'commonsense' quality which makes them readily understood by and acceptable to a wide range of clients. This also means that some of the techniques can be successfully carried out by personnel who do not have a full knowledge of the theoretical background, e.g. nursing aides. Thirdly, when compared to other therapies, the techniques tend to be more economical in the use of therapist time. In the current jargon, they are more 'cost-effective', an important if sometimes over-emphasized quality in a public service where resources are limited.

The behavioural approach makes the basic assumption that most, if not all, psychological problems are best viewed as instances of faulty learning. The client who comes for therapy is considered to have learned ways of perceiving or responding to particular, often stressful, situations which are somehow 'maladaptive'. Essentially, a maladaptive reaction is one which prevents a person from dealing effectively with their environment or which obstructs the achievement of personal goals. For instance, the inability to make conversation will clearly hamper the attainment of the goal of making friends. Equally, an obsessive concern with checking for errors would badly affect a person's ability to complete tasks and might even result in unemployment. Such maladaptive reactions are normally accompanied by persistent, unpleasant emotional states such as anxiety, anger or depression. Clients at first are often overwhelmed by such feelings and tend to be less aware of the behaviour or thoughts of which they are a byproduct.

The range of problems to which behavioural therapy can be applied is wide. Particularly common are those which are anxiety-based. Anxiety has many causes and can be provoked by a variety of objects and situations. This diversity is reflected in the types of problem referred. These can range from quite specific fears such as animal or insect phobias to more general worries such as those related to lack of confidence or low self-esteem. Depression is another typical complaint. Like anxiety it can be linked with many different kinds of life events or stresses. Other problems might include sexual or marital difficulties, alcohol or drug abuse, social interaction difficulties, obsessions and compulsions and self-control disorders, such as anorexia or bulimia.

An important point is that, although we may use labels like 'anxiety', 'depression' etc. for convenience, this does not imply that there is a standard treatment for each condition. While therapy may indeed be governed by general principles and use certain standard techniques, each case has to be considered on its own merits. For instance, anxieties which appear to be alike are often seen, on closer examination, to be quite dissimilar. Two clients may both suffer from a fear of being in large crowds. One, however, may be afraid of becoming trapped and fainting while the other is more frightened of the prospect of someone being sick. The implications for therapy are obviously different in each case.

Even when the main problem is the same, the inevitable differences in client characteristics or circumstances will affect the therapist's approach. Therapeutic strategies therefore need to be individualized or customized rather than be applied in a rigid, 'cookbook' fashion. One advantage of using books in therapy is that their wide variety and easy availability make them particularly well-adapted to the needs of such an approach.

The main task of the therapist is to offer the client a framework for understanding his problem, to explore with him possible causes and to help him develop more effective ways of coping with it. Contrary to popular belief, this does not necessarily involve a detailed analysis of childhood relationships or a strong emphasis on the development of insight. Instead, the behavioural therapist tries to arrive at an explanation in terms of what is known, in a scientific sense, about how people learn. The history of the problem is not, of course, ignored but attention is mostly given to current factors which are responsible for maintaining it.

How does this distinction work in practice? A person with agoraphobia (a fear of open or public places) who attends a traditional, 'psycho-dynamic' (i.e. non-behavioural) therapist might have their condition explained as the result of early 'separation anxiety'. In other words, the experience of anxiety which the agoraphobic person feels as he increases his distance from a 'safe' figure would be said to have its roots in the experience of panic or helplessness on being separated from a parent in childhood.

A behavioural explanation, on the other hand, would emphasize the fact that the person has learned the habit of avoiding or escaping from situations in which he feels panic and that he has become 'trapped' in this reaction because, paradoxically, it is so successful in providing short-term freedom from discomfort. He has inadvertently learnt a strategy which, though it works up to a point, is ultimately maladaptive because of the way in which it places increasing restrictions on the person's life.

There is no simple way of deciding which of the above explanations is the 'right' one. It is even possible that they could both be regarded as being correct, if partial, views of the same situation. From the point of view of effective therapy, the correctness or otherwise of the explanation is not, however, as important as it's implications for action.

Those who advocate the 'separation anxiety' explanation would be likely to stress the need for the client to gain insight into the childhood experiences which originally gave rise to the anxiety and are assumed to be the root cause of it. Treatment of the symptoms or the outward manifestations of the condition would not be expected to be very effective and might even be considered to result in the appearance of new and different symptoms. A behaviour therapist would be less concerned with helping the client come to terms with early trauma but would be keen to encourage the use of more adaptive ways of dealing with the problem as it currently presents. In this sense, therapy can be regarded as a largely educational process. The therapist acts as a kind of teacher and consciously tries to provide the conditions which will maximize the probability that the client will learn better coping strategies.

This raises the question of how we know what are the optimal conditions for learning and also which strategies are the ones most likely to produce a successful outcome. The honest answer is that we cannot always be certain what will work in a given set of circumstances. Sometimes different methods or techniques have to be tried out during therapy itself to discover which suits the client best. The sessions may develop into what might be described as a series of mini-experiments where the therapist and client collaborate to test out which ideas are most effective. In fact, the notion of treatment as a real-life experiment or an exercise in applied psychology emphasizes another major characteristic of behavioural therapy, the belief in the value of the scientific method as a way of discovering effective therapeutic techniques.

The methods which are used most commonly in behavioural therapy are usually based on principles derived from academic psychological research and have been tested out in controlled clinical studies. Such studies are essentially controlled experiments where selected groups of clients are given different 'treatments' in the attempt to find out which works best. For instance, it is now known that exposure to the feared situation is an important ingredient in the effective treatment of phobias. This fact only became clear after this method had been compared to others of equal plausibility e.g. simple relaxation, and was found to be superior. In theory, any potentially valuable treatment method can be assessed in this way.

Of course, in planning treatment, therapists cannot always wait for research to provide the right solution. If existing methods are inadequate, they often have to try out new ideas which have not had the benefit of rigorous testing. In a sense, this is where the creative aspect of behaviour therapy lies. The therapist is always free to incorporate new procedures provided that professional and clinical guidelines are adhered to and the effects carefully measured. At the present time, prescribed or directed reading could probably be said to fall within this general category. It is not yet a well-established therapeutic practice but potentially has a great deal to offer. Already research into reading therapy is beginning to appear in psychological literature.[1,2] In time, such studies may be able to identify which features of it are of most value.

Reading can be used in several different ways depending upon the focus of therapy. Although the central goal of therapy is change and most techniques are designed to generate or accelerate change in a positive direction, there are a number of areas in which change can occur. Short-term therapy will tend to emphasize one or other of these though not necessarily to the exclusion of the rest. We can develop a more concrete idea of the ways in which reading can be beneficial by identifying those areas and examining them in a little more detail.

Broadly speaking, therapy may involve change in three main areas, i.e. behaviour, beliefs and feelings. It is perhaps appropriate to deal with *behaviour* first. As the name implies, behavioural therapy has traditionally been more concerned with the factors which influence behaviour than any other aspect of human functioning. Some of its early proponents even claimed that this was the only area for valid study. Nowadays, there are few who would hold to this purist view but behaviour change still tends to be regarded as the most convincing type of outcome that can be produced by a therapeutic technique. In a sense, it might be considered the touchstone of successful therapy. What interests a behaviour therapist is not so much whether the client feels better in a general way after therapy but whether they can actually do those things which their problem prevented them from doing. Does, for instance, the agoraphobic client manage to go out shopping more often or can the couple with marital difficulties discuss their problems without violent argument? Folk wisdom supports this emphasis on what people do rather than say with sayings like 'action speaks louder than words'.

Most clients are themselves dissatisfied with their current behaviour and want to change it. The obese person wants to change his eating habits, the tense person wants to appear more relaxed, the shy person wants to behave more assertively and so on. As previously mentioned, one of the functions of a therapist is to offer explicit instruction in ways of accomplishing such changes. A prerequisite for any behavioural change is that the client acquires essential factual information relating to their problem. This is needed because, first and foremost, they have to be able to make sense of what is or has been happening to them. They need to see their problem in a meaningful context. In general, ignorance about physical or psychological functioning contributes significantly to most clients' difficulties and, in some cases, the problem may have been directly caused by a lack of knowledge.

A good example of this is the client who experiences panic attacks. These are commonly described as feelings of impending disaster which appear suddenly and unexpectedly. 'Out of the blue' is a phrase which is often used. The person experiences all the symptoms of extreme anxiety e.g. palpitations, shortness of breath, dizziness, weakness of limbs but without any of the cues or signals that might indicate real danger being present. Usually the attack will occur in a perfectly innocuous setting such as talking to a friend or walking down the street. This makes it quite inexplicable to the person concerned. Consequently, the original panic feelings become amplified as he or she strives and fails to understand what is happening to him. A vicious circle effect occurs where the person begins to 'panic about panic'. In time this may lead to a situation where whatever the cause, any symptoms of anxiety will trigger a panic reaction.

Information needs to be made available as soon as possible after the first panic attack. Firstly, the client will require reassurance that his symptoms are not the signs of a heart attack, brain tumour or other serious physical disease but an understandable, if frightening, reaction to stress. Secondly, he will also need to know something of the physiological mechanism of panic or the 'fight or flight' response of which it is a variant. This is important because it helps him to identify anxiety symptoms and feel less afraid of them. It is also essential because, without this basic information, he will be unable to make sense of any instructions he may be given to help him overcome the problem. Advice to enter situations which cause anxiety and to 'stay with' the feelings may appear incomprehensible or even malicious without the knowledge that the normal response of anxiety is to decrease or habituate, provided the person remains in the situation for long enough.

As exemplified above, it is apparent that the provision of clear, accurate information is a function which almost always needs to be addressed. How is this best accomplished? An obvious solution is simply for the therapist to tell the client during their sessions. Unfortunately, research on compliance with doctors' advice[3] tends to suggest that the amount of information which patients can take in at any one time is quite limited. Perhaps surprisingly, this has little to do with intelligence or personality factors but is more related to memory limitations. The task of conveying a great deal of information effectively is therefore likely to require a number of sessions.

This is expensive in terms of the amount of professional time involved and may not be the most efficient strategy.

An alternative solution is to use written material in the form of books or booklets to which the client can refer in the absence of the therapist. There are a number of advantages to this. It gives clients the opportunity to absorb the information at a time and at a pace which is convenient for them. It reduces the possibility that the information will be presented in a haphazard or incomplete manner. It provides material in a standardized format which will assist subsequent evaluation. Finally, it may also improve the credibility of the information in the sense that people are often more impressed by what they read in a book than by what they are told.

The provision of information is therefore one way in which reading materials can be used to assist behaviour change. This, however, really only 'sets the scene' for change. Is there any way in which reading can contribute more directly to the task of helping a person alter his behaviour? The key to this lies in the use of the concept of 'skill' as it applies to therapy.

A great deal of time in behaviour therapy is actually spent in teaching clients particular kinds of skills, referred to as 'coping' skills. These vary according to the nature of their difficulties but will often include relaxation or anxiety management techniques, social skills and problem-solving strategies. Although such skills are typically learned directly from the therapist, books can have a useful role as additional instructional aids.

In Western cultures, people are quite accustomed to the notion of learning a skill through the medium of the written word. This is a practice which usually begins in the school classroom and it carries over, to a greater or lesser degree, into adult life. A glance around any library or bookshop will testify to the extraordinary variety of the often very complex skills which books purport to teach. These range from practical skills of the 'do-it-yourself' variety through sports and hobbies to creative skills such as painting or playing an instrument. If it is possible to learn, say, the rudiments of car servicing or photography from books then it should also be possible to learn more 'psychological' skills such as how to cope with stress or overcome shyness. In fact, there is a growing demand for books within the 'self-improvement' category. The range of available books is wide. Most of the commonest psychological problems are covered such as anxiety, lack of assertiveness, child management, and self-control problems such as over-eating and smoking.[4,5,6,7,8] In addition there are more academic books which contain self-help manuals in appendix form on subjects such as overcoming agoraphobia.[9]

A problem with such a wealth of material is that only a select proportion of commercially available self-help books are well-researched and presented. The others, often accompanied by extravagant claims, appear to be written mainly to exploit a lucrative market. The effectiveness of such literature is also difficult to assess. Despite blurbs which proclaim 'this book has changed my life' it is doubtful whether reading a book on its own will result in much significant change. Reading, by itself, allows too much scope for misinterpretation and does not demand any real commitment to change, a crucial source of motivation when the going gets tough. Also, few skills can be completely represented by a set of written instructions. This is particularly true of more complex skills e.g. social skills which may be hard to define but are easier to recognize and demonstrate.

Self-help books, then, are likely to be most effective with therapist involvement. The selection of suitable material needs to be carefully made by someone with appropriate experience and knowledge. At the same time, the written instructions or guidelines will almost certainly have to be supplemented by explanation, demonstration, prompting and feedback. If these conditions can be met, the indications from recent research are that a substantial reduction in therapist hours can be made with no decrease in effectiveness.[10]

So far, we have discussed how reading can be used to facilitate change in behaviour. This is, of course, not the only area in which change can occur. More recently, behaviour therapists have begun to take an interest in the way their clients perceive the world or important aspects of it. They have become concerned, in other words, about their *attitudes and beliefs*.

A person's beliefs cannot be directly observed and measured in the way his behaviour can be. Instead, they have to be inferred from what the person says or does. This means that they are much less readily apparent than behaviour and, for this reason, may be harder to deal with in a therapeutic sense. Nevertheless, there is now a body of research and practice which suggests that beliefs can successfully be made the focus of therapy,[11] particularly in relation to negative mood states such as anxiety and depression.

The rationale for this type of approach is that these states are not caused by unpleasant or stressful events as such but by the way a person thinks about such events. For example, an event such as failing an exam will have different effects on different individuals. One person might be plunged into the depths of depression while another may be relatively unaffected after the first shock of the news has worn off. Those who cope well with exam failure are likely to have beliefs such as 'I don't have to be perfect' or 'You can't win them all'. In other words, beliefs which de-emphasize the importance of failure. On the other hand, those who become depressed will tend to have beliefs which exaggerate its importance such as 'Only the best is good enough' or 'I must succeed otherwise I'm no good'. Beliefs like these might be said to predispose towards depression because they ensure that the occasional experiences of failure which are part of living are perceived not as temporary setbacks but as reflections of the individuals' self-worth or lack of it.

Since clients are often unaware that they possess beliefs of this maladaptive nature, the first task of the therapist is to help them identify the beliefs in question. This is often done by asking them to keep a special diary in which they note down their thoughts and other reactions to stressful events in their daily lives. Once the client is clear about the link between events, thoughts or beliefs and mood state, the therapist then encourages them to try to view those beliefs more objectively by suggesting that they look for evidence which might confirm or disconfirm them. This process leads on to the final stage, when the therapist and client formulate more appropriate beliefs which fit the evidence better. The client will also be requested to 'try out' these new beliefs in situations which have produced depression or anxiety in the past.

As in the case of behaviour change, the therapist again acts as a kind of teacher. It is important to note that the aim is not to foist the therapist's own views or ideas on clients but simply to assist them to evaluate their own beliefs and draw their own conclusions. In doing so, the therapist will pose questions which will prompt the client to think critically about his or her beliefs. These will be of the 'open-ended' variety which do not suggest a 'right' answer e.g. 'What makes you think that . . .?'. Another strategy that the therapist will adopt is to suggest different ways in which the client might seek evidence for or against their views. Both of these functions, the non-directive challenging of assumptions and the search for accurate evidence for beliefs can be facilitated by the careful selection of appropriate reading material.

It is well-known that books can be a powerful means of changing people's ideas. Throughout history, authoritarian societies have sought to control or suppress any literature which challenges the prevailing assumptions of those in power. The plight of writers in the Soviet Union is but one recent example of this tendency. The rigid belief structures of such societies can only be maintained by ensuring that their members are not exposed to anything which might cause them to seriously question these structures or to look for better alternatives. Clients who come for therapy, too, often possess strong, fixed beliefs about themselves which they have been able to avoid questioning. If the right ideas presented at the right time can have a revolutionary effect on society, it may not be too fanciful to suggest that a similar, though more benign and constructive, process can occur in therapy.

The most straightforward use of reading in this context is in tackling unwanted fears or anxieties which appear to be maintained or heightened by the beliefs which a client has acquired. For instance, someone who has a strong fear of developing cancer is likely to erroneously believe that cancer is invariably painful and fatal. They are likely to use phrases such as 'everyone knows that cancer is a killer'. Their ideas about cancer may be based on a mixture of hearsay, half-digested news stories or media reports and old wives' tales. On the other hand, they may have had a close family member or a relative die of cancer in the past and have generalized from this one, painful event. Whatever the basis of their ideas, once the fear of cancer has developed it will lead them to avoid all references to it and its outcome, thus effectively maintaining the beliefs in their original, stereotyped form.

Treatment for such a fear might have to focus on changing the content of these beliefs as a first step towards anxiety reduction. In other words, the client would be encouraged to check out the accuracy of their ideas by seeing whether or not they reflected the known facts about cancer. Prescribed reading is an obvious therapeutic strategy here. The client, could for example, be asked to borrow a book containing accurate information about cancer at their local library, to read it and discuss what they have read at the next session. This, however, might leave rather a lot to chance. The book chosen might not be up to date. The style might be too difficult or clinical. The pictures might be too horrifying and make the fear worse rather than better. It may not be possible to borrow the book at the time required. These possibilities are obviously counterproductive and can be avoided if the therapist selects the book on behalf of the client. With very fearful clients, it may even be worthwhile to mark out particular passages or sections for reading within the actual session itself.

This approach might be expected to work if the person's fear is primarily based on a faulty estimate of the probability of dying of cancer. However, a better knowledge of the facts may not help if the fear is concerned with the actual prospect of dying, regardless of its likelihood. Such a client may say that they accept that the risk of death from cancer may not be great. They also accept that even if they did contract the disease, they could be treated successfully. They nevertheless continue to be obsessed with the possibility that the worst can still conceivably happen to them and cannot imagine ever being able to cope with it. Prescribed reading could still be employed in this case but it would be advisable to recommend a different kind of book e.g. one which suggests that it is possible to cope with such an experience.

There are a number of autobiographical accounts by cancer victims which provide moving, dignified descriptions of how they managed to confront the reality of a terminal illness.[12] Again, skill in choosing the right book for the client is important. From a theoretical point of view, the author could be said to be 'modelling' a set of positive, coping attitudes. Since research shows that we are most likely to imitate or identify with people like ourselves, it is necessary to try to match the authors' main characteristics such as nationality, age, social background etc. with those of the client. The wide variety of material on this subject helps to ensure that this can often be done.

The above examples show how books can be used to correct misconceptions e.g. cancer is always fatal and to challenge assumptions e.g. it is impossible to cope with cancer. In both cases, the accounts in the books form part of the 'evidence' which the therapist has suggested the client examines before concluding that his or her faulty beliefs are absolutely true.

Books, however, can also be used in a rather less directive way to prompt the client to adopt a different, more detached perspective on their problem. The best medium for this is the short story, anecdote or joke. Although this may seem, at first sight, a rather unconventional approach and perhaps even positive heresy to some behaviour therapists, the use of tales or so-called 'teaching stories' is a well-established and continuing tradition in many Eastern cultures.[13] Unlike ordinary fables e.g. Aesop's which are mainly concerned with communicating simple morals, teaching stories are designed to enable the listener to perceive situations in a new way, almost like exercises in lateral thinking. The well-known writer on oriental philosophy, Idries Shah, has published many collections of such stories some of which can be appropriately discussed in therapy.

One such concerns a man who was bizarrely throwing handfuls of crumbs around his house. When asked what he was doing, he replied that he was keeping the tigers away. The questioner protested that there were no tigers in these parts, to which came the reply, 'That's right. Effective, isn't it.' This is an admirably concise description of the self-fulfilling nature of superstitious behaviour. One possible application of it might be in the treatment of someone who suffers from an obsessional disorder. As in the story, this kind of disorder can often involve the performance of rituals (such as counting out loud) which seem absurd to an observer but are perfectly consistent with the belief system of the person concerned. Because the story is in the form of a joke, the 'message' stands a greater chance of being absorbed than if the therapist were to challenge the beliefs directly. This is not to say, of course, that therapy should simply comprise the recitation of stories but that selected anecdotes of this type can have a part to play as an element in an overall 'package' which would include standard behaviour techniques.

Sometimes, prescribed reading can be used to alter attitudes, not by challenging or by questioning, but by reassuring. It is not uncommon for clients to feel that they are fundamentally different from others by virtue of the fact that their symptoms appear strange or inappropriate. Simple verbal reassurance accompanied by explanatory handouts can often be sufficient but it can also be helpful to suggest that the client reads accounts of their condition by people who are generally considered to be adequate and competent. For instance, the popular author, Colin Wilson, has published a graphic description of his own panic attacks in the introduction to his book, *Mysteries*.[14] In his case, they were caused by trying to adhere to a punishing work schedule. His account of how the panic feelings first affected him and his attempts, latterly successful, to control them makes interesting reading. It also has the ring of truth for clients who have had similar experiences. Reading such descriptions helps people realize that anxiety need not be viewed as evidence of a basic personality flaw but rather as a condition to which almost anyone may be prone, given the right circumstances.

A similar approach can be applied with a rarely mentioned group of clients, those who report apparently 'paranormal' or extrasensory experiences. If obvious cranks or people with a diagnosable psychotic illness are excluded, there remains a small group of people who are bothered by visual hallucinations, premonitions of unpleasant events etc. Sometimes these are linked with their presenting problem and sometimes not. Understandably, these clients often find it hard to come to terms with the phenomena and are prone to regarding themselves as freaks or mad. They hope that the therapist may be able to offer a convincing explanation and may be disappointed when one is not forthcoming. In such cases, the prescription of books by reputable authors which document such experiences[15] and emphasize the fact that they have been reported by many otherwise ordinary people can do a lot to keep the matter in perspective.

Most of the interventions so far mentioned, whether directed at behaviour or beliefs, will also have had an effect on the third major area of therapy, that of *feelings*. It is in this area which clients frequently identify as their main source of distress and in which they will want to see most change occur. Put more simply, they expect, rightly, to feel better after therapy. They want to feel happier, less anxious, more confident, less depressed and so on. The therapist often has to inform them that these changes in feeling cannot be accomplished directly but will take place as a result of complementary changes in behaviour, beliefs or attitudes.

The treatment of phobias, however, is a major exception to this rule. Here anxiety has become attached to objects, situations or thoughts in such a way that simple exposure to them is enough to trigger symptoms. There is an automatic, reflexive quality about this and the phenomenon tends to be explained by saying that anxiety has become 'conditioned' to these stimuli. It can be difficult to determine exactly how the problem was first caused. With simple phobias e.g. animal fears, the client can sometimes recall an incident which may have started the problem such as being frightened by a dog. In more complex cases, e.g. social fears, the onset is more gradual, perhaps consisting of a series of minor incidents rather than a single traumatic one. However, in all phobias, whatever the cause, the final result is the habit of avoidance. This prevents the person from coming into contact with the feared object and so deprives them of the opportunity of learning that they need not really be afraid of it.

It is generally accepted that graded exposure to the feared situation is one of the most effective treatment strategies with this kind of problem. For instance, someone with a fear of spiders would be initially encouraged to tolerate contact with small, inoffensive spiders and then to touch increasingly larger, hairier varieties. This can be a fairly straightforward process in the case of animal phobias or situational fears such as agoraphobia. It is a simple matter to expose a client gradually to say, dogs or crowded supermarkets. Other fears can be less easy to approach in this way. To return to the cancer example, it is obviously not feasible to expose someone to the experience of having cancer in reality. They could, on the other hand, be asked to imagine or visualize cancer-related situations. Unfortunately, this technique has its drawbacks. Firstly, the therapist cannot fully control the scenes which the client imagines. Secondly, there are a proportion of clients who are unable to imagine any scene due to an inability to visualize or to a level of fear which is so high that even the thought of the phobic situation leads to immediate mental avoidance. Problems like these can sometimes be overcome by using written passages as stimulus material.

Reading an appropriate extract from a book can enhance poor imagery because the words act as prompts to the imagination. It also helps to provide a more controlled exposure, since the tendency to 'wander off' is restricted by the content of the selected passage. A client who fears breast cancer may therefore be encouraged to read aloud a description of a person's first discovery of a lump in her breast. She would be requested to repeat this until most signs of anxiety had subsided. Once this has been achieved, other passages which initially aroused more fear could be employed in a similar fashion. In this way, a whole book could provide useful therapeutic material for several sessions. Homework, always an important part of behaviour therapy, is made easier too since the client can take the book home and practice the same passage between sessions.

It is worth mentioning that this strategy may sometimes be required even when exposure to the feared situation is possible in reality. For example, a client with a cat phobia who could not tolerate, say, being in the same room as a small kitten might be able to cope with reading verbal descriptions of cats or their behaviour. The large, 'coffee-table' books which contain a variety of photographic studies of domestic pets can be useful in this context also.

In summary, it is clear that literature or reading matter can be used in a number of diverse ways, as part of or supplementary to the standard techniques of behavioural psychotherapy. The manner in which reading is used depends largely on the focus of therapy. When changes in behaviour are being considered, then books or manuals can be used to provide clear, accurate information about the nature of the problem or to provide explicit instruction in the techniques or skills which will help the person to cope better. If change in inappropriate or faulty beliefs is the main aim, extracts or stories can be helpful in challenging key assumptions clients hold about themselves or their problem. They can also provide some of the evidence upon which a client can construct new, more adaptive beliefs. Finally, written passages can be employed as stimulus material to produce changes in feelings such as phobic anxiety. This can be done as part of a programme of graded exposure.

It should be stressed that, in every case, reading has been only one component, albeit sometimes an important one, in a therapeutic 'package' that might include structured discussion, relaxation, role-playing or other common techniques. The way in which it is used is very much up to the discretion and judgement of the therapist and, in a sense, is limited only by his or her ingenuity. The present account has not attempted to be exhaustive but has tried to give a flavour of the possible uses and an indication of their range of application.

The decision about whether or not to use reading in therapy must, to a large extent, be based on the characteristics of the client. Literacy and attitudes to reading are obviously factors to be considered here. Also important are the therapist's own knowledge of appropriate books or other written material and their local availability. In time, a therapist can build up his own library of material which he uses most frequently. Alternatively, he can use standard library facilities in conjunction with special annotated bibliographies[16] compiled by librarians and clinicians.

At the present time, the therapeutic potential of books is a long way from being fully tapped. As is often the case with a new approach or technique, there is always the danger of making enthusiastic claims which are difficult or impossible to substantiate. It is therefore encouraging that more controlled research into the topic is beginning to appear in psychological and other literature. The indications so far are that directed reading is definitely effective in helping to maximize treatment gains and efficiency for certain problems. If present trends continue, further applications of reading in therapy will undoubtedly emerge in the next few years.

References

1 Miller, W. R. and Baca, L. M., 'Two year follow-up of bibliotherapy and therapist-directed controlled drinking training for problem drinkers', *Behaviour Therapy*, 14, 1983, 449–53.
2 Schrank, F. A. and Engels, D. W., 'Bibliotherapy as a counselling adjunct: research findings', *Personnel and Guidance Journal*, 60,(3), 1981, 143–7.
3 Ley, P. and Spelman, S., *Communicating with the patient*, London, Staples Press, 1969.
4 Marks, I. M., *Living with fear*, New York, McGraw-Hill, 1980.
5 Zimbardo, P. G., *Shyness*, London, Pan Books, 1981.
6 Patterson, G. R. and Gullion, M. E., *Living with Children*, Illinois, Research Press, 1976.
7 Peine, H. A. and Howarth, R., *Children and parents*, Harmondsworth, Penguin Books, 1976.
8 Stuart, P. B. and Davis, B., *Slim chance in a fat world*, Illinois, Research Press, 1976.
9 Mathews, A. M., Gelder, M. C. and Johnston, D. W., *Agoraphobia: nature and treatment*, London, Tavistock, 1981.
10 *Ibid*.
11 Beck, A. T., Rush, A. J., Shaw, B. F. and Emery, G., *Cognitive therapy of depression*, New York, Guildford Press, 1979.
12 Tabor, R. B. (ed.), *Reflections*, Southampton, Wessex Regional Library and Information Service, 1981.
13 Shah, I., *The exploits of the incomparable Mulla Nasrudin*, London, Pan, 1973.
14 Wilson, C., *Mysteries*, London, Hodder and Stoughton, 1978.
15 Hay, D., *Exploring inner space*, Harmondsworth, Penguin Books, 1982.
16 Tabor, R. B. (ed.), *op.cit.*

6 Therapeutic reading and personal development

Sara D. Coomaraswamy

Introduction

Reading involves a wide employment of one's imagination. This can come about within and during the therapeutic relationship, where a cognitive orientation is seen to be the preferred approach to appraising and resolving personal problems.

Whatever life may hold or lack there is always an orderly mind one can consult when one's own seems less than sensible. Reading meets great needs in us for self-understanding, for understanding others, or the events and situations that confront and baffle us. In any particular state of mind we can exercise choice as to the minds with which we wish to interact at any given time. In this way reading becomes therapeutic and spares us loneliness and isolation.

For many of us the magic of words has extraordinary power to evoke profoundly satisfying mental images. Sitting tight against one's parent the child wonders how the inked words kept the bed-time stories the same in every telling. How do feelings, images and thoughts get pinned into place as words? In time fairies, goblins and gingerbread men turn into pirates and highwaymen through the power of the words on a printed page. One feels transported as if on a magic carpet into the realms of new and high excitement exceeding all previous registers. We hear the blinding forces of thunder and lightning: we hear the drums of marching bands. Imagination takes a heady flight into the realms of the unknown. Words sweep us into the traceries of long-forgotten memories of childhood when we were wordless and inarticulate. With nostalgia we enter vicariously into the personal experiences of *Jane Eyre*[1] or *David Copperfield*.[2] The Brontës and Charles Dickens show how open, honest and passionate one's feelings can be. Such feelings become spurs to self-expression. One's personal observations become more readily available for matching with what others are searching for. In a wilderness of indecision and uncertainty, one has to choose significant trails from one's memory to obtain a coherent picture of oneself as to who one is and where one is in one's historical and personal context. This self-search comes into its own in the psychotherapeutic relationship.

In a quest for 'Who am I, where am I?' man tries to find his place in the scheme of things. One faces one's own being in terms of one's family, professional, national and historical identity. Literature provides a comprehensive and ever available framework within which individuals can initiate the search to locate oneself as a fellow human being. Each one's experience of life is unique. One is filled with admiration, wonder and compassion for the varieties of human experience which set people apart as individuals. This is how Joseph Conrad, a Polish merchant seaman, stepped straight into the centre of English literature while trying to discover his personal identity. Literature is packed with psychological clues into human motivation and behaviour.

The world we live in becomes all the more precious for knowing something of its origins, fragility, beauty and mystery. Literature gives us realistic textures of personal and family life, of how families actually behave in moments of interpersonal conflicts which turn imperceptibly into recriminatory scapegoating and insidious intrigue. Cynical patterns may emerge to demonstrate that acute insight can be sharper and more penetrating than logic as characters and situations unravel themselves.

The therapeutic value of reading in the context of my work as a clinical psychologist in a district general hospital came quite fortuitously into my awareness in the course of getting to know my patients. Some patients would glance at books lying on my table or on the shelves of my consulting room, perhaps express curiosity or interest. A dialogue would disclose shared enthusiasms for authors, topics or styles which would engender mutual exchange of enjoyment or disappointment experienced.

In 1974, when I first entered my present post I was consulted about the following persons with problems:

a) Sybil, 24, French, who fled to England to establish her personal identity and independence away from her authoritarian parents. She was highly dependent on heroin to maintain her status quo.
b) Sheila, 19+, a local drop-out from a grammar school, rebelling from parental pressures to conform to their middle-class standards.
c) Neil, 22, third-year medical student from Liverpool University, at war with his intrusive middle-class parents. Frag-

mented family life had banished Neil to boarding schools. Academic success had gone far ahead of his emotional and social development so that he felt a fraud when he came face to face with patients and he had no clue as to how to relate to them in a meaningful way.

d) Maureen, 41, disillusioned after twenty years of being a nun, besieged by deep inner conflicts needing panacea.
3) Jane, 18, anorexic, totally withdrawn from parental persuasion to proceed to university as Jane had earlier set out to do. She was too emaciated to be mobile and psychotherapy had to be offered at the bedside.

This conjunction of patients needing to launch into a search for clues to surmount their problems led me to respond to their quest by encouraging them to explore through research in the library. The active participation of the hospital librarian activated the severely anorexic Jane to help read and review books for suitability and recommendation to younger patients in other wards in the hospital.

I happened to be reading Herman Hesse's *Siddhartha*[3] at the request of my son who was negotiating his own direction into his future at this time. There was competition among my patients to read not only *Siddhartha* but the rest of Herman Hesse's work as well. This is how the slow voyage into the dark and shadowy reaches of the human personality came about, using reading as an adjunct to the psychotherapeutic venture. In attempting to mirror their research into their problems I began to recognize that we are all links in a chain of being and obtained a measure of self-knowledge while trying to read some of the books my patients recommended to me. These to and fro exchanges certainly contributed to my own development as a therapist.

I Profiles in reading and reflection

A *Simon K.* 17, starting an A-level course in English and Literature. Simon's problems arose out of a family break-up, mother's remarriage, father's prolonged retreat into the ivory towers of his Scottish University, his only sibling's withdrawal into a mould of his own choosing. Simon's sojourn to England accentuated his personal isolation among hostile peers in a strange school environment.

Simon speaks for himself,

> My feelings are alien to me. Anger, jealousy and hatred accompanied

by constant tension are pressing for analysis and understanding. I am inspired by writers like:

a) Heinlein, who wrote *Job*[4]
b) Lewis Carroll's *Alice in Wonderland*[5] and *Alice through the looking glass*,[6] as well as his nonsense poems like *Jabberwocky*,[7] because of the adventurous way he treats logic
c) Susan Cooper's *The dark is rising* series of books;[8] this sequence of books triggered my imaginary universe.

I need to create my own 'Brave new world', to integrate my own fantasy with the real and the possible to create new maps of my world. I seem to have discovered rather than invented my new universe. I have adapted and designed it to fit in with reality as I know it. I enjoy role-playing in imaginary campaigns to integrate what I want out of life for myself. My universe centres round an island I have named 'The Power'. I was nine-years-old when I started my new universe, just about the time I was migrating south to England leaving familiar Scotland far behind.

The Power fills the whole inner sea, which seems to shrink as I create Time and living matter. Hundreds of minds are created to fill this void.

'Who is the creator of this universe?' I ask. Simon continues

They are my creations. The Power is the God of my new universe. The Power generously created the Goddess Time so that love may come to exist between them. The love between their minds creates energy and new forms of life. Life has to be measured in time. Trees, birds and minds came into existence. This is the map and prehistory of my universe.

A ring of five islands symbolically unites the central power of my universe. My creation tended to run out of steam when my setting had to change from my native Scotland to the mythical south. The theme, however, has remained constant.

My memories are very selective. I tend to use the happier memories. In fact I should use the bad ones to appreciate my present and rejoice in the solutions I am discovering. This kind of nostalgia is linked to my urge to write. I compose passages as I cycle in the countryside. I need to write down my creative ideas so that the structure of my creation may not break down.

The reason why various tensions are connected with my creative urge is because I want to write them into my central character, Steven Tranter, who, in fact, is me in disguise. Will this autobiography be of any literary value?

I am really having a stab at mankind. My main theme is the battle between man and nature, the way man destroys nature. But nature wins in the end. My book illustrates that nature is everything that is not man-made. There is, however, a way man can become a part of nature.

> The ideas in my book have undergone many changes since I started to write it at the age of nine. Now I am 17 a final form is being achieved after a long period of gestation. In eight years the book has evolved in its own way to exactly how I would want it to be.
>
> Finally let me tell you that amnesia of the post-traumatic kind fascinates me. I am inserting amnesia into my central character because it makes for an interesting structure: complex perhaps because the central character me, has been mugged and lost all memory. The reader does not know this. The character walks out of hospital after the amnesic episode. He suddenly gets a *déjà vu* because his memory switches back as he walks the same street where he was mugged. It is only here that the reader discovers that the character has suffered amnesia.

Simon's emotional burdens seem to lift as he gains control over creating his own 'Brave new world'. In this solution Simon seems to discover that confidence, self-esteem and courage come to his aid.

B Christine E. 28, single, sensitive, intelligent, a high-powered secretary, interested in higher studies in English literature.

Since the age of nine Christine has been tormented by recurring episodes of clinical depression with serious suicidal intentions. She has researched into toxic and poisonous substances, making three attempts on her life at ages 15, 21 and 22, which landed her in hospital to the consternation of her parents. The need to reach oblivion from her unremitting despair became almost an obsession with Christine.

In January 1986 Christine was referred to me by her GP for psychological intervention. Christine's approach to books and research as methods of gathering information and learning to solve problems became invaluable in taking a cognitive angle in the therapeutic endeavours which followed. The therapeutic challenge posed was perceived as possibly invigorating though she could not cancel out some of her sceptical reservations and misgivings. However Christine was willing to make a commitment to examining alternative options to the oblivion poisonous substances would offer her in the management of her despair.

Christine reports

> I am the eldest child in a family of four children. We were well cared for but emotional ups and downs were not allowed with the result that the family atmosphere was generally one of emotional blandness. My emotional expression was so inappropriate in school that my peers rejected me and I experienced failures in almost all my

earlier relationships. I found myself in psychological isolation both at home and in school. By the time I was 15 I was fully rebellious, shocking my parents by drinking late in pubs and by being generally hostile and sullen at home.

I began to see imperfections all around me screaming out for explanation and quick remedy. I felt driven to the edge of the precipice of self-destruction with a compelling fascination for the oblivion that would blank out my intense anger and pain. I believed that this alone would free my mind from its high-pitched torment.

In the subsequent sessions which followed Christine proceeded to inform me

In negative states of mind I see only gloom and doom. There is dirt and grime and litter everywhere; mass media sensationalizes violence and rape while politicians lie through their teeth. I see 16-year-old single mothers feeding their unwashed babies stale chips at street corners and on the pavements. In this black mood I re-read familiar books by writers I am mentally in tune with. My mind is far from receptive to new thoughts or ideas.

The depth and intensity of my mood of despair would dictate the choice of books and writers at this given point in time. *Wuthering Heights*[9] is captivating in the intense anguish and torment of the passionate lovers which is matched only by the force of the cosmic elements. One's human status is somehow belittled and diminished by the vastness of the moors, the howling of the rampaging winds and the craggy grandeur of the monumental rocks. Yet the power of human love in the face of inevitable death is truly impressive.

Thomas Hardy's *Jude the obscure*[10] is a portrayal of a man's total irredeemable suicide. It did not give me any hope. Oxford did not provide the sanctuary that was promised. In fact Oxford turned out to be the mirage of forlorn hopes, tantalizing while Jude was most despairing. The degree was only a dream with no basis in reality.

In *Tess of the D'Urbevilles*[11] Thomas Hardy stays with the same fatalistic view. Tess lies under vast star-lit skies in the wide open fields of Dorset and sees herself as a tiny, insignificant speck in the limitless universe. How can her problem be so great? Tess gets the message not to do it. She becomes totally resigned to her impending fate. This story carries me over my crisis.

Susan Hill tells you *In the Springtime of the year*[12] how characters behave in ultimate anguish; she tells you what grief feels like. The wife is cold and hungry but she will not eat. She does not dare to find out how her husband died in case he was mutilated or disfigured by violence. His mother will not accept his death; her father will not speak about it; she leans on her younger brother. How uncomprehending the uninitiated can be! I read this book because I was so miserable.

David Ritz's book on the black American singer, Marvin Gaye,[13] who was killed by his father in jealousy over his mother conveyed to me the force of powerful emotions like jealousy. I obtained an understanding of the overgrown man of 45, who, like a baby, could take no responsibility for himself let alone his children or his two wives. Here was a great man who let himself down using cocaine for 15 years to maintain his sexy image to gratify his female fans. This story prevents me from dwelling on my black thoughts of self-destruction.

On the other hand Somerset Maugham's *Of human bondage*[14] proved to be an opiate in resisting my blackest despair. I read it so compulsively that I was able to banish my suicidal thoughts. It got me through my two darkest hours and scotched my intentions to seek permanent oblivion from my inner torment. I got so totally involved in the hero's downward spiral and his over-commitment to an unscrupulous woman, who exploited his generosity till he became so penniless he had to give up his medical education, shunning his friends and becoming homeless. He reached a position far worse than mine and yet he never considered killing himself. I couldn't understand why he didn't. Does life become a pattern, unique to individuals and yet be so diverse? Individuals are so small and so insignificant, a tiny dot on this vast planet.

Herman Hesse made me want to find ways not to die. Siddhartha goes through many inner changes in discovering for himself that good priests can turn evil while murderers and rapists can reform and become benevolent.[15] People have the capacity for good and evil and personal experience alone can change the direction we take. Siddhartha comes full circle when his son rejects him as he rejected his father, family and traditions, not accepting anyone else's teaching but setting out to find out for himself. He believes that experiences have to be first-hand. He rejects the artificial city life and overcomes his suicidal thoughts as he sits by the river. The ferryman is a good listener; he advised Siddhartha to listen to the river which had something more permanent and eternal than the human condition could offer. Life may not be brilliant but it may be worth living to 95 to find out the meaning of life.

E. M. Forster's novel, *A passage to India*,[16] has a very positive appeal for me because it develops and maintains relationships between two partners in a somewhat uneasy relationship, i.e. the British Raj and Colonial India, with well-balanced views which do not overwhelm or encroach unfairly on either culture. The heart is compared with the head in arguments.

Reading changes my experience and helps me to change direction. I read until my mind changes my black thoughts to more positive trends. When bright and positive I see fountains, roses and butterflies in the sunlight. In this happy mental state I seek out philosophy, psychology, natural history or local history in my search for brand new experiences.

Christine demonstrates that human needs can motivate

reading by seeing oneself how the mind moves, what it heeds or fears or what it brushes aside. The nature of our perceptions and hunches have the seal of our own identity. One observes one's many moods, bodily tensions, attentional shifts, impasses and the impossible choices we are presented with as well as the wishing and the hurting.

The mind that gets behind the scenes, the mind that watches the watcher is the real witness. The centre is freer and better informed and gains information processed by the brain at an unconscious level. One's awareness is raised to higher levels of integration through shifts in perception presenting one with sudden and unexpected insights.

C *Lilian Y.* 34, single, brilliant daughter of an eminent lawyer; too much was expected of her too soon. This 'golden girl's' academic promise was sabotaged by an ill-fated love affair. Lilian's search for oblivion to escape the shipwreck of her self-esteem led her to drown her mind in alcohol. Lilian's personal communication to me of her predicament was in the form of Rosie Boycott's autobiographical book *A nice girl like me.*[17] The implicit message in it was an invitation to recognize her struggle to hold on to sanity which reaches the heart of the matter and the comic edge at the same time. The alcoholic cage threatens to close: vodka is the only route to escape mental penalties.

Most children need the background of parental approval and appreciation. 'Should parents call the tune long after the children have reached the stage of adult responsibility?' Lilian questions. The experience of failure in fulfilling parental expectations is a heavy burden for Lilian to bear. A further failure in a close relationship seems to have toppled her mental equilibrium. Parents are now powerless to stop Lilian's nerve-endings from screaming as panic perches on her shoulder like a vulture. They are perceived to be ineffectual, their approval both inconsequential and unachievable.

Can Lilian confront herself to change? Hindsight cannot cancel out her humiliation. Rosie Boycott reminds her that the alcoholic's Mark of Cain would soon manifest in the tell-tale mottling caused by split capillaries to be followed by ominous mental and organic signs that will betray her to the world at large.

Lilian uses drunkenness as a shield against mental pain. The inherent deceit backfires. In seeking solace from a wasteland she senses in Rosie's revelations that the alcoholic's roles would dissolve as the love of family hardens into anger. No amount of wallowing in hung-over self-hatred would reprieve her from the descent into personal annihilation.

Lilian asks 'Can my past be sloughed off like a snake's skin? Can I develop spiritual strength to surmount moral collapse?'

Lilian knows all the answers. Her anger may counteract her despair and bestow some measure of self-esteem.

D *Maureen M.* 41, a nun for 22 years in a Roman Catholic Order, disillusioned by her own mistaken choice that rated high in the esteem of her devout parents, who also had five sons to uphold the family's unchallenged status in the life of the community. Maureen's prolonged submission to higher wills than her own made non-directive psychological intervention problematic. How does one set about building a bridge between a nun's submissive ego and her somatic and emotional tensions which instigate her unconscious upheaval?

Therapeutic reading came into its own in this scholarly nun. She began with Herman Hesse's analyses of interpersonal conflicts and proceeded to Goethe, Doris Lessing and Thomas Mann, searching for answers to her existential problems. Candour came face to face with great wells of feeling. It became possible to construct a bridge across which fresh ideas, feelings and perceptions could pass over. Two years' joint endeavour exploring the wisdom of great minds brought insight and self-understanding to both participants in the joint venture.

It was inevitable that an intuitive intimacy would develop while elucidating and clarifying the challenge of the problems being shared. Confrontations became procedurally unavoidable. The writer was prepared to question her own fallibility in entering readily into Maureen's unconscious drama. Over years of close encounters with troubled personalities one comes to realize that it is the patient who provides the script of the inner drama. Numerous clinical examples illustrate this truth. Each patient knows unconsciously what he or she wants from the analyst, who, in turn, needs to alert attention to the underlying message, to pick up the subtle cues. Listen actively to the patient and you will hear the diagnosis.

Three years later Maureen qualified to enter afresh another caring profession that met and satisfied her newly evolving needs. Therapeutic reading grew in direct ratio to diminishing psychotherapeutic encounters. The summing up finally arrived in the form of a gift, Barbara Gordon's autobiographical *I am dancing as fast as I can.*[18] Reading it the writer obtained intimations of Maureen's emergence as a vibrant personality which was profoundly rewarding.

E *Thomas R.* 37, sensitive, poetic, intuitive, attempts to explain to me the nature of his problem,

> I am profoundly disturbed. Life has passed me by at top speed. It is too late to catch up with it now. I am lost, afraid and lonely. Behind me is a trail of broken dreams. Ahead I see nothing.
>
> The life stories of creative artists, poets and composers relieve my feelings of being totally alone and unloved. Elgar's inspired compositions, such as his *Enigma Variations,* make me aware of the simple beauty of love, the affection of pure friendships. For those unfamiliar with the composer's personal history this piece would seem like a series of musical portraits of those most dear to him, his wife and friends, all drawn with the kind of affection of the highest form. The moment I sensed the significance of the music I cracked and even now I am choked when I hear it.
>
> The song *Memories* from the musical *Cats* has also pushed me close to the edge, sung as it is by an outcast of the group, looking back on her youth when she was happy, young and beautiful. I know that music, like poetry, can tap the emotions, but should my reaction be so strong?
>
> Here I bare my life to you for the first time so you may try and understand. Shared knowledge of areas of inner pain does alleviate the feelings of being an outcast on a limb.

II The unconscious and the search for meaning

What remains trapped in the unconscious controls one powerfully. The imagery which makes the greatest impact has to be dragged struggling from the deepest recesses of the most troubled minds. It is very difficult to gain insight into the unconscious forces which motivate a Yorkshire Ripper or a Stockwell Strangler. What has sexuality and fetishism to do with it?

Power relationships designed within families seem to shape the innermost 'unknown' in most of us. Fear, for example, becomes experienced as a prison long before one has the vocabulary to verbalize experience. This backs us into a corner speechless if not mute. Relationships fraught with conflict seem to carry the family signature bearing the burden of generations of maladjustment.

What distinguishes the bad from the good relationship is the loss of choice. A dyadic symbiosis is difficult to sustain. The desire to merge with one's mother is often not worked through consciously. One needs to step out of the parent-child symbiosis before one becomes ready for adult relationships. Distributing one's needs and interests more broadly in a network of relationships can be more replenishing than exclusive dyads. The mind is a composite of a vast network of interactions.

The schizophrenic personality develops in learning situations with conflicting rules. The impact of the conflicting forces affects the patient's metabolism which obeys an energy budget. Energy, in turn, is the determinant of vigorous thought and decisive action.

Apathy is the converse.

Psychotherapeutic interventions have to be timely before patients reach the point of no return. During cognitive exchanges the patient's unconscious may orchestrate his inner tumult. Changes may be noted as the therapist perceives the patient's complex cognitive and interactive styles. The black and white universe of the paranoid is not founded on certainty. It is merely compensatory. His family has reinforced his feelings of unworthiness. The courage to doubt one's own delusions grows slowly and painfully because delusions themselves have contributed to the development of perceptual distortions that produce cognitive dissonance.

A Dostoevsky's undogmatic psychological understanding connects the man and the writer to the intellectual ambience of his age and provides clues to the nature of his humanity. An incurable epileptic, steeped in suffering, mercilessly exposed to human cruelty, his literary art is a witness to the complex compassionate humanity in the writer. Humiliation and triumph are both implicit in his works. He provides astonishing insights into the dialectics of humiliation and eventual self-assertion. He explores the conflicts between the rational and irrational elements in human conduct.

In *Crime and punishment*[19] Dostoevsky delves into the subterranean currents of early emotional bonding which can fetter our thoughts and feelings throughout our lives. His intimate confessional tones make readers privy to the character's struggles to survive as a reasonable human being.

Therapeutic reading may render the overhanging psychosis into a voyage of discovery to return with insights. As an extension of this activity the therapist may recommend keeping a journal similar to H. D. Thoreau's *Diary of a thinking man*.[20] The literary diarist becomes his own source of remarkable insight into his inner life. Unconsciously and imperceptibly the diarist's views of life can change. The calendar of thoughts gives patients an opportunity to observe the operations of the thinking, feeling mind. Gradually the diffuse thoughts develop a crisp, cutting edge.

The patient learns to communicate with the therapist and to receive reflections as the therapist invites the patient to clarify, to explore problems and to track them down through the daily record of things seen, felt and thought about.

The therapist says 'Your problem is your experience. Make it obvious to me, as I am trained to see the connections. I can work actively to obtain a grasp of your problem.' Accurate verbalizing can proceed without expanding the patient's guilt or hopelessness. The therapist can emphasize the fact that what he has is a problem and not a defect.

Individuals alienated like Kafka's Gregor in *Metamorphosis*[21] agree that man's existence can become a prison and the work environment soul-destroying. As a beetle Gregor retains his human awareness and yet could not communicate with his hitherto parasitic and presently alienating family. Kafka presents a paradox of submission and revolt. Gregor has failed to make meaningful relationships. All his human contacts are humiliating. Readers become able to identify with Gregor the 'Outsider', whose bid for revenge plunges him into psychosis and final oblivion.

B Sexual morals come up for clarification in self-questioning within innumerable permutations of love relationships fraught with conflict, guilt and lack of emotional staying power.

Adolescent anorexic crusades, symbolic acts of violence and emotional blackmail carry the trail of inner chaos.

Nathaniel Hawthorne's *The scarlet letter*[22] reflects the Puritan sexual morals of 1630 Boston. Hester, a woman of pride and dignity, refuses to be humbled by the Puritan morality which debases womanhood. Bearing the scarlet letter for life gives Hester a moral stature with a sensibility which enables her to recognize hidden guilt in others. Her sin is not described but the implication of the man in Holy Orders is implicit. One wonders whether the ostracism would sow the seeds of maladjustment in her child. Does the fate of mothers like Hester psychologically cripple their daughters?

George Eliot, at the more genteel Victorian level, provides a brilliant analysis of her experience of sexual morality and arrives at solutions that are valid for our time. Many of her readers have gained insight and understanding into individual dilemmas and derived the courage to evolve their own personal and sexual morality in our present context.

III The long view

The past, present and future merge into the human drama in the search for personal harmony. Strong human emotions are the bedrock from which genuine cognitive changes and personal morality may come about.

Camus dwells on *The outsider*'s[23] need to understand the meaning of the life into which he has been thrust. This need remains unsatisfied because the world which confronts him is absurd. Is suicide the solution to a meaningless life? The mind leads one to the edge of the cliff but the body shrinks from annihilation.

Man wants and needs to comprehend the world he inhabits through a unifying principle of absolute knowledge and certainty. Neither are achievable. Life is a complete trial and no one knows why. Camus concludes, in *The myth of Sisyphus*,[24] that man can never fully know the world: neither can he know himself. He illustrates how a lack of connection between humans can and does banish empathy. On a deeper, less negotiable level, one may not know oneself or one's next of kin to unravel the deeper mysteries of each other's personality.

Literature, like art, music and psychotherapy, offers a variety of alternative view-points to meet our many needs and ultimately to set us free. Self-knowledge is the key that can unlock our minds from the stranglehold of our long-established false assumptions upon which our unhappiness rests. We need new beginnings.

The courage we need to start anew is not a chance gift of Nature like Intelligence. Courage is thought out with feeling and it takes action to know by finding it.

References

1 Brontë, C., *Jane Eyre*, London, J. M. Dent, 1983.
2 Dickens, C., *David Copperfield*, Harmondsworth, Penguin Books, 1969.
3 Hesse, H., *Siddhartha*, London, Pan Books, 1974.
4 Heinlein, R. A., *Job: a comedy of Justice*, London, New English Library, 1985.
5 Carroll, L., *Alice in Wonderland*, London, J. M. Dent, 1954.
6 Carroll, L., *Alice through the looking glass*, London, J. M. Dent, 1979.
7 Carroll, L., *Jabberwocky and other poems*, London, Macmillan, 1981.
8 Cooper, S., *The dark is rising* series, London, Chatto & Windus, 1965.
9 Brontë, E., *Wuthering Heights*, London, Chatto & Windus, 1947.

10 Hardy, T., *Jude the obscure*, London, J. M. Dent, 1985.
11 Hardy, T., *Tess of the D'Urbevilles*, London, J. M. Dent, 1984.
12 Hills, S., *In the Springtime of the year*, Harmondsworth, Penguin Books, 1971.
13 Ritz, D., *Divided soul: life of Marvin Gaye*, London, M. Joseph, 1985.
14 Maugham, W. S., *Of human bondage*, London, Pan Books, 1975.
15 Hesse, H., *op.cit.*
16 Forster, E. M., *A passage to India*, Harmondsworth, Penguin Books, 1985.
17 Boycott, R., *A nice girl like me: a story of the Seventies*, London, Chatto & Windus, 1984.
18 Gordon, B., *I am dancing as fast as I can*, London, Bantam Books, 1981.
19 Dostoevsky, F. M., *Crime and punishment*, Harmondsworth, Penguin Books, 1970.
20 Thoreau, H. D., *Diary of a thinking man*, Dover Publications distributed by Constable, 1960.
21 Kafka, F., *Metamorphosis*, Harmondsworth, Penguin Books, 1970.
22 Hawthorne, D., *The scarlet letter*, Harmondsworth, Penguin Books, 1970.
23 Camus, A., *The outsider*, Harmondsworth, Penguin Books, 1983.
24 Camus, A., *The Myth of Sisyphus*, Harmondsworth, Penguin Books, 1975.

7 The clinical use of self-help manuals

Stephen Hunt

Browsing through any high street bookshop you are likely to come across any one of the following books: *Living with Fear* (Isaac Marks), *'Relax and Enjoy It'* (Aleph One Ltd), *Programme Practice for Agoraphobia* (Matthews *et al.*), *Migraine Relief: A Personal Treatment* (Kohlenberg), *Treat Yourself to Sex* (Brown & Faulder), *Living with Children* (Patterson & Guillion), *Kick the Smoking Habit* (Aleph One Ltd), *Trouble with Tranquillizers* (Release). Chances are, these can also be found in public and hospital libraries. Many more never reach publication but are nonetheless used by a wide range of health care professionals. These are self-help treatment programmes that present readers with a specific set of therapeutic procedures. They aim to treat a wide range of clinical problems: psychological, emotional and physical. As such they form an important and rapidly expanding subset of reading therapy. So rapid is their growth that early review studies covered a broad range of manuals dealing with fear reduction, phobias, smoking, obesity, sexual dysfunctions, assertiveness, child behaviour problems, study skills and physical fitness.[1,2] Within only a couple of years it was necessary to restrict reviews to specific problems tackled using specific kinds of self-help manuals, c.f. *Training Parents in Child Management Skills*.[3]

In an effort to keep up with this rising tide of material, self-help resource files have begun to appear in the UK. One such file is run by the Exeter Health Authority, Department of Clinical Psychology. It lists over 150 books, pamphlets, manuals and cassettes imparting specific advice to help with adult mental health problems.[4] A similar file exists at the Department of Clinical Psychology, Grampian Health Board.

Clearly it is beyond the scope of this chapter to review all this material, or indeed all the problems with which self-help manuals have been used. Instead we will concentrate on self-help manuals that have been empirically tested, that deal with clinical problems and are based on behaviour therapy. A large proportion of self-help manuals are based on behaviour therapy.[5] This may be because behaviour therapy is often considered prescriptive in that it involves a systematic assessment and application of specific procedures made explicit to clients in therapy. These procedures tend to be easily understandable and based on empirically validated theories of human learning. This chapter will consider what kinds of manuals are currently available, their advantages and disadvantages. In addition we will briefly consider how material should be designed and evaluated, and present a detailed example of one such self-help manual. This is not offered as a shining example of how best to use self-help manuals, more to illustrate some of the practicalities and problems involved in using and evaluating specific written instructions to achieve specific therapeutic goals.

A taxonomy of self-help manuals

These materials can be described and differentiated on the basis of at least four different variables. Each variable can be seen as a continuum.

a) Fictional versus factual manuals

Fictional material, when used therapeutically, seeks to achieve its aim through processes such as catharsis and insight. Factual, instructional manuals give information and specific instructions to change dysfunctional skills and attitudes. Most self-help manuals are factual, they impart factual information. However, in an effort not to produce written material that is too 'dry' some manuals use a combination of factual and fictional material to achieve therapeutic aims. Beselal *et al.*[6] produced a manual to treat bed-wetting in children. It was over 100 pages long and very 'wordy and intellectual for families who are not literature oriented'.[7] In addition it was written in a dense textbook style recounting an instructional bed-time story with a fictitious child. It also included general guidelines on how dry beds could be achieved. Its evaluation showed that it was less effective than the same approach delivered using a therapist and no manual.

McMahon and Forehand[8] distinguished between manuals that have a broad versus a narrow focus. In making that distinction they appear to have compounded separate variables, namely whether the manual offers general information versus specific guidelines on achieving change, and whether the manual addresses multiple versus single components and problems.

b) General versus specific

General manuals have their greatest use in imparting information about a particular problem. For instance a number of researchers have found that adults and children who suffer from diabetes are disturbingly ignorant about their condition.[9] In common with other doctor/patient communications, advice about treatment is recalled much less well than diagnostic information.[10] Diabetes is a lifelong disorder and requires complicated treatment regimes including dieting, self-injection and regular testing of blood sugar levels. Although Hulka *et al.*[11] found no correlation between memory for information transmitted and either compliance with prescribed medication or metabolic control, the systematic presentation of selected information will form a central part in any multicomponent package to help diabetics improve compliance and metabolic control.[12] At the other end of the continuum lies self-help manuals imparting specific guidelines on change, an example of which is provided in the second part of this chapter.

c) Multicomponent versus single component manuals

Manuals that aim to produce specific therapeutic change in target behaviours can be considered on the continuums of whether they have many components and seek to change a number of target behaviours or are more selective, targeting single behaviour problems or suggesting a single self-help procedure. *Living with Children*[13] is an example of the multicomponent variety offering specific advice on how best to manage children who refuse requests, fight, are over-active, dependent, frightened or withdrawn. They suggest the use of over fifteen different management strategies to combat these difficulties. More recent child-parenting manuals offer fewer strategies to change fewer behaviours. These include; coping with children on shopping trips[14] and problems with whining.[15] Multicomponent manuals are often more readily available to the public, with single component manuals being more often used as a part of a treatment programme guided by a clinician.

d) The level of therapist contact

Glasgow and Rosen[16,17] identified four levels of therapist contact when using self-help manuals.

(i) Self-administered manuals These form the sole basis for treatment where clients administer the programme themselves without therapist contact (apart perhaps from evaluative data

collection). These include manuals available in bookshops and through the post.

(ii) Minimum contact manuals These retain some contact with the therapist, usually through infrequent meetings, telephone conversations and written communication. The intervention relies primarily on the written material.

(iii) Therapist administered programmes These are based on regular contact with the clinician, the meetings focus on clarifying or elaborating information presented in the manual.

(iv) Therapist directed programmes These are where regular contact occurs between clinician and patient but no manual is used.

As Nimmo and Koch point out,[18] many clinical interventions have confined themselves to only the last category and show how narrowly clinicians' roles have been defined until very recently. Articles reviewing the relative merits of these different types of manuals, when applied to a wide range of clinical problems, are available elsewhere (Glasgow and Rosen,[19,20] McMahon and Forehand,[21] Bernal and North[22]).

Advantages and disadvantages of self-help manuals

Given that self-help manuals are becoming more widely used it is very important to consider their limitations as well as their potential benefits in clinical practice. Bernal and North[23] suggest self-help manuals are most useful with circumscribed problems. As problems become more complex incorporating more facets, or become more generalized across settings, people or time, greater involvement from the therapist is likely to be necessary.

a) Advantages

The problem facing clinicians in almost every branch of health care is that of numbers. Among mental health professionals particularly, there will never be enough therapists to meet the need from the community. Goldberg and Huxley[24] have estimated one year period prevalence for psychiatric morbidity in the community; in other words the number of people in a population with diagnosable psychiatric problems during the course of the year. Their suggested figures is 250 per 1000 adults at risk per year. This does not count distressing but less discreet clinical problems and is only an estimate based on the median of community surveys. Obviously not all these people will consult their GPs, and of those that do, not all will be recognized as having marked psychiatric problems. On the basis of these potential filters Goldberg and Huxley estimate that some 230 per 1000 will be detected and 140 per 1000 referred on to secondary services. Clearly, it is impossible to offer services to all these potential clients at either the GP or secondary referral stage. It then becomes necessary to consider how best to use limited resources. Group work and the training of other professionals in psychological skills are two options. Perhaps the careful use of self-help manuals might provide a third. This issue demands the analysis of relative cost effectiveness. This will be discussed in more detail later but at face value it would appear that self-help manuals might offer a cost effective alternative treatment option. This is a tentative statement, as terms like cost effectiveness and cost benefit assume some assessment of benefit in personal and financial terms, as well as cost. Whilst that would seem obvious it appears to have eluded many publishers and producers of self-help manuals.

There may also be some therapeutic advantages in such an approach, as Nimmo and Koch[25] point out. There is a growing body of evidence to suggest that behaviour change that is attributed to oneself is more likely to be maintained than behaviour change where an individual believes it has been caused by external factors such as his therapist, medication or the mere passage of time.[26,27]

b) Disadvantages

In treatments in which therapists and clients have face to face contact, the relationship itself creates non-specific ‘effects’. These effects, common to all therapist-directed therapies, are said to contribute to the effectiveness of the treatment but are not the therapeutically potent procedures themselves. They are an important determinant of treatment outcome. Such non-specific variables include the expectations of treatment, the expectations of outcome, talking to someone who cares and will listen, talking to people who do not judge, being understood, receiving encouragement, etc. These might well be missed from self-administered manuals and may dilute effectiveness as a consequence. Conceivably they may be part of minimum contact or therapist-directed delivery modes and it may be possible to design a text to accommodate some of these issues, such as matching the content of the manual to an assessment of the expectations of potential users.

Glasgow and Rosen[28] noted that as many as fifty per cent of subjects dropped out from self-administered fear reduction programmes. Comparable drop-out rates have been reported in other self-help treatment studies. Subject attrition is not a problem limited only to self-help manuals, it plagues many therapist-directed treatments. Without specific research and the reporting of subjects and treatment variables associated with drop-out, it will not be possible to refine manuals and delivery systems to minimize this apparently unavoidable problem. It is possible, for instance, that a minimum level of therapist contact may be needed in all manuals dealing with clinical problems.

Drop-out can be considered as the most extreme form of non-compliance in treatment. Less extreme non-compliance is also a major problem for behaviourally based self-help manuals.[29] Nimmo and Koch (in press) present a model to explain the relationship between understanding the content of manuals and participation in manual-based treatments. They simplify the model by treating each of the above as dichotomous variables. They argue that clients using manuals can either:

i) Fail to understand the information and participate in the programme.
ii) Understand the information and fail to participate in the programme.
iii) Fail to understand the information and not attempt to participate.
iv) Understand the information and participate in the programme.

They suggest how each of these combinations relates to the predicted outcome of the programme. Following this model begins to allow therapists to understand why a treatment is not working and may give a guide as to how to tackle the problem. Reasons why a manual is not understood or followed are very complex and may be a combination of factors associated with the manual, e.g. text design, or factors associated with the client, e.g. motivational levels or beliefs about the treatment being undertaken. Haynes and Sackett[30] indicate that what you believe about a treatment is a powerful determinate of compliance. For example it is better when a client regards a problem as serious and considers him/herself personally at risk.[31] It is also important that he or she believes the treatment is effective, although evidence of this component is less strong. This has obvious implications for the context of the text.

Text design

If self-help manuals are to be effective they must be easily understandable as a minimum requirement. Nimmo and Koch (in press) recommend that self-help manuals should be designed around the 'programmed text' format since this has been found to speed learning.[32] The programmed text includes the clear identification of goals, which can be measured easily. The client reads through the text at his own speed following a carefully ordered sequence of short items. Each item normally requires the client to respond in some way and feedback on his response is given. Hartley[33] provides other guidelines in text design and suggests the use of simple sentences without subordinate clauses, assertive and active sentences rather than negative and passive ones and the avoidance of technical data. Layout and the use of colour and special cues are also recommended to aid comprehension and recall. Figure 7.1 shows two examples of the same text using contrasting styles of layout.

How to tie the Epankylotos Brokhos

Place the cord across the palm of the left hand between the thumb and forefinger. Allow at least twelve inches to hang over the back of the hand. Wrap the other part of the cord around the back of the hand, over the thumb and across the palm. Grip it firmly between the little finger and the adjacent finger. Holding the left hand flat and, using the right hand, pass the loop nearest the wrist under the other loop. Holding the first loop tightly, pull both loops off the hand.

How to tie the Epankylotos Brokhos

Place the cord across the palm of the left hand between the thumb and forefinger.

Allow at least twelve inches to hang over the back of the hand.

Wrap the other part of the cord around the back of the hand, over the thumb and across the palm.

Grip it firmly between the little finger and the adjacent finger.

Holding the left hand flat and, using the right hand, pass the loop nearest the wrist under the other loop.

Holding the first loop tightly, pull both loops off the hand.

Fig. 7.1 *Above:* text presented without reference to its structure. *Below:* the same text with material grouped systematically on both the horizontal and vertical axes.

(Figure courtesy of E. Brown)

Of even greater significance, is the clarity of the written word. Readable texts are read for greater lengths of time with greater understanding and by more people than less readable texts. A number of readability formulae are available. Some are based on the number of words per sentence and syllables per 100 words[34] and others count the number of multisyllable words in a given number of consecutive sentences.[35] Nimmo and Koch criticize these formulae as being too narrow in their focus and being of questionable validity, given that different formulae produce different readability levels with the same texts. Nevertheless, they are important attempts to judge the clarity of written material and should be much more widely adopted as part of the evaluation process. O'Farrell and Keuthen[36] assessed the readability of 124-page self-help manuals available in America and reported that the median reading level of the manuals required greater reading capabilities than could be expected from 35 per cent of U.S. adults who had completed less than twelve years of schooling. Flesch[37] reported that people like and choose to read material from a reading ease category one level below their actual ability, suggesting even fewer people would choose, use or understand those manuals. In 1978 the American Psychological Association recommended that reading levels should be provided for all self-help manuals but this remains the exception rather than the rule.

Evaluation

Repeatedly, authors and reviewers have argued that self-help manuals must be carefully evaluated before being widely used in clinical practice, or made available to the public. Turvey[38] offers a powerful reason for this. He warns of the 'Benzodiazepine trap'. When first introduced Benzodiazepine drugs (Valium, Librium, etc.) were heralded by over-optimistic claims. Their subsequent inappropriate use and increasing evidence of questionable effectiveness turned public opinion against them. This generalized to other medical treatments and in some cases to the medical profession itself. It is important that this does not happen to the promising but under-evaluated area of self-help manuals.

Glasgow & Rosen[39] suggest three levels of validation:

i) Techniques used in manuals based on theories shown to be effective by research. Here, manuals based on behavioural procedures have an obvious advantage.

ii) The treatments used are shown to be effective in a therapist directed context.

iii) The manual itself is evaluated under conditions of clinical usage, and shown to be effective.

McMahon and Forehand[40] suggest more specific guidelines for the evaluation of manuals themselves. These include assessing the readability level, the use of appropriate controls or comparison groups, follow-up assessments, cost effectiveness data and the use of clinical subjects and settings. Too often manuals are evaluated in non-clinical settings using volunteer university students as subjects.

By way of illustration the following small pilot study describes the use and evaluation of a minimum contact self-help manual for the treatment of childhood bed-wetting.

Using and evaluating a self-help manual

Childhood nocturnal enuresis – the persistent wetting of the bed at night in the absence of organic problems, is one of the most widespread of childhood disorders;[41,42] i.e. it affects some twelve per cent of all school age children. As such, it constitutes one of the most common referrals to the paediatric clinician.

Unlike enuresis that is secondary to organic or psychiatric problems, the majority of bed-wettings are considered to be the result of the child's failure to learn bladder control at night. More specifically the failure to learn to wake up to the sensations of a full bladder. When the child has never learned bladder control, it is termed primary nocturnal enuresis and has been treated successfully for many years using methods taken from behaviour therapy. The most prevalent form of behavioural intervention is the urine alarm, or bell and pad. This is a simple apparatus which consists of an alarm box placed at the foot of the child's bed. It is connected to a urine detector pad located beneath the sleeping child. When a bed-wetting accident occurs the presence of the urine on the pad completes an electrical circuit and this triggers the alarm box. A loud alarm sounds, waking the child, who must then turn off the alarm and go to void the remaining urine in the toilet. In time, waking and the inhibition of urination become conditioned responses to the feelings of a full bladder.

It was first introduced as a treatment for bed-wetting in 1938. Since then the explanatory theories and procedures themselves have gone through a number of changes. However the procedure remains highly successful, at least in terms of the initial arrest of bed-wetting. The results of using this approach have been extensively documented and the literature has been reviewed elsewhere.[43,44] Of the primary enuretic children treated by the orthodox urine alarm, approximately 70 per cent achieve initial dryness.

Why use a self-help manual?

Three main problems exist with the urine alarm. Namely, the length of time it takes for dryness to be achieved, the high drop-out rate and the high relapse rate following initial treatment success. Relapse is a problem for all treatments, behavioural or otherwise.[45] A number of modifications to the procedure reduce relapse rates and reinstatement of the treatment itself is successful in retraining 80 per cent of those who relapse.[46] However these benefits occur at the expense of further increasing treatment duration. In the studies reviewed by Doleys,[47] average treatment duration ranged from five to 16 weeks. In other studies times of 30 weeks and even 12 months have been reported. It has been suggested that the lengthy treatment duration contributes to the high drop-out rate.

One response is to increase the amount of clinical supervision families receive during treatment. This is done in an attempt to increase their cooperation and perseverance, lack of which is found to be the principal cause of treatment failure.[48] This increased expenditure of clinical time is itself a problem for service delivery given the high prevalence of the problem.

Another behavioural approach was introduced to reduce treatment duration. Dry bed training (DBT) is a complex treatment package involving the urine alarm, intense first night training, rewards for dry beds, repeated practice in using the toilet and involving the child in changing and remaking the bed when an accident has occurred. There is evidence that DBT is as effective as the urine alarm, with the added bonus of being significantly faster.[49] In a study of 12 chronic enuretics average treatment duration using DBT was four weeks.[50] However, DBT is a more complex procedure and requires close clinical supervision to help unravel the complexities of the treatment package, as well as providing support for carrying out the procedure.

Thus in DBT, clinicians have a rapid and successful treatment approach based on empirically validated procedures but which make large demands on clinical resources. These demands are increased because it is such a commonly referred disorder. This seems an ideal clinical problem for a self-help manual. Using a manual, would it be possible to reduce the amount of clinical supervision involved, whilst retaining DBT's success rate?

Previous attempts to use a self-help manual to treat enuresis had a number of theoretical, procedural and methodological shortcomings.[51,52] In addition, both manuals were self-administered with no ongoing involvement from clinicians. Given that some support and assistance is necessary to ensure perseverence and compliance, even with DBT, any manual would have to be delivered under minimum contact conditions.

The manual itself

A 30-page illustrated booklet describing a self-help dry bed training package was professionally illustrated and printed (Griffiths[53]). It was based on the DBT procedure initially evaluated by Azrin, Sneed and Fox.[54] Minor variations in procedure were introduced. This modified procedure was then evaluated using 12 severe chronic nocturnal enuretics.[55] One subject withdrew, all the remaining 11 children achieved dryness (defined as 14 consecutive dry nights). Median treatment duration was four weeks with a training period ranging from two to 20 weeks. Subsequently two children relapsed and at the nine month follow-up 73 per cent of subjects were completely dry. Thus, before embarking on an evaluation of the techniques when delivered through a minimal contact manual it was clear that the techniques were successful under therapist directed conditions.

The text of the manual was organized as a step by step sequence and directions, leaving little or no room for misinterpretation by the parents. Virtually no demands were made on memory and the text was aided by a simple to follow lay-out, pictorial cues and colour coded sections (see Figure 7.2).

Separate sections printed on different coloured paper provided an introduction to the procedure, a nightly wetting diary and instructions on how to set up the urine alarm. In addition the training programme itself was explained in three colour-coded sections: the first training night, from the second training night to the seventh consecutive dry night, from the seventh to the fourteenth dry night. Figure 7.2 shows three pages from the second treatment section.

The manual was tested using the Flesch measure of readability. Results indicated that 86 per cent of the standardization sample would be able to read, understand and act upon the instructions contained in the manual.

To help explain how to use the manual a 14-minute video was produced. In the video, each step of the treatment programme was modelled in detail by a young mother and her seven-year-old son (the boy had been treated successfully for

Page Eight

ONGOING TRAINING:
THE SECOND NIGHT AND THOSE FOLLOWING UNTIL THE SEVENTH CONSECUTIVE DRY NIGHT

At bedtime

- Place the urine detector pad on the bed

IF your child was wet the night before, he/she must now do the Ten Times Toilet Practice (See Page Three)

- Give your child a half glass of his/her favourite or usual bedtime drink
- Remind your child that he/she should do his/her best to stay dry and that if he/she is wet then he/she will have to change the sheets and do the Ten Times Toilet Practice
- Ask your child what he/she must do if the need to urinate comes on during the night (Your child should reply that he/she must wake up immediately and go quickly to the toilet)
- Switch on the alarm
- Let your child go to sleep. Do not wake him/her unless the alarm sounds and the bed is wet

IF AN ACCIDENT OCCURS GO TO PAGE NINE

IF YOUR CHILD REMAINS DRY THROUGHOUT THE NIGHT GO TO PAGE TEN

Page Nine

ONGOING TRAINING:
THE SECOND NIGHT AND THOSE FOLLOWING UNTIL THE SEVENTH CONSECUTIVE DRY NIGHT

At any time throughout the night

What to do if your child wets the bed:

- Switch off the alarm
- Waken your child and show your disappointment in him/her for wetting the bed
- Send him/her immediately to the toilet to finish urinating
- Have him/her change his or her nightclothes if wet and take the wet bedlinen to the dirty laundry
- Wipe the pad dry and replace on the bed
- Get your child to remake the bed with clean sheets
- Get him/her to do the Ten Times Toilet Practice (See Page Three)
- Reset the alarm
- Return your child to bed

Repeat this procedure for subsequent accidents during the night

In the morning

★ Make a note in the Diary that your child was wet and show him/her the record

FOR THE NEXT NIGHT GO BACK TO PAGE EIGHT

Page Ten

ONGOING TRAINING:
THE SECOND NIGHT AND THOSE FOLLOWING UNTIL THE SEVENTH CONSECUTIVE DRY NIGHT

In the morning

After a completely dry night:

- Make your child feel the dry sheets
- Praise your child for not wetting the bed both in the morning and during the day
- Make sure other members of the family praise him/her as well

★ Make a note in the Diary that your child was dry and show him/her the record

FOR THE NEXT NIGHT GO BACK TO PAGE EIGHT

WHEN your child has achieved seven completely dry nights in a row....

GO ON TO PAGE ELEVEN

Fig. 7.2. (Figure courtesy of P. Griffiths)

bed-wetting). Many studies have attested to the superiority of guided modelling over written material in teaching new behaviour.[56] Thus, the video was likely to enhance the learning of new procedures for parents and children. In addition, similarity to the model increases the effectiveness of modelling. At the bottom of the video picture a coloured bar matched to the colour of the appropriate section of the manual which reminded parents which part of the programme they were watching. Superimposed on the colour was the time at which different stages were to be executed. A narrative also gave parents a simple commentary on what the mother and her child were doing and which page of the manual they were watching being enacted.

Where was the manual tested?

As McMahon and Forehand[57] suggest, self-help manuals should be evaluated under conditions of intended clinical usage. The Cambridge Enuresis Clinic is a NHS clinic run by a clinical psychologist. It takes referrals from GPs, school nurses, paediatricians and health visitors. The standard clinic procedure is as follows: After a physical check and urine test by the GP, referrals are seen for an assessment interview and a treatment plan is formulated. If this is to include the urine alarm, it is issued and the child is seen at home every week to ten days by school nurses. If complications arise the child is seen again in the clinic. Children are not referred under six years of age and they tend to be chronic and severe night-time wetters, with whom previous treatments have failed.

Who was the manual tested on?

If a self-help manual is to be used for a clinical population there is little point evaluating it with a non-clinical client group. Effects gained with the latter group cannot be assumed to apply to the clinical population. Subjects for this study were selected from referrals to the clinic. From a total of 23 screened, 10 (eight males and two females) were selected and consented to take part. All were offered either the urine alarm or manual-based DBT. Only one mum chose the former, saying that as she was the 'bread winner' she considered the latter too demanding. Day-time wetters or those with wetting secondary to other problems were screened out and this left 10 subjects all with chronic primary nocturnal enuresis, wetting the bed at least six to seven nights a week before treatment started. Their ages ranged from five years eight months to 10 years four months and all had previous treatment failures with lifting, fluid restrictions, drugs or the urine alarm.

How was the manual evaluated?

Each subject acted as their own control in that they were asked to keep a record of wet and dry nights for four weeks between the first and second interview. These baseline wetting frequencies were then compared with their weekly wetting frequencies following the implementation of the manual-based package.

At the second interview a principal trainer was selected (this turned out to be the mother in all cases). The principal trainer and the child were then shown the video and they were then asked to set up the urine alarm on a bed in the clinic. Having been corrected when necessary, they were given an alarm and manual and told that they would be telephoned at home after the first intensive night's training and weekly thereafter. During these phone calls a checklist was used to monitor progress and help with any procedural difficulties. Clearly, without being in the house to observe the procedures being carried out there is no reliable way of assessing compliance to the package. Home visits were not considered as they would have significantly increased the amount of clinical involvement with each family.

The family was seen in the clinic at the conclusion of treatment. A treatment satisfaction questionaire was given to parents to investigate the acceptability of the package. Where subjects dropped out the questionnaires were sent and returned by post. Each subject (including those who dropped out) was followed up by telephone twelve months after treatment had finished. Throughout, all face to face clinical contact and telephone contacts were timed and recorded. Details of the treatments used are outlined in the treatment manual[58] and these have been published in detail elsewhere.[59]

Did it work?

Of the ten subjects who were treated using this approach 80 per cent reached the criterion of 14 consecutive dry nights. This was achieved with a mean treatment time of seven weeks and one day, with a range from two to 14 weeks. Figure 7.3 shows the wet nights per week for all the subjects over the baseline and treatment periods.

The drop-out rate from this small study was 20 per cent. Those were the two youngest wetters and in the latter case

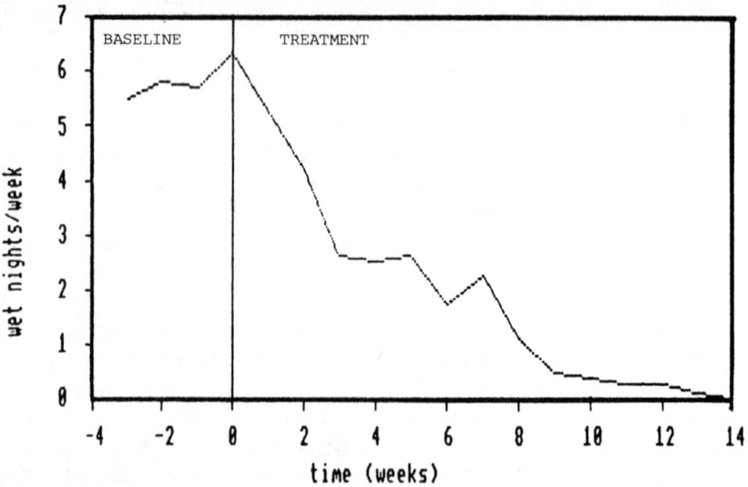

Fig. 7.3 Mean wet nights/week for baseline and treatment conditions

the child's mother, contrary to the programme's instructions, continued to wake him hourly after the first night. This presents a problem, as even with a clearly understandable manual and explanatory video there are a number of complex procedures to follow and at least one mother from the 10 did not follow an important part of the procedure. This is a reminder that whilst we think we make procedures easier to understand they may still be too complex or presented in such a way as to confuse. It is unclear why this subject's mother had difficulty following the procedure but during the second interview she had her three young children with her whilst she watched the video and it is possible that she was distracted by this. The two subjects who had dropped out of the treatment were still wetting at follow-up.

Of those who had successfully completed treatment two subjects did relapse during the 12-month follow-up period.

At first glance it would appear that the treatment package delivered through a minimum contact self-help manual is as effective as a therapist-directed urine alarm. It would also appear that these effects have been produced as quickly as any therapist-directed DBT package. Although the initial remission, relapse and drop-out figures for this study appear impressive they must be considered with caution. To begin with, the sample size of this study was very small and although selected from a severe and chronic clinical group can not be considered to be representative of all nocturnal primary enuretics. Enuretics who wet during the day as well as those who were not on the telephone were screened out of the study. It would be necessary to repeat these findings with a larger more heterogeneous group before claims of 'wonder cure' can be made.

When compared with themselves, prior to undertaking the treatment, the groups' frequency of nightly wetting dropped markedly. It cannot be concluded however that it was the treatment *per se* that produced the change. For instance it may have been the expectation of treatment on the part of the parents (and/or the child) that produced renewed motivation to become dry. Alternatively it could merely have been the passage of time. Forsythe and Redmond[60] have shown that the spontaneous remission rate for enuretics is between 20 and 25 per cent, depending on age. In order to screen out these possibilities a different experimental design would have to be considered. Matched or randomly assigned subjects could be allocated to two groups, one of which received treatment whilst the other remained on the waiting list. Empirically this would allow us to be more certain about the causative link between treatment and improvement. However this approach could be criticized on ethical grounds as it might be seen as improper to withhold treatment from clients who might otherwise benefit from it. This is particularly important when undertaking research within the NHS. An alternate experimental design which also increases the likelihood that changes in wetting were produced by the treatment package would be what is known as a 'reversal design'. This has the advantage of needing fewer subjects than group comparisons and does not involve waiting list control groups. Here, as with the present study, children act as their own controls. An initial baseline period is followed by the intervention period. At a certain stage the intervention is stopped and a 'no treatment' baseline period reintroduced. If the decrease in wetting seen during the intervention stops, or is reversed once the baseline is reintroduced, then we are in a stronger position to claim that it is the treatment package that is producing the reduction in wetting. If reinstatement of the intervention again produces a marked decrease in wetting for the group the case is further strengthened. Of course we still do not know what component of the treatment package has produced the change and that would need the examination of components in isolation.

There is another difficulty with the study in its present form. On paper the speed of treatment and various measures of success appear comparable with other evaluations of therapist-directed dry bed training. Unfortunately we cannot make that claim because the present and other studies differ markedly on a number of variables. The number and types of subjects involved differ, for example the severity of wetting reported in different studies varies from six nights a week to once a month. Evaluations were undertaken using different therapists with follow-up periods ranging from six weeks to 12 months, outcome criteria ranging from seven consecutive dry nights to 21 consecutive dry nights. In order to claim comparability between two different treatments (or of more relevance to the evaluation of self-help manuals) to similar treatments under the differing modes of delivery, group studies would need to be reconsidered. In these, the modes of delivery might differ whilst trying to hold stable as many other variables as possible. Such an evaluation might involve randomly assigning incoming clinic referrals to one of two treatment groups with the same therapist and procedure but differing only in the way that the treatment was delivered. Once again the question of control groups might have to be considered.

After considering carefully what the present study does tell us we are left with the rapid and effective treatment approach for a small number of older, severe but motivated bed-wetters. In other words we can answer the question 'does the treatment work?' with 'yes, for a small, selected group of enuretics'. We are not able to answer the following questions: 'Does the approach work as well as other approaches?, or the same approach delivered under therapist-directed conditions?', or 'which component of this treatment approach is the therapeutically powerful ingredient?' The main aim of this study was to see if an approach to bed-wetting could be developed that was effective in reducing bed-wetting whilst also allowing a major saving in clinical supervision. It might be useful to consider clinician's time within the more general context of a cost effectiveness analysis, as the relative cost effectiveness of a self-help manual is, in many cases, a *raison d'etre*.

Cost effectiveness analyses

Cost effectiveness analyses are seldom reported when treatments are evaluated. McMahon and Forehand[61] reviewed 21 studies of self-help manuals in parent training and noted that none had attempted a cost effectiveness analysis. A few studies do report the measurement of some subjective client costs using consumer satisfaction questionnaires but this does not constitute a full cost effectiveness analysis, nor does the more commonly reported cost accounting analysis in which the financial costs of two or more treatments are compared without attempting to evaluate outcome. It is not surprising that such analyses have not been regularly undertaken. First it is often very difficult to define and measure all the components necessary for the full analysis. Secondly it is a very time-consuming task as we found out when attempting such an analysis for the enuresis self-help manual. Thirdly it is rather a chicken and egg situation as it is of limited use until other modes of delivery are evaluated in the same way, enabling clinicians and service planners to compare the relative cost effectiveness of a number of approaches. Finally, only recently has such a model for such analysis become available.[62,63]

Cost effectiveness analyses require the measurement of both the amount of resources consumed with the outcome produced. Yates[64] lists the kind of resources necessary to enable the full analysis to take place. He differentiates between resource costs and client costs both objective and subjective. McMahon and Forehand[65] provide examples of these variables which are particularly relevant to the evaluation of written materials. These include:

i) the amount of professional time involved,
ii) the cost of the manual or other equipment,
iii) client costs such as the cost of the manual to them, time taken to implement the manual, perceived usefulness and difficulty of the programme, etc.

The subjective client costs are particularly important with self-help manuals because they may well determine how closely procedures are followed by the client. In therapist-directed treatments these variables can be assessed and addressed continually within sessions. With the absence of ongoing contact they could be missed and the effectiveness of the intervention would suffer accordingly. Applying a simplified cost effectiveness model to the present study it could be said that the critical resource cost under examination was the amount of professional time involved in the treatment programme.

1. Resource costs

The treatment results were achieved with an average input of two hours 21 minutes professional time spent on each subject. This involved three interviews each of approximately 30 minutes' duration (the last one being necessary more for research than clinical purposes). The remainder of the time was spent in weekly telephone contact with the subjects. This represented a major saving of approximately five hours professional time per enuretic child when compared with the standard urine alarm procedure as used in the Enuresis Clinic. However the latter is only an estimate of professional involvement and would need to be confirmed with more detailed time recordings. Nevertheless this approach appears to produce significant savings in professional time. As before, caution is necessary in the interpretation of these data as no other study has measured professional time and few studies give clear enough procedural details to make estimates possible. Thus, further research is needed here too.

Other resource costs in this programme include the use of a bell and pad apparatus but this is common to most behavioural treatments. Where such an apparatus is not used the outcome is often adversely affected.[66,67] New materials involved the self-help manual itself which would cost £3.95 if commercially available to a service or parents. In addition the video took two months part-time work using trained technicians, the author and expensive video production facilities. This however is a capital cost and would not recur.

It could be argued that the major saving in clinical time has been produced at the expense of a subjective client cost.

2. *Client costs*

There are no financial costs involved for the clients, other than funding travel to the Cambridge clinic on three occasions. The subjective costs were assessed using the treatment satisfaction questionnaire. The questionnaire was based on one used by Fincham and Spettell[68] to measure the acceptability of bed-wetting treatment packages. It requires parents to rate how acceptable they found the treatment, whether they would recommend it to a friend and the extent to which the treatment caused stress in the family. In addition the questionnaire used here broke down the treatment package into its component parts and parents rated how difficult and useful each component was on a 0-4 scale. This provided measures of subjective cost and perceived benefit for each of the treatment components. Results showed that parents found the approach both difficult and demanding. This is the additional client cost mentioned above. Sorotzkin[69] concludes that therapist-directed dry bed training places considerable demands on parents and children. It is likely that providing a similar approach for a minimum contact condition will make the procedure more demanding and potentially more stressful.

By examining each treatment component in isolation it was possible to discover which components were perceived as the most difficult and contributed most to the perception of the overall package as difficult and demanding. Three discreet components were consistently rated as 'very demanding'. Two components provided aversive consequences to the child for wetting, namely 'positive practice' and 'cleanliness training'. The third was the waking schedule used during the first night of training. Could these not be dropped from future programmes to make the approach less demanding? Before answering that we need to understand how much these components effect overall outcome. In a component analysis of therapist-directed DBT Bollard and Nettlebeck[70] reported that positive practice and cleanliness training did not add significantly to the effectiveness of the urine alarm on its own and concluded that they could be dropped from the package with a little difference to outcome. In the same study the authors found the waking schedule to be the most important single procedure next to the alarm itself. The alarm with the waking schedule was almost as effective as the full DBT procedure, thus it should be retained in the programme. In the present study parents reported the procedure as difficult but because it only occurred on one night, tolerable. Some parents also rated the waking schedule as useful because they felt it was responsible for producing the first dry night their children had had for many years. This they felt provided the boost for subsequent training nights.

3. *Benefits*

The major benefits of this programme to both the service provided and the subject alike is the percentage who achieve initial dryness and the speed with which this is achieved. In common with many self-help approaches the subjects and their parents perceived themselves as the main agents of the change as measured by a visual analogue scale on the Treatment Satisfaction Questionnaire. This shift in 'locus of control' away from the clinician and the treatment and towards the clients may have beneficial effects in terms of the durability of the treatment.[71] However this would need to be supported by closer experimental examination. The small pilot study reported here has clear methodological shortcomings which restrict the claims that can be made about manual-assisted dry bed training. However it does enable us to modify the treatment components to better facilitate delivery through a self-help manual. It also suggests further areas of research as all pilot studies should.

It would seem that the behavioural treatment of choice for primary nocturnal enuresis can be delivered using a self-help manual with a marked saving in clinical time. That is not to say that this is a new wonder cure. It is most effective with an older motivated subgroup of bed-wetters. As Fielding points out,[72] children who wet the bed do not form an homogenous clinical group. Therefore a variety of treatments are likely to be necessary. By providing a rapid and cost effective approach for this subgroup it may leave more time for clinicians to devote to treating families with more intractable problems.

References

1 Glasgow, R. E. and Rosen, G. M., 'Behavioural biblio-therapy: review of self-help behaviour therapy manuals', *Psychological Bulletin*, 85,(1), 1978, 1–23.
2 Glasgow, R. E. and Rosen, G. M., 'Self-help behaviour therapy manuals: recent developments and clinical usage', *Clinical Behaviour Therapy Reviews*, 1, 1979, 1–19.
3 McMahon, R. T. and Forehand, R., 'Self-help behaviour therapies in parent training' in Lakey, B. B. and Kazdin, A. E., *Advances in Clinical Child Psychology*, New York, Plenum, 1980.
4 Miller, J., 'Self-help skills resource file', Exeter Health Authority, 1985.
5 Glasgow, R. E. and Rosen, G. M., *op.cit.* (1)
6 Beselal, U. A. *et al.*, 'Evaluation of a parent manual for training enuretic children', *Behavior Research and Therapy*, 18, 1980, 358–60.
7 Griffiths, P., 'Behavioural treatments for primary noctural enuretics', *The Scottish Child*, 11, 1986, 9–11.
8 McMahon, R. T. and Forehand, R., *op.cit.*
9 Watts, F., 'Behavioural aspects of the management of diabetes mellitus: education, self-care and metabolic control', *Behaviour Research and Therapy*, 18, 1980, 171–80.
10 Ley, P. and Spelman, S., *Communicating with the patient*, London, Staples Press, 1967.
11 Hulka, B. S. *et al.*, 'Doctor patient communications and outcomes among diabetic patients', *Journal of Community Health*, 1, 1975, 15–27.
12 Watts, F., *op.cit.*
13 Patterson, G. R. and Guillon, M. E., *Living with children*, Illinois, Champion Ill, Research, 1968.
14 Greene, B. F., Clark, M. B. and Risley, T. R., *Shopping with children*, San Rafael, Academic Therapy, 1977.

15 Forgatch, M. and Monning, E., *Training for child management: early intervention and prevention*, Oregon, Oregon Research Institute, 1976.
16 Glasgow, R. E. and Rosen, G. M., *op.cit.* (1).
17 Glasgow, R. E. and Rosen, G. M., *op.cit.* (2).
18 Nimmo, J. and Koch, M., 'A methodology for self-help booklets', *Clinical Psychology Forum*, No. 4, 1986.
19 Glasgow, R. E. and Rosen, G. M., *op.cit.* (1).
20 Glasgow, R. E. and Rosen, G. M., *op.cit.* (2).
21 McMahon, R. T. and Forehand, R., *op.cit.*
22 Bernal, M. E. and North, J. A., 'A survey of parent training manuals', *Journal of Applied Behaviour Analysis*, 11, 1978, 533–4.
23 *Ibid.*
24 Goldberg, D. and Huxley, P., *Mental illness in the community: the pathway to psychiatric care*, London, Tavistock Publications, 1980.
25 Nimmo, J. and Koch, M., *op.cit.*
26 Valin, S. and Nisbet, R. E., 'Perceiving the causes of one's own behaviour', in Jones, E. E. *et al.*, *Attribution, perceiving the causes of behaviour*, London, General Learning Press, 1972.
27 Bandura, A., *Social learning theory*, Englewood Cliffs, N.J., Prentice Hall, 1979.
28 Glasgow, R. E. and Rosen, G. M., *op.cit.* (1)
29 O'Farrell, T. J. and Keuthen, N. J., 'Readability of behaviour therapy self-help manuals', *Behaviour Therapy*, 14, 1983, 449–54.
30 Haynes, D. L. and Sackett, R. B., *Compliances with therapeutic regimes*, Johns Hopkins University Press, 1976.
31 Becker, M. H., 'Sociobehavioural determinants of compliance', in Haynes, D. L. and Sackett, R. B., *ibid.*
32 Hartley, J., *Designing instructional texts*, London, Kogan Page, 1978.
33 Hartley, J., *The psychology of written communication*, Oxford, Pergamon, 1980.
34 Flesch, R. F., 'A new readability yardstick', *Journal of Applied Psychology*, 32, 1948, 221–33.
35 McLaughlin, G. H., 'SMOG grading a new readability formula', *Journal of Reading*, 12,(8), 1969, 639–46.
36 O'Farrell, T. J. and Keuthen, G. M., *op.cit.*
37 Flesch, R., *How to test readability*, New York, Harper, 1951.
38 Turvey, A., 'Treatment manuals' in Watts, F., *New developments in clinical psychology*, Leicester, B.P.S. Publications, 1985.
39 Glasgow, R. E. and Rosen, G. M., *op.cit.* (2).
40 McMahon, R. J. and Forehand, R. 'Suggestions for evaluating self administered materials in parent training', *Child Behaviour Therapy*, 3, 1981, 65–8.
41 de Jonge, G. A., 'Epidemiology of enuresis: a survey of the literature', in Kolvin, I., Mackeith, R. C. and Meadows, S. R., *Bladder control and enuresis*, London, Heinemann, 1973.
42 Foxman, B., Valderg, R. B. and Brook, R. H., 'Childhood enuresis:

prevalence, perceived input and prescribed treatments', *Paediatrics*, 77,(4), 1986, 482–7.
43 Doleys, D. M., 'Behavioural treatments for nocturnal enuresis in children; a review of the recent literature', *Psychological Bulletin*, 84, 1978, 30–54.
44 Sorotzkin, B., 'Nocturnal enuresis: current perspectives', *Clinical Psychology Review*, 4, 1984, 293–316.
45 Bollard, J., 'A two year follow up of bed-wetters treated by dry bed training and standard conditioning', *Behaviour Research and Therapy*, 20, 1982, 571–80.
46 Sacks, S. and DeLeon, G., 'Training the enuretic child', *Behaviour Research and Therapy*, 16, 1978, 276–9.
47 Doleys, D. M., *op.cit.*
48 Dische, S. *et al.*, 'Childhood nocturnal enuresis: factors associated with outcome of treatment with an enuresis alarm', *Developmental Medicine and Child Neurology*, 25, 1983, 67–80.
49 Bollard, J., *op.cit.*
50 Griffiths, P., Meldrum, C. and McWilliam, R., 'Dry bed training in the treatment of nocturnal enuresis in childhood: a research report', *Journal of Child Psychology and Psychiatry*, 23, 1982, 483–95.
51 Houts, A. C., Leibert, R. H. and Padewer, W., 'A delivery system for the treatment of primary enuresis', *Journal of Abnormal Child Psychology*, 11, 1983, 513–20.
52 Beselal, U. A. *et al., op.cit.*
53 Griffiths, P., *A training method for the prevention of bed-wetting in childhood: parents manual*, unpublished, 1984.
54 Azrin, N. H., Sneed, T. J. and Fox, R. M., 'Dry bed training: rapid elimination of childhood enuresis', *Behaviour Research and Therapy*, 12, 1974, 147–56.
55 Griffiths, P., Meldrum, C. and McWilliam, R., *op.cit.*
56 Bandura, A., *op.cit.*
57 McMahon, R. J. and Forehand, R., *op.cit.* (40).
58 Griffiths, P., *op.cit.* (53).
59 Griffiths, P., Meldrum, C. and McWilliam, R., *op.cit.* (50).
60 Forsythe, W. I. and Redmond, A., 'Enuresis and spontaneous cures', *Archives of Disease – Children*, 49, 1974, 259–67.
61 McMahon, R. J. and Forehand, R., *op.cit.* (40)
62 Yates, B. T., 'Three ways to improve the cost effectiveness of behavioural programmes for obesity reduction', *International Journal of Obesity*, 2, 1978, 249–66.
63 Yates, B. T., 'The theory and practice of cost utility, cost effectiveness and cost benefit analysis in behavioural medicine: towards delivering more health care for less money', in Ferguson, M. and Taylor, C. B., *The comprehensive handbook of behavioural medicine*, New York, S.D. Books, 1987.
64 *Ibid.*
65 McMahon, R. J. and Forehand, R., *op.cit.* (40)
66 Bollard, J. and Nettelbeck, T., 'A component analysis of dry bed

training for treatment for bed-wetting', *Behaviour Research and Therapy*, 20, 1982, 383–90.
67 Nettlebeck, T. and Laugeluddecke, P., 'Dry bed training without an alarm', *Behaviour Research and Therapy*, 17, 1979, 403–4.
68 Fincham, F. D. and Spettell, C., 'The acceptability of dry bed training as treatment of nocturnal enuresis', *Behaviour Therapy*, 15, 1984, 388–94.
69 Sorotzkin, B., *op.cit.*
70 Bollard, J. and Nettlebeck, T., *op.cit.*
71 Bandura, A., *op.cit.*
72 Fielding, D., 'An analysis of the behaviour of day and night wetting children: towards a model of micturition control', *Behaviour Research and Therapy*, 22, 1982, 49–60.

8 Special reading materials for handicapped children

Margaret R. Marshall

Reading therapy used with children often has aspects not common to therapy with adults. There are two obvious constraints, that children are still learning to read and their varying degrees of fluency have to be taken into account, and that the children's stage of conceptual development and experience affects understanding of what is read by or to them. Additional dimensions, possibilities and problems are present in reading therapy with children handicapped by mental or physical disability and the growing number of children who have multiple handicaps. One dimension, with its attendant possibilities and difficulties, is the parents and family of the handicapped child and examples of both direct and indirect therapeutic help to parents and siblings are given later in the chapter.

At the most basic level the question of what reading does to or for any reader is brought to the fore when faced with children who have difficulty in seeing print or picture, hearing the spoken word, understanding meaning in 'normal' vocabulary and sentence structure or physically turning the page. What are they missing, these children who have a visual handicap, hearing impairment, mental handicap or physical disability that affects reading?

If we believe that reading is a good thing we tend to believe that it offers the reader amongst other benefits – stimuli for emotion, imagination, language, self-awareness, conceptual and perceptual development, vicarious experience, identification of situation or emotion, vocabulary growth, information in terms of facts, values and attitudes, stimulus to conversation, enjoyment.

It follows then, that children and young people whose handicap affects reading are denied these benefits unless special books be created or ordinary children's books are identified as suitable. Intermediaries in the form of all those who connect handicapped children with books, such as librarians, teachers, psychologists, psychiatrists, therapists, social workers, care workers, parents and publishers, also need to be aware of books appropriate to the needs, what is available, where to get it and how to use it.

When the National Library for the Handicapped Child[1] opened in 1985 it became clear that the need for such knowledge was widespread. Visitors and postal and telephone enquiries came from all the professions mentioned so far, plus representatives of organizations concerned with handicapped children and from the professional associations of those who work with handicapped children. Overseas visitors indicate that the need for such knowledge obtains in their countries also.

Reading therapy assumes ability to read, to be read to, to share reading. It assumes an identification of need, but before books can be used by or with children with handicaps, the would-be therapist must select materials that can physically and technically facilitate ease of reading. The following outline of requirements indicates the kinds of special attention needed when selecting books to facilitate both reading alone and reading with children with special needs.

Visual impairment is part of, or in addition to, the disability of many children. Partially-sighted children need large print or clear, black, even typeface in short lines with plenty of white space and good margins. Non-glare paper helps to avoid distracting reflections. The illustrations, whether full colour or black and white pictures should have clear outlines, pinpoint the salient features, be informative rather than decorative and representational rather than abstract.

It is helpful if the picture is not taken to the edge of the page and if it is placed on the same opening as the text being illustrated. There should be no overprinting of text on the picture as this impairs the clarity of both print and picture.

Large print children's books from Chivers Press (Lythway series) include in the 24 titles so far, authors such as Judy Blume,[2] Philippa Pearce, Enid Blyton and Gene Kemp. Clio Press offers in the Windrush series *The Secret diary of Adrian Mole aged 13¾*[3] and its sequel[4] and the Narnia books of C. S. Lewis.[5] Adult books in large print but suitable also for young people can be found amongst the lists of Ulverscroft, Magna Print, Mills and Boon, Chivers and Isis (Clio Press). Some of these are indicated in Margaret Marshall's *Seeing Clear; books for the partially sighted child.*[6]

For the blind child learning to read braille is not necessarily any easier than learning to read print is for a sighted child. The finger tips become the 'eyes' and need to learn the feel of the braille dots, to decode them and then to understand the meaning of the decoded word. The psycholinguistics of learning to read braille or print for visually handicapped children is clearly shown in a readable Australian book by Ena Danielson and Gayle Lamb,[7] where the importance of pre-reading activities and experience is demonstrated and stress laid on the need to read to and with visually handicapped children, using tactile objects stuck onto the page, toys and hand puppets in the form of characters from books e.g. Paddington Bear, Little Red Riding Hood, a witch, and real objects.

Fluency is difficult to achieve and there are not the visual clues to the text provided by the pictures in most reading schemes or picture books for sighted children. Books with tactile raised surface pictures are available and more are being developed.

A boon for sighted people who read with blind children or blind adults to read with sighted children, are the Twin-Vision books available from the American Brotherhood for the Blind.[8] There are hundreds of titles available for loan throughout the Library of Congress service to the blind and physically handicapped. But in Britain just a few titles of Two-way books for children can be obtained on loan from the National Library for the Blind in Stockport via public library services. The books have normal print and pictures with in addition a braille version of the text. The RNIB in Britain inserted braille on clear plasticized sheets into some picture books and had them on trial in 1987–8. Thermoplastic raised surface picture books are available in some countries and take several forms. Virginia Allen Jensen's *Red Thread Riddles*,[9] *What's that?*[10] and *Catching*[11] incorporate printed words, some braille and raised shapes of differing textures e.g. rough and smooth, in plasticized material on the page. Philip Newth's *Roly goes exploring*[12] has pages of cut-out shapes to feel as the story progresses in braille and print.

A picture book for sighted children, *The very busy spider*[13] by Eric Carle, has a raised surface for the spider, spider's web and fly, thus encouraging both sighted and blind children to 'feel' the story.

Physical difficulties in handling a book can be eased by selecting where possible, books that are not overlarge to handle, have a strong safe binding or a soft pliable one. Board books and block books should have rounded corners for greater safety and all materials should be non-toxic where possible.

Books that lie flat when open are particularly helpful to children who cannot use hands to keep the book open, for children in wheelchairs, for those who read with the book laid on a table or reading stand and for the partially-sighted who need to open the book wide to see the text nearest to the inside margins or who hold the book close to the eyes. The same principle is involved in braille books for blind children, in twin-vision and in other books with tactile surfaces, where the reader's fingers do the reading, the brain interprets what is felt and the reader then responds to what is understood.

A book that lies flat is also easier for the therapist who may need to hold child and book, or to lay the book on the table for the child to read or point to, or to hold the book face out for group use.

Group reading or paired reading is increasing and a variety of specially prepared books is available. For example there is the enormous book for a teacher to show to a class while a set of the same book in a smaller version is used by the children, as in the *Story Chest*[14] sets from Arnold-Wheaton. The Ladybird *Puddle Lane*[15] series is designed so that the story is told in very simple language on one page and more complex on the facing page. Others such as Bill Gillham's *Paired Reading Storybooks*[16] are simple picture books with instructions to parents on how best to share the book with the child.

An experiment with children with special needs is described in an article in *Maladjusted and Therapeutic Education,*[17] where Keith Topping paired children aged five–14 with adults, having pretested the children's reading levels. Accuracy, fluency, comprehension and motivation all improved. These findings are supported also in my own experience some years ago with one-to-one story reading with 12-year-old boys in an ESN school, paired with undergraduate and postgraduate students of librarianship one afternoon a week for one term.

For those whose physical disabilities make it difficult to handle books there are reading aids such as book holders for supine and sitting reading, page turners both independently and electrically operated. For those who need the print to be enlarged there is a variety of magnifying aids from bar and dome magnifiers to closed circuit television aids such as Visu-altek which can magnify up to 45 times.

'Reading' the computer is another aspect of particular value to severely handicapped children. Visispeech software for deaf children, the Vincent Workstation system for visually handicapped children, early learning programmes and more advanced reading programmes using adventure story games are available for children who find books physically difficult or impossible to use. These and many more are described in the

BBC's booklet *With a little help from the chip.*[18] Other aspects are dealt with in the *Learning to cope* magazine.[19]

For children who cannot handle the book format there is the alternative of stories on cassette, disc or film. Children with hearing impairment are overjoyed when they can understand books on film, particularly those without words such as *Harold and the purple crayon* (Weston Woods)[20] and Raymond Briggs' *The Snowman.*[21] Other films of children's books, with words but with clear visual information and sequencing include *Rosie's Walk*[22] (Weston Woods) and Eric Hill's *Where's Spot?*[23] (Ventura). For some children the filmed book is a familiar medium, is relaxing and can reduce hyperactivity.

There are many children's books on cassette but not all are read at a speed suitable for less able children to listen to or for following the story in the book while listening. However for the children whose hearing and mind are unimpaired but who are physically unable to hold a book, the use of talking books either via headphones or ordinary speakers can ensure that the benefits of reading independently or otherwise are open to them.

Understanding what is read can be facilitated by a number of technical and editorial measures. Advertisers know that the layout of the advertisement is half the message; page layout can contribute to quicker understanding. Familiar vocabulary and new vocabulary in known surroundings, short lines, sensible line breaks and simple sentence structure help the mind to take in the meaning. Sequencing of information in both fiction and non-fiction provides a framework and gives momentum to reading by propelling the reader along the line of thought or action – an aspect of picture books much sought after for instance by speech therapists.

Freedom from ambiguity and abstraction can help the deaf reader, the mentally handicapped reader and others whose fluency in reading and knowledge of words are not sufficiently developed to cope with having to search amongst several possibilities for the relevant meaning.

Hearing impairment in both pre-lingually and post-lingually deaf children may be accompanied by language, communication and comprehension problems. Cerebral palsy, brain damage and mental handicap may also produce those problems and reading 'ordinary' books is difficult if not impossible. Special books and non-book media can help such children to enjoy stories and information books by providing them in a form that *can* be read, understood and therefore enjoyed. The therapeutic effect of having access to the same book, film or story as other children should not be underestimated.

In addition to specially written books incorporating sign language by special organizations, e.g. *The travels of Polo Bean*[24] from the Donaldson School for the Deaf in Edinburgh and *Can elephants fly?*[25] from the Paget Gormon Society, some ordinary children's books have been given special treatment, as in *Where's Spot?*[26] which is now available in a special edition with British Sign Language diagrams, published by the National Deaf Children's Society in cooperation with Heinemann.

Makaton and Blissymbolics are communication media employed with some speech handicapped children and adults and which appear in some reading materials prepared by individual teachers for particular groups.

Books intended for all children but on themes indicating the joys and tribulations of a child with a disability are indicated in the section dealing with children's books about handicapped children at the end of this chapter.

The reading ability of a handicapped child may be well below the chronological age of that child, well below the average reading age for that age group. For some children it may be significantly below the interest age. This means that for reading independently such children need a high interest/low vocabulary content. In practice this becomes most obvious with prelingually hearing impaired children and teenagers and with mentally handicapped teenagers and adults.

There is a dearth of attractive interesting books for the older age range, a fact emphasized at a 1986 conference by Leicestershire County Library Service on books for mentally handicapped adults and attended by 200 people from every profession concerned with mental handicap and by carers and parents.

Some of the series for less able teenage readers are manageable by some deaf or mentally handicapped young people. Most school library services stock them all and selectors could browse for the most suitable. But most are too complex in sentence structure and vocabulary for the 'average' deaf or mentally handicapped teenager. Special books have been created by Jean Satterthwaite[27] and Barry Noble[28] of the Continuing Education Unit in Leeds, with residential care backgrounds and in the Gatehouse series with simple themes of interest to teenagers and adults who need high interest/low vocabulary content. Imogen Smallwood created the *Jane*[29] books specifically aimed at young teenage readers needing a match between picture and words and simple sequential progress through the book.

The range of simple text, pictorial children's non-fiction is increasing and much of it has possibilities for the older less able reader.

Subject content in the context of reading therapy is vital, but basic selection procedures apply to the reader first as a child or young person and then as a reader with a disability or a problem. This requires a knowledge of whether the subject is of interest to readers within given age bands and then of whether the scope of the subject in a particular book is within the capabilities of that age group. An assessment is needed of whether the book's style of treatment of the subject, theme or genre, is suitable for the intended reader's age, conceptual ability and reading ability.

Then comes the question of relevance of the theme and the 'whole' book to the intended therapy objective, whether the book is for independent reading, reading by, assisted reading or for reading to the child. Reading therapy with a known child takes into account all those plus the known interests, capabilities and needs of that child, but in general it is obvious that some criteria pertain more to one disability than another.

An example of reading therapy evolving out of the ordinary materials underlines the multiplicity of ways in which 'reading' can be used. Susan Beckley, a Carmarthenshire archivist, invites mentally ill and young offenders with their day centre staff to the Archives Services to look at and use documents of local history for bibliotherapy purposes. Print, picture and photograph play a part in this carefully planned activity.[30]

Obviously few books meet all the criteria mentioned so far and compromise is necessary until tailor-made books are created, for independent reading. But the selection of books to be used *with* children for therapy purposes allows further compromise in that the therapist as the intermediary can pinpoint appropriate aspects, words or pictures to stimulate response, where necessary avoiding the irrelevant, ambiguous or too-difficult aspects.

It is clear that the child with one or more senses impaired or missing may be further handicapped if not linked up with books one way or another; handicapped in imagination, language, speech, visual perception, psychological development, social skills, conceptual knowledge, self-knowledge and environmental awareness. These are part of developmental therapy and self-actualization and they are part of, in combination or individually, milieu therapy, psychotherapy, occupational therapy and speech therapy. So how are children's books used in reading therapy with handicapped and/or disturbed children and young people?

The use of books with disturbed and disadvantaged young people as a catalyst for discussion is well known in USA and Scandinavia where there is a large volume of fiction for teenagers and in the UK where school and public libraries stock the American teenage novels and an increasing number of British-centred teenage novels and teenage oriented non-fiction.

Doris J. Robinson in an article entitled 'Talking it out; the use of books in discussion for developmental bibliotherapy with children',[31] separated literary discussion, which is intended to 'enhance the child's knowledge of the art of writing, words, sentences, plot etc.,' from bibliotherapy which she defined as enabling the child to gain 'insight into life and how to cope with it,' acting as a catalyst. She cites the 'problems' that seriously disturb many young people, such as looking after siblings, anger at being abandoned/neglected/ill-treated by parents, death, fostering, abuse, obesity, drugs and aspects such as love, self-esteem, prejudice, loneliness. These aspects are also looked at in Pardick's *Young people with problems; a guide to bibliotherapy*.[32]

Many secondary school librarians and librarians of teenage libraries could cite examples of relief, insight and release obtained for young people to whom they recommend particular books on themes known to be relevant to the teenager's needs. Therapists who work with young people also liaise with librarians in hospitals and educational services to identify appropriate books.

At one time I had a group of mixed age children with mixed problems. Fifteen-year-old Roy came from a disturbed, disadvantaged and violent background and he was under assessment after stabbing a teacher at his school. Two therapeutic activities were provided for the one hour a week for five weeks in which I was involved with him. I gave him the responsibility of reading to five-year-old Dawn who was at the assessment centre to uncover why she was hyperactive and completely out of the control of parents and teachers. When I discovered that she would sit quietly for three or four minutes if she sat beside Roy he was invited to share a picture book with her. He responded well; seemingly he felt that the task made him feel needed and trusted. The second aspect came when I lent him my paperback copy of *The cross and the switchblade*[33] by David Wilkerson, which, though not an 'easy-read' he sat down to read for the rest of the session. He was allowed by the centre staff to take it to his room and required to remember to bring it with him to the next week's session. The subject content struck a chord, he was engrossed in the book and very disappointed when he came to the last page.

From being sullen and unresponsive, though arrogant and abusive when he did speak, he developed in that short space of time during those sessions, into a smiling, more talkative and less aggressively anti-everybody young man.

At its most general children's fiction is useful for providing enjoyment, fun, escapism and motivation to read, whether a child has a problem or not. The good book is not about problems or good experiences but about characters for whom life has some problem or experience. The concern is with reactions to these and can provide insight or information or simply a means of identifying with the character's experience – a sharing.

For some children fiction can be offered as a form of therapy. Adults and children alike tend to think that no one else has this difficulty, this disability, this worry or fear and, paradoxically, it can be comforting to talk to or read about others who have gone through a similar experience; for example Jill Krementz's books for young people, *How it feels when parents divorce* and *How it feels when a parent dies*,[34] in which young people describe their own experiences of these.

Naming the fear in a fictional form can also be releasing and fears can fade if the reader sees a possibility of controlling what is frightening him. Trying it out, experiencing vicariously, knowing someone has been there before you, seeing how it was tackled, can be comforting, informing, reassuring, releasing by externalizing the internal problem.

The fear/problem in story form is shown in manageable portions for the younger or older child, in an ordered way, with cause and effect and has the potential for animating inner speech, talking inside oneself, and for promoting conversation to talk about the text or the pictures. For example some young children and many mentally handicapped children are frightened of holes, such as bath plug holes. A book that deals very effectively with the subject is Ann Jonas' picture book *Holes and peeks*.[35] Older readers with emotional problems can be helped by one or more of the short stories and articles by some excellent writers in *Is anyone there?*[36] edited by Monica Dickens and Rosemary Sutcliff.

A useful aid to identifying an appropriate theme in children's fiction and poetry is the quarterly computerized index on floppy disk *Junior Fiction Index*,[37] an extremely detailed thematic index.

Whether the matching of book to reader's need is done by teachers, librarians or others there is potential in selected fiction for this therapeutic objective.

Over many years I have proved time and again the emotional value of using playacting of well-known stories with disturbed and handicapped children. The principle is role-playing of course, where the child forgets self by taking on another's character. Rather than create a situation where the child has to work out what to say or do, which can be demanding or threatening initially, the use of a familiar story with much repetition, or with characters with whom the disturbed child can identify, enables the child to be taken out of himself. He has an identity he has *chosen* to adopt for the play acting or for which he has been selected by the therapist who believes it will enhance self-esteem and/or public esteem.

At a special school one very pale withdrawn, undernourished, undersized and battered girl aged 12 was thrilled to be selected as Snow White because she had blonde hair. She, who had been abominably treated at home, became 'somebody' in the character of Snow White and the happy ending to that story. Every time I saw her at her school over the next three years I called her Snow White and she responded with a brilliant smile.

David is another example of the value of story to unlock emotions, stimulate speech and release fears, in a pleasurable unforced way. He was one of a group of 12-year-old boys who came to a weekly session for which I invited the help of librarianship students on a one-to-one basis. David was withdrawn and had not spoken to anyone, teachers or pupils, at school for a whole term. For four weeks he came with the other boys but sat on the window sill behind the curtain. On the fifth week I had finished the session with a story to all the boys, accompanied by pictures in the book, the story of the Wooden Baby who was whittled from a piece of wood by a childless elderly couple, only to come alive and be very badly behaved. At the end of the session when all the other children and students were leaving the room, David came out from behind the curtain and stood in front of me. He said, 'I can whittle' and took from his pocket a penknife and a piece of wood whittled into the shape of a dog. In both cases these happenings were relayed to the appropriate staff in the school and formed part of the total picture of the child's development towards wholeness.

Children who have speech impairment requiring therapy often need systematic progressive word and sentence catalysts to encourage vocabulary pronunciation, sentence patterns and links between thoughts and words. Some speech therapists use flash cards, worksheets, sets of photographs or pictures. Others look for children's books or interesting pictorial information books. Differing causes of communication disorder and the incidence of differing accompanying handicaps e.g. mental handicap, deafness, cerebral palsy, may also affect the choice of content, structure or format of reading material to be used, in terms of concepts and vocabulary understandable by the child.

Speech therapists make use of several kinds of children's books in their work with children and young people. Examples include the following;

a. Very simple books with one object per page are useful for identification and naming of the object, restoring lost memory, releasing memory to encourage speech e.g. Kratzmeir and Fay's *My big picture word book.*[38]
b. Books showing progressive action, to relate the object to sentences with 'doing' words e.g. Satome Ichikawa's *Let's play,*[39] Carol Watson's *The shop*[40] in which progressive shopping includes nouns, verbs and humour, Byron Barton's *Building a house*[41] which is suitable for a wide age range and has clear pictures and the sequences in building a house.
c. Narrative picture books relating objects to actions and providing new words to encourage speech and provoke reaction; e.g. Campbell's *Henry's busy day,*[42] Ahlberg's *Help,*[43] Collen Bare's *Guinea pigs don't read*[44] which has colour photographs, large print and repetitive sounds, and, for older children, Smallwood's *Jane shops at the supermarket.*[45]
d. Picture books without words help to stimulate the child to identify what *he* gets from the pictures and to put that into words, e.g. Briggs' *The Snowman,*[46] McTrusty's *Rabbits,*[47] the latter an information book showing the life of wild rabbits in colour scenic drawings.
e. Picture strip books or comics which show sequences and promote progressive sentence structure, e.g. Briggs' *Father Christmas.*[48]

For two years I spent one afternoon a week at an assessment

centre for a city's disturbed, disabled or problem children. For a period of between a week and six weeks the children, who were hyperactive, maladjusted, had physical or mental disabilities, were tested at the Centre. They were at schools where staff were very concerned about the need to identify and treat the difficulties. Some of the children had been withdrawn from the schools and were temporarily attending the Centre from their homes. Others were at the Centre on a temporary residential basis. I saw about eight of the children in a group each Friday.

One boy aged eight had a cleft palate, was diffident in speaking in front of the other children, was short-sighted and had behaviour problems. He loved the children's books read to the group and the book-related activities. I decided to use one story in particular to get him to participate and to try out sounds especially difficult for him with a cleft palate. The story of the three little pigs who built their house of straw, wood and bricks has a bad wolf who says, 'I'll huff and I'll puff till I blow your house down'. I told the story using the picture book version to add visual understanding. Then we practised huffing and puffing with Darren as the big bad wolf. He waited eagerly until the time came for him to say those words and he proudly huffed and puffed until I decided that the house had been blown down. The next two houses were similarly treated to huffs and puffs, two difficult words for Darren but successfully declaimed in a context where the fun overcame the potential effort involved.

On another occasion I had a group of eight children aged five to 15 but there had not been time to tell me about their background in advance of my session with them. After the children had each selected a picture book from the box in which I had a pre-selection of books for various ages, abilities and interests, and I had read each, I told them we were going to do a play about Goldilocks and the Three Bears. I read the story aloud using the picture book face out to show the pictures and then asked for volunteers to play the parts, with me telling the story and the actors saying the spoken parts. One boy put up his hand in answer to a request for Father Bear. When the story reached the points at which Father Bear looks at his porridge, his chair and his bed, the boy loudly declaimed the questions – 'Who's been eating my porridge, who's been sleeping in my bed?' At the end of the story/drama he and the others lined up to take a bow and applause from the others. After the session I described this to the assessment centre staff who were sure I had mistaken the boy. He – they said – is here because he has a gross stutter.

Using the senses to aid understanding is necessary for many children who cannot use the usual sense for the usual purpose or who need to develop a sense to make up for an impaired sense. Using other senses in reading therapy involves for example psychotherapy and physiotherapy, to relate senses of smell, touch and even taste in reading therapy.

The use of books in a physiotherapeutic way is exemplified by block books and board books to encourage the use of fingers and thumbs, hands and the mind. To encourage touch, manipulation, digital dexterity, direction, movement and rhythm, there are many examples of useful books.

Block books are square, small, chunky books such as Rodney Peppe's series, *Numbers, People, Animals* and *Colours,*[49] the latter showing Mary in varying progressive stages of dressing, naming the clothes and the colours, and providing thick cardboard pages hinged to make a double spread. Other chunky small board books include Richard Scarry's *Colours*[50] with rounded edges, Collins *My house,*[51] with clear coloured illustrations and words and Tony Tallarico's *What's opposite?*[52] with flaps and rounded corners encouraging children to lift flaps to find the opposite of the object or event in pictures. Eric Hill's *Play with Spot*[53] in board book format, has an edge shaped to facilitate opening by fingers and thumbs.

Using the fingers to lift flaps and the voice to answer questions asked in the text is enjoyable in the flap edition of *Play with Spot* which is also available in 60 languages, in British Sign Language and in dual language editions e.g. Gujerati, Bengali, Hindi, Urdu and Chinese. Rod Campbell's *From Gran*[54] shows a present from Gran being progressively opened on each page while Zeifert's *Nicky's noisy night*[55] employs flaps within flaps, asks questions and promotes speech and conversation.

Using fingers to scratch and the nose to sniff, is the basis of a range of books mostly available from toyshops, some bookshops and from Franklin Watts. Fleming's *It feels like Christmas; a book of surprises to touch, see and sniff,*[56] Miller's *Sniffy the mouse*[57] and Audean Johnson's *Soft as a kitten*[58] all have tactile materials on the pages, microdot fragrances to smell when the page is scratched and words to read or hear. Though intended for very young children they have a use with older children and even produced delighted interest from a blind television presenter.

Toy books to touch include Rod Campbell's *Speed,*[59] which is a board book on plastic wheels, with pictures and names of wheeled objects. Crowther's *The most amazing hide and seek alphabet book*[60] requires the reader to do things rather than just to look.

Cloth or rag books have a place also in reading thereapy e.g. Purnell's range of rag books, non-toxic and washable, such as *A cat on the mat*[61] with simple words and phrases and clear outlines and colours.

Finger play rhymes are also part of this kind of sensory 'reading' and good examples can be found in Elizabeth Matterson's book *This little puffin; finger play and nursery games*.[62]

I was involved recently with a Toy Library to which about 20 handicapped children came regularly with parents, foster parents and siblings. A good toy collection was well used but the small collection of books on loan from the county library service was rarely touched until I arranged for the above kinds of books to be included in the choice. I began to use books specifically with two children, an eight-year-old autistic girl and a seven-year-old girl with Downs Syndrome.

The autistic girl did not speak but used noises and physical signals to communicate both pleasure and displeasure. For periods of up to a minute she would stand beside my chair as I deliberately looked at a picture book. She would glance at the pictures but not give me time to read the words before she turned the page. Then at or before the end of the book she would move away to roam the room or go to interrupt her mother who was sitting chatting with other mothers about the toys, the children, the problems and the attempts at solutions.

Autism tends to make such children avoid physical contact with people though they may be obsessive in touching objects or themselves and Mary (not her real name) deliberately avoided touching me by simply moving away or shrugging off any contact. One book proved to be a breakthrough – a book of things to be touched, a tactile book. While leafing through the book, cursorily touching the pages with her finger tips we came upon a page depicting a biscuit on a plate, the biscuit having a rough surface not unlike a ginger biscuit. She lingered, refusing to turn the page, her fingers going round and round the outline while I talked to her. Eventually she abruptly moved away. On her next visit to the Toy Library I showed her the book and the same thing happened. On the third occasion she leaned against me as she stood beside the chair. On the fourth occasion she picked up a biscuit from the plate put for parents, found the book on the little wire book rack and brought it to me, leaned against me and waited patiently as I read each page until we came to the biscuit which she then lingered over with her fingers though her eyes were not looking at it. I followed this with other tactile books and books with very clear one object pictures. It seems that by having something to touch, by using another sense in addition to sight and sound, Mary's brain was able to make more sense of what she saw and heard and that she found the experience pleasurable.

Realistic pictures, relevant and recognizable, plus the possibility for participation with tabs, flaps or tactile materials on the page, produce a marked increase in length of concentration, in evidence of pleasure, in understanding and in motivation to read more. In addition to the previously mentioned benefits of reading there can be seen to be the benefit of physical therapy in literally 'handling' these books.

These examples may appear to give a simplistic view but they are not one-off incidents, nor were they in isolation from the team work involving each child. When passed on to the relevant people they provided an insight or aspect not hitherto seen.

Reading stories one to one or to a group of handicapped children is not new, nor is the recognition of its great value. Throughout the country many parents and families share books with their handicapped children and many attend public library story hours, enjoying stories read to them in the classroom or playschool.

Using stories as a springboard for other therapeutic work is also common. In many cases handicapped children are encouraged to write/tell their own stories and to draw pictures arising from the story. Craftwork, topic work and drama are used both as a spin-off from reading and as an integral part of the story or information book work.

Puppetry is a recognized form of therapy in its own right but is also often used with reading and storytelling. Many storytellers working with mentally handicapped and disturbed children and with hospitalized children find that a glove puppet breaks any reserve or hostility and acts as an intermediary between the adult human and the book.

But many handicapped children are not exposed to books and reading at home. In homes where books are not the norm for anyone, parents of children with hearing impairment or multiple handicaps find it particularly difficult to read to or with such children, partly the result of low concentration span, partly the difficulty of finding the right book and in the case of severely handicapped children with little or no communication, the problem of getting no response to what is read: an example is given here to encourage parents to read with such children.

A three-year-old girl, severely disabled by cerebral palsy, was resident in a hospital and her mother visited her daily. The little girl could not communicate and appeared to be mentally handicapped also. The mother had been a librarian and had looked forward to the time when she could read to her children. She was sad that she could not read to her little daughter and that there was never any response from her attempts to talk to her. She came to me at the end of a lecture I had given on sharing books with handicapped children and with tears in her eyes said she was now going to sit by her daughter's bed, read to her and show her the pictures exactly as she would with an able child. I asked her to keep in touch with me and she phoned a few weeks later to say that she was still reading daily to the little girl and felt that she was 'doing something positive' rather than sitting helplessly looking at her child. The effect on the child is not known but there is no doubt that the therapy in this case was effective for the parent.

That leads me to the last aspect, children's books *about* children with handicaps.

There is some misunderstanding about children's books, fiction or non-fiction in which the subject is a handicapped child: one viewpoint believing, wrongly, that they are advocated only for handicapped children says that handicapped children don't want to read about handicapped children. Many other children and young people, however, find interest, identification and information in the books and parents and families of children with disabilities frequently ask social workers, health visitors, librarians and booksellers for such books.

Two examples were given to me by Janet Bower, a social worker with the Dr Barnardo's Keighley Project in West Yorkshire, 'a community based social work project for children and young people with varying handicaps, and their families'.

Talking about the use of such books she said

> I developed the use of books further when working for Bradford's Social Services' 'Give Mum a Break' – a respite care service for families with handicapped children. Much of my time was spent recruiting and working with voluntary carers who would look after a handicapped child to give the parents some time off. I found that it was not uncommon for married couples to come forward as carers with thoughtful concern and interest for the task ahead and then worry as to how they would deal with the topic of handicap and special needs children, with their own children. Obviously this

would have to be dealt with properly as inevitably their own children would be involved in the care of the handicapped child.

Mrs Bower obtained a few books about handicapped children which were used successfully with the carers' children and once that became known, parents of handicapped children asked to borrow them for use with their children, both handicapped and siblings, relatives' and neighbours children.

The Project has now developed a Children's Book Resource at the Project Headquarters in Keighley and contains about 50 factual children's books about handicap. There are plans to extend the stock into children's books that explore for example the emotional aspects of handicap in fictional form. Intended initially for use by the families known to the project and by the Project's staff, it is hoped to widen the scope to other professionals in the area.

Parents of handicapped children are often themselves in need of support and information for the emotional and practical problems or fears arising from their child's disability. Many also find that by discussing the content of such a book with a professional, with another parent or with other children in the family, it is a catalyst for discussion about their own child or their own state of mind. Sometimes teenage members of the family are resentful or ashamed about their feelings towards that child, about how others might react to them having a handicapped brother or sister, about the tasks they have to do for them or about parental neglect because the handicapped child takes up so much time. They can discover they are not alone, others have been there before them and survived, as in *My brother Steven is retarded*,[63] *What about Me?*,[64] *Welcome home Jellybean*,[65] all novels for young people in which the subject of handicap in the family is described with understanding, humour and constructively.

An important function of books with a handicapped child as the main character is to enable non-handicapped people to understand that a child or young person is that first and the disability comes second. The good books are those in which such a child's *abilities* and normality are stressed as in Rachel Anderson's *Tim walks*[66] (teenage boy with Downs Syndrome), *Anna*[67] (infantile eczema and psoriasis), *I can't hear like you*,[68] (hearing impairment) and *Mundo and the weather child*[69] (hearing impairment). Other books for older children and teenagers include *Sweet Frannie*[70] (paraplegic teenage girl), Ivan Southall's

Let the balloon go[71] (cerebral palsy) and *What difference does it make Danny?*[72] (epilepsy).

In this sense the therapeutic effects of the books lie in their potential for developing or changing attitudes towards handicap, a kind of behaviour modification of the 'normal' adult or child reader. Though such books, and others, can be specifically used by therapists with particularly disturbed siblings of handicapped children, in general the books are of interest to families, siblings and others in their normal reading.

It is clear that in many countries those who live with or work with handicapped children work in isolation from each other, with insufficient transfer of information and experience between them. To build up a 'whole' picture of reading therapy with children with special needs there is a need for team work between publishers, librarians, pre-school staff, teachers, residential and care workers, social workers and health visitors, specialists and therapists and the organizations concerned with handicapped children, to include also the children themselves. Whether the child needs special books or ordinary books, reading therapy requires the 'right' books.

References

1 National Library for the Handicapped Child, University of London, Institute of Education, 20 Bedford Way, London WC1H 0AL. Tel. 01–636 1500 ext. 599.

2 Blume, J., *Are you there God? It's me, Margaret*, Bath, Chivers Press, 1985, Lythway large print edition.

3 Townsend, S., *The Secret Diary of Adrian Mole Aged 13¾*, Oxford, Clio Press, 1985 (Windrush large print children's books).

4 Townsend, S. *The Growing Pains of Adrian Mole*, Oxford, Clio Press, 1985 (Windrush large print children's books).

5 Lewis, C. S., *The lion, the witch and the wardrobe*, Oxford, Clio Press, 1986 (Windrush large print children's books).

6 Marshall, M. R., *Seeing clear: books and materials suitable for the partially sighted child*, Swindon, School Library Association, 1985, (large print edition)

7 Danielson, E. and Lamb, G., *Beginning reading/writing for braille or print users: a teacher's guide to the psycholinguistic viewpoint*, Melbourne, Royal Victorian Institute for the Blind School, R.V.I.B. Australia, 1983 (Available in UK from the National Library for the Handicapped Child).

8 American Brotherhood for the Blind, 18440 Oxnard Street, Tarzana, California 91356, USA.

9 Jensen, V. A. and Edman, P., *Red thread riddles*, London, Collins, 1980.
10 Jensen, V. A. and Haller, D. W., *What's that?* London, Collins, 1978.
11 Jensen, V. A., *Catching*, London, Collins, 1984.
12 Newth, P. *Roly goes exploring: a book for blind and sighted children in braille and standard type with pictures to feel as well as see*, London, Collins, 1981.
13 Carle, E., *The very busy spider*, London, Hamish Hamilton, 1985.
14 *Story Chest* reading sets, Exeter, Arnold Wheaton.
15 McCullagh, S., *Puddle Lane reading programme*, Loughborough, Ladybird Books.
16 Gillham, B., *Awful Arabella*, London, Methuen, 1986, (Paired Reading Storybooks).
17 Topping, K. and others, 'Paired reading', *Maladjusted and Therapeutic Education*, 3, (3), 1986, 52–5.
18 Heddell, F., *With a little help from the chip: how microtechnology can help disabled people to lead more independent lives*, London, BBC TV, 1985.
19 *Learning to Cope*, 1985/6 no. 4, London, Educational Computing Ltd. (Journal).
20 Johnson, C., *Harold and the purple crayon* (video), Henley on Thames, Weston Woods Ltd, 1985.
21 Briggs, R., *The Snowman*, (video) Henley on Thames, Weston Woods Ltd, 1985.
22 Hutchins, P., *Rosie's walk* (video) Henley on Thames, Weston Woods Ltd. 1986. Captioned for use with deaf children.
23 Hill, E., *Where's Spot?* (video) London, Ventura Publishing, 1986.
24 Montgomery, J. *The travels of Polo Bean*, Donaldson School for the Deaf, West Coates, Edinburgh 12, 1985.
25 Fuller, P. and others, *Can elephants fly?* Association for Experiment in Deaf Education. Paget Gormon Society, 3 Gipsy Lane, Headington, Oxford OX3 7PT. Also *The Elephant's day out*.
26 Hill, E., *Where's Spot?* London, National Deaf Children's Society and Puffin, 1986, (dual language British Sign Language edition).
27 Satterthwaite, J., *Roy and the chocolate bar*, Printed Resource Unit for Continuing Education, Leeds, 1979. Also six other titles.
28 Noble, B., *Trail Bikes*, Printed Resource Unit for Continuing Education, (PRU), 27 Harrogate Road, Leeds 7, Yorkshire, England.
29 Smallwood, I., *Jane telephones her friends*, London, Collins, 1986, (Handi-Read Book).
30 Beckley, S., 'Archive therapy in Carmarthenshire', *Journal of the Society of Archivists*, 7, (4), October 1983, 245–6.
31 Robinson, D., 'Talking it out; the use of books in discussion for developmental bibliotherapy with children' *Top of the News*, 41, (2), Winter 1985, 151–5.

32 Pardick, J. A. and Pardick, J, T., *Young people with problems: a guide to bibliotherapy*, New York, Greenwood Press, 1984.
33 Wilkerson, D., *The cross and the switchblade*, Lakeland Publications, 1964.
34 Krementz, J., *How it feels when a parent dies*, London, Gollancz, 1983. and *How it feels when parents divorce*, London, Gollancz, 1985.
35 Jonas, A., *Holes and peeks*, London, Julia MacRae Books, 1984.
36 Dickens, M. and Sutcliff, R., eds., *Is anyone there?* Harmondsworth, Penguin Books, 1978. (Puffin Plus).
37 *Junior Fiction Index: quarterly index to author/title/theme of junior fiction, poetry, short stories*. (on floppy disc for use with BBC B microcomputer). Wheel Publications, 144 Leeming Lane South, Mansfield Nottinghamshire NG19 9BE.
38 Kratzmeier, J. and Fay, H., *My big picture word book*, London, Collins, 1981.
39 Ichikawa, S., *Let's play*, London, Heinemann, 1981.
40 Watson, C. and King, C., *The shop*, London, Usborne, 1980. (Picture Word Books.)
41 Barton, N., *Building a house*, London, Julia MacRae Books, 1984.
42 Campbell, R. *Henry's busy day*, London, Viking Kestrel, 1984.
43 Ahlberg, A., *Help*, London, Walker Books, 1985. (Rednose Readers).
44 Bare, C. S., *Guinea pigs don't read*, London, Hippo Books, Scholastic Publications, 1986.
45 Smallwood, I., *Jane shops at the supermarket*, London, Collins, 1986. (Handi-Read Book).
46 Briggs, R., *The snowman*, Harmondsworth, Penguin Picture Puffin, 1980.
47 McTrusty, R., *Rabbits*, London, A & C Black, 1976.
48 Briggs, R., *Father Christmas*, Harmondsworth, Penguin Books, Puffin, 1975.
49 Peppe, R., *Colours*, London, Methuen, 1985. (Block Book.)
50 Scarry, R., *Colours*, London, Collins, 1982. (Chunky Board Book.)
51 *My House*, London, Collins, 1983. (My First Chunky Board Book.)
52 Tallarico, T., *What's opposite?* London, Methuen, 1986. (Little Hands.)
53 Hill, E., *Play with Spot*, London, Heinemann, 1985. (Little Spot Board Book).
54 Campbell, R., *From Gran*, London, Blackie, 1984.
55 Zeifert, H., *Nicky's noisy night*, Harmondsworth, Penguin, 1986. (Picture Puffin Lift the Flap Book.)
56 Fleming, D., *It feels like Christmas: a book of surprises to touch, see and sniff*, New York, Random House, 1984.
57 Miller, J. P., *Sniffy the mouse*, New York, Random House, n.d. (Sniffy Books.)
58 Johnson, A., *Soft as a kitten*, New York, Random House, 1982.
59 Campbell, R., *Speed*, London, Blackie, 1984. (Little People Pocket Wheels.)

60 Crowther, R., *The most amazing hide and seek alphabet book*, London, Kestrel Viking, 1977.
61 Purnell, *A cat on the mat*, Bristol, Purnell, 1985.
62 Matterson, E., *This little Puffin . . . finger play and nursery games*, Harmondsworth, Penguin, 1969.
63 Sobol, H. L. and Agre, P., *My brother Steven is retarded*, London, Gollancz, 1978.
64 Rodowsky, C. F., *What about me?* London, Franklin Watts, 1976.
65 Shyer, M. F., *Welcome home, Jellybean*, London, Granada, 1982.
66 Anderson, R., *Tim walks*, London, C I O Publishing, 1985.
67 Wadhams, M., *Anna*, London, Bodley Head, 1986.
68 Althea, *I can't hear like you*, London, Dinosaur, 1985.
69 Dunbar, J., *Mundo and the weather child*, London, Heinemann, 1985.
70 Sallis, S., *Sweet Frannie*, London, Heinemann, 1981.
71 Southall, I., *Let the balloon go*, Harmondsworth, Penguin Books, 1972.
72 Young, H., *What difference does it make, Danny?* London, Deutsch, 1980.

Further Reading

Enderby, P. and Philipp, R., 'Speech and language handicap; towards knowing the size of the problem', *British Journal of Disorders of Communication*, 21, 1986, 155–65.

Hallworth, G., *My mind is not in a wheelchair; books and the handicapped child*, Hertfordshire Library Service, UK, 1982.

Marshall, M. R., Simonis-Rupert, S. and Holst, S., *Books for the mentally handicapped; a guide to selection*, The Hague, International Federation of Library Associations, 1983. (Available in UK from Margaret Marshall, 6a Harmer Green Lane, Digswell, Welwyn, Hertfordshire AL6 0AD, UK.)

Marshall, M. R., *Libraries and the handicapped child*, Aldershot, Gower, 1981.

Marshall, M. R., *See all, say all; a selection of books for the language deprived child*, 1BBY British Section, 1985, (Available from Burchell & Martin Ltd., 34 Granville Street, Birmingham B1 2LJ or the author.)

Smyth, M., comp., *Count me in: books for and about disabled children*, London, Library Association Youth Libraries Group. Pamphlet no. 23, 1981.

Thatcher, J., *Teaching reading to mentally handicapped children*, Bromley, Croom Helm, 1984.

9 Children's fears about hospital: how books can help to overcome them

Jocelyn Rodin and Pauline Shelley

It is hard enough for an adult to have to go to hospital but even worse for a child. Imagine what it is like for a child who suddenly finds himself in hospital. He is likely to be sick and in pain, probably frightened about what is going to happen to him, perhaps wary of the many strangers who will need to touch him and certainly suspicious of the strange hospital environment. This was expressed graphically by nine-year-old Shulan who wrote:

> I lost count of how many X-rays I had
> I lost count of how many times I felt sad here
> I lost count of how many days I've been here
> I lost count of how many injections I had.[1]

For many children and their parents, this dreaded event too often becomes the reality. Every year, around three million children are brought in to the accident departments for emergency treatment and nearly one million children have to stay in hospital.[2] Added to this are the many children who come to hospital to see the paediatrician and other specialists or to have medical investigations such as X-rays or blood tests. Undoubtedly this causes tremendous stress because in most families, life revolves around a child who is happy and healthy. However, if the child has an accident or if the child is ill then normal life is suddenly shattered. For the parents this will probably be the most difficult and worrying experience that they have ever been through. Their child is sick and depending upon their loving support more than ever before. Yet they are nervous and anxious themselves. At such a time parents need encouragement too. Hospital staff realize this and do all that they can to help.[3]

The purpose of this chapter is to convince other professionals – such as librarians and teachers – that they have an equally valuable role to play by providing information which will enable children and their parents to cope better with the strange hospital world. The traumatizing effects on a child of a bad hospital experience are widely recognized and we should all strive to ease the child's adjustment to illness and hospitalization.

How do children react to hospital?

Every child is an individual and will respond to new things in his own way. Obviously a child's reaction to the experience of going into hospital will depend upon his age and temperament.[4] Yet of greatest importance is whether or not the child will have to face up to this strange and frightening place on his own or will he get continuous support from someone close to him, preferably either mum or dad?

For the young child who finds himself in hospital, the main problem is that he feels confined and insecure. This is probably the first time that he has ever been out of the familiar home environment which he knows so well. Perhaps his only experience of being away from home will have been to stay with friends or relatives. This, of course, is a pleasant event for the child. He knows the house, the bedroom, even the bed he will sleep in. He can take his own clothes and toys. He knows just what kind of food he will get, indeed probably all his favourite things. He will be loved and cuddled just the same as at home because this other house is just an extension of his own home and is a place where he feels safe and secure.

How different it is for the child who suddenly finds himself in hospital. Imagine what he sees and how he feels. An enormous building with long corridors, waiting rooms, lifts and large rooms with lots of beds; many strange people wearing unusual clothes; noises from ambulances, trolleys, telephones, bleepers; mysterious hospital smells; unfamiliar and threatening machinery and equipment; doctors and nurses who have to touch and examine him, take tests, give injections; other children who look pale and ill, walking with crutches, sitting in wheelchairs, lying in bed on traction or with drip tubes attached to their bodies. Nothing is the same as at home; even the food, the lights, the beds, the bathroom and the lavatories are different. To a small child everything in hospital is unfamiliar, bewildering and potentially threatening. The impact of seeing all these new things at once must be something like having a nightmare when you find yourself on a desert island where no one speaks your language. One child said 'you are frightened of what is going to happen to you and terrified of getting lost because then no one will ever find you and you will never get home again'.

Added to this is the pain and misery of illness which a young child simply cannot understand. He might even think he has been sent to hospital as a punishment because he has done something naughty, something so bad that no one wants him any more and then how long will he have to stay? He probably has no realization of time; to a toddler three days in hospital will seem much the same as three months.

Needless to say, older children will not be so disturbed by the strangeness of the hospital and its differences from home. Hopefully, they will have gained some idea of what it is like from books and television. One of the main problems for school age children is that they quickly get bored in hospital. They miss their usual routine of going to school and playing with their friends. Unless mum and dad can visit often, they tend to lie in bed listlessly or wander around the ward looking for something to do and someone to talk to. They ask a lot of questions about what is going to happen to them and worry about whether they will be given injections or have an operation. Some of them have remarkably vivid imaginations and begin to think quite wrongly that all sorts of horrid and painful things will be done to them.

How can parents help?

It is obvious that most families will have to overcome problems of one kind or another when their child is in hospital. The most important thing is that parents should be with their child as much as possible; they are the vital link between hospital and home providing an ever present stimulus to the child's recovery.

Certainly this was confirmed when Rodin[5] asked groups of parents, paediatricians, paediatric nurses, teachers, playgroup leaders and health visitors, who they thought should tell a child about hospital? Parents were overwhelmingly chosen as the most suitable group to give information to the child. It was reasoned that although hospital staff can provide accurate information, parents are particularly able to interpret that information. Parents have the unique position of knowing their child better than anyone else and no amount of general knowledge about child development by the medical professionals can substitute for the specialized knowledge of the parents. Only parents will be able to relate preparation material to things which the child understands; they are likely to have more idea of what sort of things worry their child and just how the child is likely to react. This is obviously important especially when medical staff might only have time to tell the child what they think he should know, rather than discussing all the things which are actually going on in his mind and therefore worrying him.

However, if parents are to be involved in preparing their children, it is important that they themselves should be given adequate information. Yet those studies that have looked at the information given to parents reveal much dissatisfaction. Even twenty years ago, Vernon *et al.*[6] showed that lack of information is a prime cause of anxiety and that anxious parents are less capable of providing adequate support and security for their child when they too are under stress. This was backed up by Rodin who also showed that the anxiety of the child who is undergoing a medical procedure is directly related to the anxiety shown by the parent.

It becomes apparent that all parents should be given as much information as possible as a matter of routine. Yet Harris[7] showed that lack of information caused many parents to feel frustrated by their consequent inability to answer their child's questions. Nearly all the parents that she spoke to said that they had no idea of what their children would face in hospital. Even more surprisingly, many did not think they could ask the doctor for information. They were put off because he usually seemed too busy to be questioned especially when there was a long queue of other people waiting to see him! Indeed, this feeling of not wanting to bother the doctor for advice is fairly widespread. Every year, more than half a million people write to the 'agony aunts' who are employed by national newspapers and women's magazines asking for information about health matters.[8] Claire Rayner, alone, estimates that in 1979 she personally received 40,000 such letters[9] and four years later this had risen to 50,000; clear evidence that people increasingly want and need information. Some of the requests are for surprisingly simple information and many of the parents who write seek advice about their child who is going to hospital, asking such things as 'Will I be able to stay?', 'Can I take my other children with me when I go in to visit?', 'Will I be allowed to visit on the day of operation?'

Certainly, one of the most frequent requests from parents is for straightforward information on how to prepare themselves and their child for hospital. The usual advice is that parents should contact NAWCH (National Association for the Welfare of Children in Hospital) for one of their advice leaflets, the most recent one being, *Children in hospital – an action guide for parents* which was published in cooperation with the Consumers'

Association.[10] This booklet aims to tell parents how children should be treated in hospital. It takes the parent through what is likely to happen during the stay and gives practical advice on how to share in the child's care. It covers all aspects from the mundane problems of what to pack if a child needs to go into hospital right through to what parents need to know if their child is to have surgery and what to do on the day of operation. The booklet encourages parents to play hospital games and to read suitable stories to their children, all of which helps them both to understand and to accept what is likely to happen to them.

Should children be prepared for hospital?

Regard for the feelings of young children is a relatively recent occurrence in our human history and hospitalized children have been no exception to this. Becker[11] described this well when he reflected on the achievements of medicine over the past 25 years. He pointed out that for no other patients have the changes in outlook been as dramatic and profound as they have been for the paediatric patient. Quite often, sick children can now be restored to health with new confidence and offered potentials for recovery which were previously impossible. Unfortunately this is often achieved at great expense to their emotional well-being. Nevertheless, those directly charged with the medical, surgical or nursing care of children are beginning to understand and treat disease in the broadest and most enlightened terms, adopting a bolder and more innovative approach to their young patients. Becker believed that the real problem is one of honest communication. He said that unfortunately what to tell a child about his diagnosis, illness or imminent surgery is an assignment too frequently left to the least experienced staff member. When a child comes to hospital he is not just the incidental carrier of a disease that is to be cured. He is not measles, rheumatic fever, asthma or a sore throat. He is an impressionable human being and a member of a family which is very interested not only in his blood sugar curve or leucocyte count but, very profoundly, in the person that he is.

One of the concerns of the professional working in paediatrics today is not to allow this failure of communication with the child to continue. Indeed, it is now considered a standard of good practice for hospital personnel to provide information whenever possible, either by giving out explanatory leaflets or by using other methods of preparation. These have varied from such things as showing informative videotapes to helping a child to prepare for a forthcoming medical procedure by encouraging him to play and talk about it beforehand.

A review of all the various methods of preparing children for hospital and medical procedures was made by Rodin[12] and she found that the overall effects are beneficial in reducing anxiety; children who were prepared in any way coped better than children who were not prepared. However, some of the methods demanded a lot of time for already busy staff, diverting them from their important medical duties. This was confirmed when Rodin went on to look at the effect of preparing children for a specific medical procedure. She discovered that most people believed that preparation of the child and telling him the truth about what is going to happen will probably help him to endure treatment in hospital. Indeed many professionals recognized that preparation makes the child more cooperative and their job then becomes much easier. However, excuses were continually made for not giving information to the child. For the professional, it was lack of time and for the parent and teachers it was because they did not know what to tell a child. By comparing three groups of children, only one of which received preparation, Rodin's study showed that if a child is told the truth about what is going to happen to him, then the child will cope better and his anxiety will be reduced. She suggested that material such as books which are designed for the purpose of informing about hospital and medical procedures, provided that they are accurate, realistic and attractively prepared, can be of great benefit when used by parents and children together.

Using books to prepare a child for hospital

Clearly books which familiarize a child with hospital can be very useful in preparing the child to cope with his medical treatments. Books have the added advantage of being widely available to all children in their homes, schools, libraries and hospital. A good book which is attractive to the child is read frequently and has the advantage of involving parents and teachers who also then learn about the medical procedure so helping them to support the child. It is usually considered that the best person to read a book about hospital with a young child is the parent. Together, they can raise questions, clarify areas of confirmation, and touch on additional points which are particularly pertinent to themselves until the child gradually becomes at ease with the idea of going to hospital. Usually, it is best to let the child set the pace for receiving new information.

In the view of Altshuler[13] a good book can provide a jumping off point for discussions of a forthcoming hospital stay. It can help prepare a child for unfamiliar routines, equipment and personnel. It can stimulate questions and expressions of feelings about the child's body, the illness or defect, and the treatment measures that have been prescribed. It can also be used to assure the hospitalized child that his questions and reactions are normal. Rereading of such books after returning home can help a child to integrate the hospital experiences into his life in a growth-producing way.

Nevertheless, books to prepare a child for hospital experiences should be selected carefully. To be properly prepared, children need information not only about the facts and what will happen to them but also about their feelings. Obviously facts help children to understand reality. They help clear up fantasies and distortions. For example by explaining that when you have a blood test, you don't lose all your blood; or that the big X-ray machine is firmly fixed to the ceiling and will not fall on your head. Facts prepare the child psychologically for medical routines, by anticipating strange or new procedures, so making the treatment less frightening. They can also draw on a child's coping abilities perhaps by saying such things as 'if you make your arm go floppy, the injection hurts less'. However, the best books promote discussion between the adult and the child by talking about feelings as well as facts. Children should know that it is normal to feel anxious and fearful in unusual situations. They should understand that sometimes sick people get cross and angry when everything seems too much for them. They should also learn that crying is not babyish but a natural reaction to stress. It becomes clear that books, if wisely used, can be of real benefit to a child. Equally an inappropriate book could lead to confusion and conflict. Therefore, in selecting books to help a child learn about hospital, several questions should be considered.

Firstly, does the book meet the child's special needs? Many myths have been unintentionally perpetuated through books that portray hospital experiences inaccurately. For example, injections do not feel like mosquito bites. Children rarely walk hand-in-hand with their doctors to the operating room. Ice cream does not necessarily taste wonderful to a child whose throat is sore after a tonsillectomy. Nurses in a children's unit are not always dressed in white uniforms and caps. Also. books that imply good health is entirely under the child's control may deepen the sense of guilt in a school-ager who already blames himself for the illness. Yet these misconceptions and others do appear in books for children – even books written or approved by doctors and nurses.

Equally, books about hospitals should prepare children for the potentially pleasant aspects as well as for frightening and uncomfortable experiences. Obviously, any book used to explain hospitals and illnesses to children should present an accurate, fair and balanced picture of hospitalization.

Fortunately there are now a number of truthful and sensitively produced books which deal with children undergoing treatment or operations for specific illnesses. It is certainly helpful for a child with a chronic illness such as asthma or diabetes to hear a story that he can identify with because it tells about someone with the same problems that he has got. Equally the child who is going to have his tonsils out will want to know what will happen to him when he has his operation. However, it is also necessary to realize that a hospital, like all other institutions, revolves around a daily routine that is common to nearly all patients. So most children should be able to involve themselves with a generally descriptive storyline provided that it is clear and well-told. From this kind of book, they will learn such things as children in hospital usually sleep in a big ward with lots of other children and that they have their own bed and locker; that mum and dad can stay all the time; that there are lots of doctors, nurses, playworkers, teachers and many other people who are concerned with making them well again; that hospital food is brought on a trolley and that there is always a rest time after lunch.

It is also valuable for the child to understand why some of these routine medical procedures are being done. That he is being weighed and measured so that the correct dosage for his medicines can be calculated; that his temperature is taken to find out how hot he is; that the doctor listens to his chest with a stethoscope to hear how his heart is beating; that he has given the nurse a specimen of his urine so that she can test it. To a young child, if it is done without any explanation, even the simplest procedure can seem quite unnecessarily alarming. For example, psychologists tell us that small children can get very distressed at having to wear a hospital identity bracelet if they are not prepared for it. Yet why is this when it is an apparently non-threatening and painless occurrence? Obviously, for most children, this is probably the first time that they have ever needed to be labelled because in their own home environment, everyone knows exactly who they are. Could it be that the identity bracelet merely serves to emphasize their anxieties about this new and enormous place called hospital and increases their worries about whether they will get lost? Certainly a book can usefully introduce the child to the idea that he will need to wear an identity bracelet. It could point out that everyone in hospital has to wear some kind of name badge – not only the patients but also the staff who work there. Prepared in this way, the child might well decide to play out this new concept in games about hospital, perhaps by making badges and identity bracelets for his toys and everyone in his family. A good book could also go on to point out to the child that he will be able to take his identity bracelet home afterwards and show it to all his friends. The joy of recounting tales about 'what happened to me in hospital' is not just confined to adult patients. Children like to do it too!

Another important aspect that should be considered when choosing a book about hospital is to ask if the illustrations will appeal to children? Obviously all children's books should have imaginative and attractive pictures which add to the story. However, when the aim is to use the book to tell a child what is going to happen to him, then how realistic should the drawings be? A NAWCH research project[14] tried to find the most appealing illustrative style for conveying medical information to children aged five to seven years. It was found that there was a highly significant preference for real photographs with the second most popular being the cartoon style. From an evaluation of the verbal responses made by the children to the question asking why they preferred a particular style, it was clear that the style of the graphic representation was much more important than the subject matter of the pictures. The colour of the pictures was a very important factor and many children thought it was important for the picture to make things seem real.

Examples of types of books

Some books give adequate facts about illnesses and hospitals but are written in such a stilted, formal style that children soon lose interest in reading them. Fortunately, there are others which present imaginative, lively and well-written stories that capture a child's interest in addition to supplying information about the hospital settings. These books can be described best by dividing them into four types:

a) the purely factual

b) the story of a particular child, inviting identification
c) complete fantasy
d) books dealing generally with stress, not specifically hospital.

a) The purely factual style is well-represented by the Althea books. In these, both text and illustrations are simple and accurate which is reassuring for children and parents alike, making her books very popular. In *Going into Hospital,*[15] Althea sensitively thinks of the details that may particularly upset a child and points them out in a matter of fact way. She explains that you sleep with lots of other children and that some of the beds have sides like cots; that there is a special potty to use when in bed; that hospitals smell different from home; about the 'nothing by mouth' sign. Althea also describes the blood test when the child responds with a realistic 'ouch'.

These details, some of which occur in very few other books remind the parent of what to discuss with the child in order to avoid confronting the child with the unexpected. Another good thing for young children is that the style of writing often involves them actively such as when the text say 'Everyone is having lunch – can you see what it is today?'. This Althea book is also nice to handle – small, cosy and compact – a good addition to the child's bedside locker; to be used repeatedly as needed.

In *Talk about going into hospital*[16] the book has a double text, a simple one for the child and a more difficult text in italics for the parents. The readers are guided through the hospital from the accident and emergency department to becoming a patient on the ward and having an operation. Details are given of the staff, medical procedures, tests, ward routines, meals, play and school. Each page features one of these and there are lots of details in the picture which the child is invited to discuss, with the reminder to the parent of things to ask and explain to the child. It is particularly good in that the staff, parents and children are multiracial and mixed in sex. This is most important in reflecting reality and encouraging all children to identify with role models in their play about hospitals both before and after the event.

b) The story of a particular child is undoubtedly one of the most popular formats with publishers. Some of these are excellent, many using the photographic style which children have been shown to identify with more easily.

Going into Hospital, by Camilla Jessel,[17] is written for tiny children and it features Jamie, aged about three or four. Jamie's feelings fluctuate beautifully. Either he feels uncooperative: 'Can I look in your ear?' says Dr Liz, 'No!' says Jamie, obviously cross. Later he hides under his cot pretending to be a lion, quite chirpy and cheeky again. He also plays at doctors with his teddy which is an important reminder of the value of play in helping children master stress.

In *Linda goes to hospital* by B. Wade,[18] Linda, aged eight, has her tonsils out. The book has a nice mixture of feelings and facts such as when Linda gets a bit scared and wishes her mum was there. However, there is lots of family reassurance: her mother is there as much as possible, sister and grandpa visit and it is her father who takes her home. The identity bracelet is introduced most effectively when a nurse gives Linda a wrist-band with her name on. Her teddy bear and her doll have labels stuck on them which say 'I belong to Linda'. This truly is an excellent book which covers the doctor's examination, pre-medication and going to the theatre in a realistic but reassuring way.

For older children, *Paul in hospital* by Camilla Jessel,[19] is a wonderful evocation of a boy's thoughts, feelings and curiosity about his hospital experience, although the book's dense text and black and white photographs may be initially offputting. A wide range of feelings are expressed about the routines that many children face in hospital such as when Paul suddenly felt panicky – 'Mum must I stay?' he asked. Further on in the book, Paul is disgruntled about having so many injections especially when the other children are given pills. Sister explains that Paul's injections are the quickest way to make him well. Nevertheless, she does try to cheer him up by offering him the empty syringes so that he can show his friends at school just how many injections he had. Obviously, this helps Paul to cope because much later, when he is feeling better, he and another boy have a water fight with the empty syringes, displaying a piece of impudence that makes the nurse a bit cross. He also pretends to 'stick up' the doctor with a toy gun. In both incidents, Paul is permitted his outlet of cheek where he gets the better of the medical staff and feels in charge again. Paul also expresses anxiety about other children in the ward when he wonders will another boy always need food through a tube? Through such questions, the reader is focused on various potentially alarming incidents and reassurance is given by the staff. Reassurance is also provided by his family, such as dad waiting while he sleeps – and when Paul surfaces from sleep occasionally he feels happy at dad's watching presence.

In addition to expression of feelings, there are also many explanations given from why and how blood is taken to the mundane need to wee in a bottle when he is confined to bed. The value of this book is in Paul's expression of anxiety, fear, doubt and anger and in his mastery of these negative emotions, through his own resources and through reassurance of parents and staff. It also appeals to the intellectual curiosity of children who want to know 'why?'

A prolific writer of children's individual medical experiences is Nigel Snell who specializes in simple books for younger children, cheerfully illustrated in cartoon style. Two are *Ruth goes to hospital*[20] and *Lucy loses her tonsils*.[21] Both books are notable for their honest explanations of simple procedures. When Ruth has her cut leg cleaned 'it stung a bit!' but later the reader is reassured to learn that under the X-ray machine she 'didn't feel a thing'. Snell uses little touches of humour such as when Lucy's toy penguin goes to hospital with her and has a label put on his flipper. Lucy is happy to eat ice cream when her tonsils come out, but her penguin would prefer fish. This allows the child to laugh while still giving the necessary reassurance and comfort.

c) The use of fantasy to describe hospitals to children seems to be on the decline. For many years one of the few books available for children was *Zozo goes to hospital*,[22] the story of a monkey who swallows a piece of jigsaw puzzle. This is now out of print having been superseded by the more realistic publications mentioned above. However, still available are the Crocodile Books by Marjorie Anne Watts, – *Crocodile Plaster*[23] (in print), *Crocodile medicine* (OP)[24] and *Crocodile teeth*[25] (1986). In all these a child called Julie, bored, fed up with hospital life is plunged into excitement with the arrival of a crocodile on the ward. The fact that Julie and the other kids are unvisited by any grown ups is a curious feature especially as there are very few long stay institutionalized children these days in hospital. However if you accept the situation as entirely fantastic, there is a lot of value in the material. In all three books, Crocodile feels sorry for himself: he fusses, moans and refuses to cooperate. At one point, he 'roared and yelled and turned and pulled up all the bed clothes over his head'. Julie's role is rather like that of a play specialist; she coaxes him into good humour, distracts him with play, comforts him and explains procedures. She even identifies where his pain is in *Crocodile plaster*, seeing that it is a broken tail and not a broken foot or back. The stories are reminiscent of a child playing the role of a caring adult. They allow the child to take charge for a while, but always with humour. By laughing at and debunking frightening images the child's tension is also released in a way that could be especially valuable for children who have already been in hospital or face repeat admissions.

d) It could also be helpful for parents and children to use books that focus on fears that are not directly related to hospital. For example *Away for the night*, by Camilla Jessel,[26] portrays a small child staying at a friend's house and coping well with help from the friends. Other books such as Snell's *Martin feels Lonely*[27] or *Danny is afraid of the dark*[28] might help a child and parent focus on specific fears and receive comfort through reading and discussing them. *Mummy goes into hospital*[29] is another example of a different angle. Does the child remember mother being in hospital (or any other relatives) and are there any sad memories of separation left from that time? How did the family manage without her? In this book the family cope but miss her till her return just as the child will be missed – although in his case perhaps mother will stay in hospital with him.

Conclusion

It is obvious that when we are talking about preparing children for hospital we are really often talking about preparing the parent or caring adult, to prepare the child. Factual information for parents, which is clearly written such as the NAWCH book,[30] mentioned previously is an important part of that preparation. Children's books are another vital means. By reading these books with their children, parents gain a better understanding of their child's possible reactions to hospitals and so become more sensitive and helpful. As for the children, the benefits of reading are manifold. Reading helps to anticipate unexpected events and feelings, encouraging more realistic play about hospital and discussion of fears which might otherwise be hidden; it convinces children that parents do not abandon them in hospital and that hospitalization is not a punishment, it shows children the reasons for strange procedures and encourages them to think that they will be able to cope.

Everyone realizes that children will be upset by going to hospital and having to undergo medical or surgical procedures. It is part of life, of growing up, and of surviving. Equally, many people are aware that preparation of the child and telling him the truth about what is going to happen will help him to endure the procedure. A well-written and suitable book does just that.

References

1 Children of Bellevue Inc., *Calendar*, The Child Life Program, Bellevue Hospital Center, New York NY 10016, 1980.
2 NAWCH Keypoint 5, *Statistics on children in hospital*, London, NAWCH, October, 1980.
3 Jolly, J., *The other side of paediatrics: a guide to the everyday care of sick children*, London, Macmillan, 1981.
4 Muller, D. J., Harris P. J. and Wattley, L., *Nursing children: psychology, research and practice*, London, Harper and Row, 1986.
5 Rodin, J., *Will this hurt?*, London, Royal College of Nursing, 1983.
6 Vernon, D. T. A., Foley, J. M., Sipowicz, R. R. and Schulman, J. L., *The psychological responses of children to hospitalization and illness*, Springfield, Illinois, Charles C. Thomas, 1965.
7 Harris, P. J., 'Preparation of parents and their children for a planned hospital admission', *Nursing Times*, 77, 1981, 1744–6.
8 Gann, R., and Knight, S., *Consumers' guide to health information*, London, The College of Health, 1986.
9 Rayner, C., 'Reality and expectation of the British National Health Service consumer', *Journal of Advanced Nursing*, 4, 1979, 69–77.
10 Consumers' Association and NAWCH, *Children in hospital*, London, NAWCH, 1985.
11 Becker, R. D., 'Children in Hospital', *The Israel Annals of Psychiatry and Related Disciplines*, 14, 1976, 240–65.
12 Rodin, J., *op. cit.*
13 Altshuler, A., *Books that help children to deal with a hospital experience*, Washington, DC, U.S. Government Printing Office, U.S. Department of Health, Education and Welfare, 1974.
14 NAWCH Research Project, *Preparing children for hospital*, London, NAWCH, October, 1980.
15 Althea, *Going into hospital*, Cambridge, Dinosaur Publications, 1980.
16 Wells, P., *Talk about going into hospital*, Loughborough, Ladybird Books, 1985.
17 Jessel C., *Going into hospital*, London, Methuen Childrens Books, 1983.
18 Wade, B., *Linda goes to hospital*, London, Adam and Charles Black, 1981.
19 Jessel C., *Paul in hospital*, London, Methuen Childrens Books, 1983.
20 Snell, N., *Ruth goes to hospital*, London, Hamish Hamilton, 1985.
21 Snell, N., *Lucy loses her tonsils*, London, Hamish Hamilton, 1984.
22 Rey, M. & H. A., *Zozo goes to hospital*, London, Chatto and Windus, 1974.
23 Watts, M. A., *Crocodile plaster*, London, Andre Deutsch, 1978.

24 Watts, M. A., *Crocodile medicine*, London, Andre Deutsch, 1977.
25 Watts, M. A., *Crocodile teeth*, London, Andre Deutsch, 1986.
26 Jessel, C., *Away for the night*, London, Methuen Childrens Books, 1981.
27 Snell, N., *Martin feels lonely*, London, Hamish Hamilton, 1983.
28 Snell, N., *Danny is afraid of the dark*, London, Hamish Hamilton, 1985.
29 Elliott, E., *Mummy goes into hospital*, London, Hamish Hamilton, 1985.
30 NAWCH Research Project, *op. cit.*

For further information about the National Association for the Welfare of Children in Hospital (NAWCH) or to subscribe to *NAWCH Update*, a regular journal for everyone concerned with children in hospital – please contact NAWCH, Argyle House, 29–31 Euston Road, London NW1 2SD or telephone 01–833 2041.

10 Using library materials with elderly psychiatric patients

Heather George

In recent decades, the proportion of elderly people in the population of countries in the Western world has increased, and rising numbers of old people are supported by services in day care or residential facilities. From the 1960s there has been growing concern among workers with the elderly in the United States and in Britain about the quality of life for their clients.[1] Although the quality of care is often good, with physical needs being well met, there is little attention paid to psychological needs. Observers of care settings have commented on the pervading atmosphere of sterility and boredom and are left with the feeling that for most of the time nothing happens. Research data supports the impression that many individuals spend a great deal of their time in isolated inactivity e.g. in a 1975 study McClannahan and Risley observed the activities of elderly people in an American nursing home from 7 a.m. to 7 p.m., and found that on average 87 per cent of residents were not engaged in any form of social interaction at any given time.[2]

Low levels of purposeful activity are particularly common in residential settings, many of which resemble the 'total institutions' described by Ervine Goffman,[3] where the individual's identity and personal freedoms are eroded by rules and regulations. By providing staff with routines to cope with the physical needs of a group of elderly people, institutional care often reduces the need for residents to engage in many practical activities of daily living, and fails to provide a chance to engage in recreational activities: one American study by Kurasik found that only 33 per cent of private hospitals and 20 per cent of nursing homes in New York provided any active recreation programmes.[4] Where recreational facilities do exist, these may become so stale and routine that there is little attention paid to personal choice or creativity. Even when staff talk to patients, topics are frequently impersonal: work studies of nurse/patient interaction indicate that nurses spend very little of their working day in purely social contact with patients, and that when conversations take place they tend to be about tasks and things related to physical care rather than personal thoughts or feelings.[5]

'Disengagement' and old age

Some authors have suggested that there is a tendency for elderly people to become more solitary, introspective and generally withdrawn from everyday life. Cumming and Henry saw limited social contact and increasing inactivity as 'disengagement' which occurs as an important aspect of normal ageing.[6] With such images of the elderly in mind, many young people fear old age as a time of loneliness, dependence and confusion. Some see old people as dull and boring, with an irritating tendency to 'live in the past' and dwell on old times.

More recent authors reject the disengagement hypothesis and present alternative perspectives on why many old people tend to lead isolated and different lives from the young. Dependence and confusion may be a reflection of the environment rather than (or in addition to) failing intellectual processes and declining physical health. Inactivity and social withdrawal may be related to lack of opportunity or encouragement. Reminiscing is perhaps an enjoyable part of growing old, both for those recalling their past and for others who listen to their memories and learn more about an individual's experiences and about life in times gone by. These theories are more optimistic in giving reasons for why a lonely and separate existence need not necessarily be characteristic of the last years of life, and have practical implications in showing how we can maximize personal choice, independence and pleasure in old age.

Reality orientation (RO)

Changes in our intellectual abilities occur as part of normal ageing. 'Benign forgetfulness' (a tendency to be unable to remember names and other details) is common; creative problem-solving involving abstraction and speed of processing new information usually becomes more difficult; and adapting to novel situations takes longer. Not all aspects of intellectual functioning decline; well-practised skills and verbal abilities hold or even improve with age. However, other losses are common in old age. Rates of physical illness, disability and sensory loss (e.g. eyesight, hearing, touch) increase sharply each decade after middle life, particularly after about age 70 years. Retirement means a loss of work routine and professional identity. Hospital or other residential care can deprive individuals of their homes and neighbourhood. Family members may have long since moved away and be geographically distant. Friends and contemporaries may die. Such losses frequently precipitate depression and temporary confusion. If depressed people are cared for in unstimulating environments, they may withdraw further, lose existing skills, and become more dependent and confused.

A minority of elderly people suffer global intellectual decline and increased physical dependence as a result of organic changes in abnormal ageing. Severe memory disorder, disorientation, confusion and personality changes occur in dementia, and there are no cures; functioning gradually slows and eventually the person dies.

Reality orientation (RO) is an approach to working with confused elderly people which aims to compensate for temporary or permanent deficits by altering very basic aspects of the environment, providing cues, aids and encouragement to ameliorate the effects of mental disorientation, failing physical senses or depressed mood. As early as 1958, Sommer and Ross showed how the very arrangement of furniture may inhibit social interaction on geriatric wards.[7] If things are arranged so that patients may sit in small groups rather than chairs being placed around the sides of a large day room, social interaction increases. Una Holden and Bob Woods comment further on normalizing institutional practices to foster independence and activity e.g. by allowing as many personal possessions as possible; using large, clear, unambiguous signs and labels around the ward or home; and providing sessions to stimulate communication and maintain habitual interests and skills.[8] An important part of RO is the emphasis on using every encounter with staff to give individuals information about their surroundings, but in addition group sessions provide materials and to further encourage elderly people to express themselves and mix together.

Other programmes for stimulating activity

Another approach to increasing levels of activity and social interaction is to apply behaviour therapy, where verbal utterances or other behaviours are encouraged by rewarding individuals with tangible reinforcers such as sweets, tokens or money, or with increased attention from staff.[9,10] These methods may be readily applied to increase independence in terms of personal care and to promote social contact in withdrawn people, but there is a problem. Aside from the ethical considerations inherent in all behaviour modification programmes, these techniques present the paradox of further externally prescribing detailed aspects of life in environments where the rigid routines of institutional care may have been in part instrumental in the development of withdrawal among clients.

In a British study by Jenkins and others the effects of introducing regular recreation sessions without extrinsic rewards were examined in two Social Services Department Homes where the average ages of the residents were 85 and 80 years respectively.[11] During 'free time' in the lounge, residents each were asked if they wished to use materials (these had been selected and packed so that they could be used easily by residents sitting in armchairs e.g. magazines, jigsaws, puzzles). Residents were observed and recordings of engagement – defined as interacting with others, using equipment provided or everyday materials e.g. a comb – were made for each 45 minute session over 18 days. The results showed that residents' levels of activity were considerably higher than baseline recordings taken before materials were introduced. The authors comment on how elderly, institutionalized people may become significantly more active by simply providing materials and minimal encouragement from staff. They conclude that self-initiation of purposeful activity may be a problem for old people in residential settings, but that low levels of engagement are in part due to lack of opportunities and assistance provided to them, rather than their specific disabilities or inherent lack of interest. Other evidence supports the view that elderly people may be active given adequate opportunities and encouragement.[12]

Reminiscence therapy

Another form of group work emphasizes the discussion of past life experiences. Typically, regular sessions are held using materials from the past to stimulate conversation, and life events are discussed in chronological order up to the present time.[13] Such groups have developed with the growing interest among psychologists and psychogeriatricians in the function of reminiscence.

Professional opinion about reminiscence has changed greatly from when, in 1963, Butler wrote:

> The prevailing tendency is to identify reminiscence in the aged with psychological dysfunction and thus to regard it essentially as a symptom . . .
>
> . . . In consequence, reminiscence becomes a perjorative, suggesting preoccupation, musing, aimless wandering of the mind.[14]

Butler postulated that far from being a sign of psychopathology, reminiscence is characteristic of the elderly, occurring with greater frequency than among younger people due to the process of 'life review' i.e. an attempt at resolving conflicts in preparation for death. Butler's observations and ideas were congruent with Erikson's psychosocial theory, where the development of generativity in middle adulthood represents the individual's need to gain a sense of having contributed to the future, and may be thus manifested by recollection of past experiences and knowledge to younger listeners; and in the final stage of life the task is one of developing 'ego integrity', the individual accepting his life as appropriate and meaningful in preparation for death.[15]

The conceptual frameworks of Erikson and Butler were adopted in a number of studies in the 1960s and 1970s, which investigated reminiscence via structured interview or experimental techniques. The general findings were supportive of Butler's proposals – reminiscence occurred in a greater proportion of people than had been previously suggested, and appeared to serve some adaptive functions. In survey by questionnaire, Havighurst and Glasser found a 67 per cent report of silent reminiscence and a 79 per cent report of reminiscing with others among respondents, the majority of whom were aged 70 to 79 years.[16] An interview study of war veterans (average age 84 years) found men who spontaneously reminisced to be less depressed than those who did not.[17] From the findings of an experimental study of self-concept, Lewis observed that identification with the past was a healthy mechanism by which the elderly maintain self-respect when faced with current threat or stress, and he concluded that reminiscence was a 'psychologically healthy form of communication'.[18]

Butler conceded that there may be some dysfunctional manifestations of reminiscence (e.g. despair, anxiety and depression) among the isolated aged. Several authors have distinguished between various types of healthy and pathological reminiscence. For example, Lo Gerfo identified 'informative' and 'evaluative' reminiscence as leading to gains in self-confidence and energy among elderly people, whereas 'obsessive' reminiscence was seen as withdrawal into obsessive ruminations (e.g. excessive guilt over past deeds).[19] Fallot suggested that in some instances past oriented talking may be a defensive avoidance of present anxiety or expected future stress.[20]

Clinical reports of using reminiscence therapeutically in group settings indicate a low occurrence of such negative aspects, and have yielded promising results. Norris has illustrated how reminiscence may increase responsiveness among the institutionalized elderly; may lead to greater involvement among their families; and may change the attitudes of care staff towards a more psychological perspective.[21, 22, 23, 24] Langley and Corder asserted that after reminiscence therapy elderly people are 'less depressed, less intellectually disabled and therefore able to cope both personally and socially'.[25]

In the 1970s Help the Aged sought to design some material to stimulate reminiscence groups, and in 1981 the Education Department produced an audiovisual package (*Recall*) which comprised photographic slides and audiotaped material of events dating back to the turn of the century.[26] An investigation into the value of such audiovisual aids found trends towards decreases in apathy and undesirable social behaviour in 30 elderly, mentally frail residents in an old people's home.[27]

Reading therapy

Reading therapy in its widest application includes the use of information booklets, self-help manuals, and reading as a preventive tool for child behaviour problems.[28, 29, 30, 31]

The therapeutic value of books and library materials has long been recognized in the USA and early studies there included work with elderly populations e.g. Pomeroy, a hospital librarian, published a paper on the topic in 1927.[32, 33, 34] The use of books in general hospitals and psychiatric settings began to receive attention in the UK in the 1970s. Sara Coomaraswamy has used books in her work as a clinical psychologist to provide a means of communication with her psychiatric and psychogeriatric patients.[35, 36] Following Sweeney's American work, Marr used the approach in both day care and long stay psychiatric settings and found similar beneficial effects of restoring morale and increasing active participation in clients, whilst fostering more positive attitudes towards caring for the elderly among staff.[37, 38]

The positive applications of reading therapy with the aged have been demonstrated by the work of Stephen Hoy, who, as Principal Librarian for Specialist Groups, Leicester County Library, has worked with Age Concern to provide library club programmes – weekly sessions using public library resources to bring together people, many of whom have few other opportunities for stimulation and company, and who spend most of their time alone at home.[39] The library club maximizes the potential of public library and voluntary services. During the sessions, library staff give advice on requests for books and information, and an opportunity for borrowing and returning books; Age Concern operates an advice surgery to deal with practical problems; and guest speakers give presentations and readings. Reading aloud exploits the book stock by introducing new authors and topics to regular borrowers; by restimulating interest among lapsed readers; and by making printed literature available to those people who are unable to use books themselves because of sensory or physical handicap.

Development of reading therapy in a psychiatric hospital

In 1984 I started a one-year placement in the Clinical Psychology Department of a psychiatric hospital. Whilst working with elderly and long-stay patients I was able to use many ideas and practical implications generated by the approaches discussed above.

The hospital was old (it opened in 1905) and large (with 904 beds). Like many hospitals situated some distance from town centres, the grounds and surrounding countryside were pleasant, but the hospital buildings were rather run down, and felt cold and impersonal. There were a few acute wards for young and newly-admitted patients, but the majority of wards were for elderly and long-stay patients. Many patients had lived most of their lives there, having been diagnosed as schizophrenic in the 1940s or 1950s; they had grown old (and institutionalized) within the hospital. Others were admitted as psychogeriatric patients; their diagnoses were chronic conditions, and so most were expected to spend the rest of their lives at the hospital. Wards tended to have a mixed population of old and new long-stay patients, with perhaps a few newly admitted confused old people. The atmosphere was typical of many residential settings – often people would be sitting, staring into space or slowly shuffling around, apparently aimlessly. The radio or television may have played (sometimes simultaneously in the same room), but few or no people would be attending, and perhaps no other patients would be using other recreational materials or talking together. Nurse to patient ratios were poor, with a great deal of staff time taken up by basic physical caregiving to the more dependent patients. On some wards the situation was eased and atmosphere improved by more able patients being involved in the domestic routine, for instance helping with setting the tables or tending the plants.

The hospital was not without recreation facilities. For several years stimulation programmes had been undertaken by the

Occupational Therapy (OT) and Industrial Therapy (IT) departments, but most took place in the OT rooms or IT workshops, away from the wards. A wide range of facilities was provided by the voluntary services, which tended to be irregular (e.g. seasonal events like Christmas singsongs or Easter parades) and run by a succession of constantly changing volunteers. A very good variety of outings and events was available, offered on a hospital-wide and often 'first-come-first-serve' basis. Consequently, a few sufficiently motivated and socially able patients gained maximum benefit. There was a need for regular ward-based activities for those patients who were more dependent, withdrawn or institutionalized.

American work on reminiscence therapy by Lesser and others suggested that the approach may be successfully used with psychotic geriatric in-patients, who construe reminiscence as less threatening than traditional group therapy. In a 22-week study where reminiscence followed group therapy, there was increased spontaneous verbalization, receptiveness and patient to patient communication.[40] An early American study used short-term reading therapy with a group of chronic schizophrenic patients in a large state psychiatric hospital, and found trends towards more active participation among very withdrawn patients.[41]

At the present hospital reminiscence groups using the Help the Aged *Recall* tapes and slides had already formed part of the psychological therapy for patients on two wards, and the package had been used on occasion by the OT department and volunteers. Staff impressions of the groups were favourable, but there had been no systematic studies of the effects of using *Recall*. Books and magazines were used occasionally as stimulus materials during OT and by ward staff. There was an excellent library offering a lending service to patients sufficiently mobile and motivated to visit the collection in the stacks, and library staff and volunteers took reading materials to a small number of wards. However, the librarian felt there was potential for much greater use. The stock, like a public library resource, included a very good hardback and paperback selection (fiction and non-fiction), newspapers and magazines and a small record collection. A good deal of lending was to the staff. A few patients used the materials, but most saw the Library as a common room, a change from the wards, a shelter from the grounds in bad weather, and a good place to 'cadge' cigarettes. Opening hours were limited and clashed with OT, IT or mealtimes. The library was some distance from many wards. Ten years previously the stock had been quite actively used by a fair number of able patients, but by this time the population had aged; mobility and motivation were limited for many, and almost all were institutionalized, their lives an unchanging routine which did not include regular trips to the library.

By examining the resources in the hospital it was clear that more ward-based activities were required for non-ambulant and more isolated patients; that congruent with other findings, reminiscence therapy and using library materials in groups were well-received by staff and patients when they occurred; and that the library and its materials were under-used in therapeutic application. Finance for additional input was very limited – what was needed was a review and reorganization of existing resources.

New developments

Via regular contact with patients and staff on the wards I was able to work with library staff and volunteers to introduce a number of new projects. The librarian wished to extend the trolley round services to cover most wards, but some nursing staff feared that books would be lost, damaged or destroyed, or they felt that they had litle time to provide encouragement and so believed books would fail to be used by patients. By recruiting regular volunteers to take deposits to the wards and stay for some time to promote use of the materials and by keeping records of returns, requests and losses, the service could be monitored and easily integrated into existing ward routines. A typical deposit collection comprised about 20 items – picture books; *Reader's Digest* and other magazines; romances and large print novels or short stories; and occasionally scrapbooks of pictures and magazine cuttings. The exact composition would depend on the interests and abilities of each ward population.

Reality orientation had been introduced to several wards during the previous year by a former psychologist. Patients on these wards tended to be highly dependent and quite severely intellectually deteriorated. Training in the application of RO techniques had been given to the ward staff, and some changes had been made e.g. clearer signs and notices to show locations of the bathrooms, more personalized items around beds in the dormitory, and RO sessions for a small group of patients which were held in a side room comfortably furnished to resemble a homely sitting room. The aim was for sessions to take place on a daily basis, Monday to Friday. In practice, they often were 'squeezed out' of the basic care routine of the day. Furthermore, in the past deposit collections from the library had been locked in the ward offices because staff believed patients would 'spoil' them.

As an additional member of staff, I was able to spend time re-establishing enthusiasm for RO and the use of books by regularly leading RO sessions and training volunteers to take sessions on days when I was not available. Topics for a week of sessions were planned in advance so that materials could be gathered from the library. Few of these patients were able to read themselves, and their concentration was too poor to listen to stories or passages read aloud. However, books with large, clear illustrations were used as very basic stimuli, patients identifying objects (e.g. their name, colour, shape, function) and perhaps spontaneously giving a few remarks about how they liked or used them, or some other memory elicited by the visual images. For example, one 85-year-old Scottish lady who was frequently confused about the time of day, where she was or even who she was had moments of lucidity when she would enjoy looking at photographs of places in Scotland, or browsing through illustrated recipe books. 'Conversations' with her may consist of just acknowledging her comments as she pointed and identified places she recognized, or foods she liked, or at other times she would give information about her past related to the pictures e.g. how she had worked as a cook in service. The use of books in this way is not at a sophisticated level, but library materials can be elegant tools to provide an enjoyable activity for both patients and staff. On these wards, the RO approach demonstrated to staff how to use the deposit collection or other books to stimulate and make contact with patients with failing intellectual capacities.

Another development was the use of the library once a week to hold an evening story reading. This was initiated by a volunteer who had an interest in drama. During the day he worked with patients in OT and IT, and was able to recruit an audience by reminding patients that a story reading would be given, and drawing their attention to posters giving relevant details which he placed around the hospital. Obviously, this was a service for more able patients, although some long-stay institutionalized patients regularly participated; response was much better than expected. Thus the library was used by people who had formerly not used their free time in purposeful activity.

The Help the Aged *Recall* package was already available, along with a wealth of other materials in the library stock. Some wards had requested more psychological input, particularly in the form of running groups. The final development at this time was to introduce an experimental study of reminiscence, comparing different stimulus materials and examining whether such activities have general effects on increasing levels of engagement on the wards.

A systematic study of reminiscence and reading therapy

The aims of the study were to increase the quality of life for some patients by acknowledging psychological needs (e.g. social contact, personal choice, recreation) and providing more activities to meet these; to increase levels of engagement among patients who would enjoy a more active recreational programme; to improve ward atmosphere by increasing staff involvement in ward-based activities and stimulating staff and patient interest in the library and the past; and to examine how the library could be modified to cater for the large number of patients who never or rarely used the service.

More specifically, the effectiveness of the *Recall* package was compared with using books from the library as stimulus material in reminiscence groups. This was achieved by looking at four groups, each of six patients who wished to participate and comparable in age (average 71 years), length of stay (average 28 years), and diagnosis on admission (for the majority, schizophrenia), but where each group was from a different ward and was subject to one of four different conditions. The group from the first ward received reminiscence therapy using the *Recall* package; in the second books were used as the stimulus material; in the third group, both *Recall* and books were used; and the fourth group received no reminiscence sessions but acted as a 'control'. On all four wards a trolley round service was supplied every week, and during a 30-minute period when a volunteer encouraged use of the materials, collected the deposit from the previous week and took requests for other books, the behaviour of each patient in the study was observed and monitored, recordings being made of whether or not he or she was 'engaged' (using books or other materials, or having a conversation with other patients or staff) or non-engaged.

The study was conducted over a 14-week period. Initially, all patients were rated by staff for individual communication ability (using the Holden Communication Scale – details are given in Holden and Woods, 1982).[42] Staff also rated ward atmosphere using a standardized scale.[43] From the first week all four wards received the trolley rounds and patient levels of engagement were recorded as well as numbers of books borrowed, lost or requested. The trolley service was the only intervention for the control group ward. In addition the other three groups received 14 sessions of reminiscence therapy over eight weeks using different materials as outlined above. The sessions were audio-taped for analysis of content. After eight weeks all patients were rated again by staff, who also completed a second ward atmosphere scale. The same ratings were taken again after a further six weeks as follow up data.

Conducting the reminiscence groups

A number of objects (e.g. a Coronation mug, a ration book, photographs of the hospital during the First World War) were used in all three reminiscence groups. For the 'books only' and '*Recall* and books' groups I worked with the librarian to develop a range of materials from the library to parallel the *Recall* package topics (*viz.* childhood, the Great War, the 1920s, the 1930s, the Second World War, and post-war times). A selection of extracts from literature (fiction and non-fiction) and photographs and pictures from books were collected, the latter being cut out and mounted on card or used as complete books to pass around group members. There was no problem in assembling these materials – the library had a wide range of novels and non-fiction books to cover aspects of everyday life and special events in the twentieth century e.g. Ronald Blythe's *Akenfield* and *The Triple Echo* by H. E. Bates. Some pictorial books were obtained on interlibrary loans. During the 1970s and 1980s there was a growing interest in oral history and events of the present century, resulting in the publication of photographic albums depicting daily-life activities. These form excellent reminiscence materials, and two such books were purchased as new stock.[44,45] Further details of the books used are given in the Bibliography.

The groups took place on the wards, run by myself and a male volunteer with any ward staff who wished to attend. Each group lasted for one hour. There was an introductory session during the first week, then sessions followed the *Recall* topics twice weekly for six weeks, and finally there was one review session. In the *Recall* only group, the tapes and slides were used with stimulus questions as suggested in the *Recall* handbook. In the books group, passages were read aloud by the presenters, and pictures circulated among the group. In the *Recall* with books group both types of presentation were used.

Results of the reminiscence and reading therapy study

Overall there was a good response to the trolley round service, with levels of interest and activity higher than were expected. Although not all patients used the deposit collection there was some interest on all four wards. The range of requests was much wider than expected (e.g. one patient wanted a book on the peaceful uses of nuclear power!) and book losses and damage were low.

There were no trends towards increases in levels of engagement over time. This suggested that introducing the deposit either did not change activity levels at the trolley round times, or that a change occurred during the first week and remained the same. However, activity levels were only monitored during the 30-minute round; anecdotal reports from ward staff indicated an increase in engagement for some patients at other times e.g. in the evenings, when they would read or look at the books. There were no differences between groups in terms of activity – any increases which occurred during the reminiscence groups did not generalize to trolley times on the ward. Measured staff ratings of patient communication and ward atmosphere remained constant.

Within the reminiscence therapy sessions there were measurable changes. Analysis of the audiotapes showed that patient participation increased, with fewer contributions from the presenters and more utterances from patients over time. The level (i.e. amount) and quality (relevance of conversation and development of discussion) were highest for the group receiving both *Recall* and books, and lowest for *Recall* only, suggesting that a combination of materials is most stimulating, but that using books is better than use of tapes and slides alone.

There were problems in using a traditional experimental design to evaluate the groups. For example, for purposes of comparison it was important to limit the composition of the groups to the first six able patients who expressed an interest in attending a reminiscence activity, but once the groups had been established for a few weeks several other patients wanted to join but had to be disappointed because group numbers were held constant. Analysing verbal utterances probably gave some idea of participation, but some authors have noted the preference among some elderly people for private review and reflection; it would be difficult to measure such 'silent reminiscing', but it is quite likely that some patients in the study preferred this to talking openly about their memories.[46] For the purposes of systematic evaluation, the study was time limited, but more positive measurable effects may have resulted from a longer term intervention – findings from other studies have suggested that reminiscence is only effective as a long-term therapy, since attenders of the group may need to develop trust and feel secure with the presenters and staff who are much younger than themselves.[47, 48, 49] Finally, the study looked for group effects which may have failed to recognize individual changes in behaviour e.g. one 63-year-old lady in the 'books only' reminiscence group had been very depressed and withdrawn before the therapy started. She had stopped going out, and only considered participating in the groups because they were ward based. She became much more cheerful and responsive during the treatment period. When the groups ended, she was taking more care in her physical appearance and relied less on the nursing staff for her basic personal care. She returned to attending OT sessions, from which she had excluded herself when she became depressed.

Long-term effects and later developments

Although the study failed to produce many measurable positive effects, it was felt that many patients did benefit as a result of the intervention, which was something of a surprise to members of staff who considered them 'unpromising' subjects.

The groups were obviously enjoyed by most patients. The reminiscence approach proved successful even though many patients had been in the hospital for several decades – they recalled how life there had changed, including some memories of difficult times. No patients became distressed about bringing their past to mind. In fact, the atmosphere during most sessions was very cheerful; people would laugh about old times, they would compare different experiences, or even sing a favourite song. Several asked if the groups could be continued. There were other short-term effects. By request from both patients and staff, the trolley rounds continued. Staff and volunteers became more interested in using *Recall* and the reading materials, and new library and ward-based activities have been developed.

The secondary effects on staff are possibly the most significant outcome. The interventions described above acted as a springboard for new ideas, all of which have contributed to adopting a more holistic approach to patients and a less pessimistic attitude towards long-stay residential care.

From spontaneous responses by staff and patients, it appeared that the general aims of the study were met. Activities were developed for patients of different levels of communication and intellectual ability. Nurses and volunteers felt more supported, their morale improving via sustained interest and cooperation from the library and psychology department staff and because working with the patients became more rewarding. Programmes began to take place on the wards, and the library became a venue and resource centre for regular and special events such as a Christmas story reading.

An important aspect of work at the hospital was the cooperation and collaboration between the librarian and myself as a psychologist. In a long-stay institution it is difficult to implement change, but by working closely together we were able not only to bring different skills to the problem of introducing new activities, but also to offer support to each other when our ideas were 'blocked' (temporarily or permanently) by long established rules and regulations. By persisting with these original projects, an avenue for further changes was opened as more other staff became interested and involved.

Major later developments were the establishment of more deposit collections; the creation of a special reminiscence section in the library stock, and purchase of more photographic and picture books for use by less able patients; the introduction of a creative writing group; the involvement of patients as workers in the library; the development of a leaflet for nursing staff describing the library services; and the adoption of a no smoking policy in the library. The last of these is a major achievement – smoking is a habit which is extremely resistant to change but is a primary pleasure and reward for many psychiatric patients. Many staff felt that the library would not be used if patients were prevented from smoking, but the outcome is a positive one and provides a pertinent conclusion.

A number of projects were introduced to illustrate how books and other library materials may be used therapeutically in an old, large psychiatric hospital with even very intellectually impaired and behaviourally dependent patients. Putting into practice therapeutic approaches from stimulation programmes, reminiscence and reading therapy increased interest among staff and patients, changing the library's function from an under-used 'smoking room' to a valuable hospital-based resource providing activities from very basic 'memory jogging' to sophisticated reading and creative writing.

To the outside observer unfamiliar with large institutions, these results may seem insignificant and the study of reminiscence therapy simplistic. However, in the context of a setting where rules, routines and restrictions can generate apathy or pessimism changes such as increases in activity, interest and motivation and secondary effects on staff are great achievements.

Acknowledgments
I wish to express my thanks and appreciation to Penny Shapland, Hospital Librarian for all her help in developing these ideas, and for continuing to show the important role a patients' library can play in enhancing the quality of life for psychiatric patients.

References

1 Folsom, J. C., 'Reality orientation for the elderly mental patient', *Journal of Geriatric Psychiatry*, 1, 1968, 291–307.
2 McClannahan, L. E., and Risley, T. R., 'Design of living environments for nursing home residents: increasing participation in recreation activities', *Journal of Applied Behaviour Analysis*, 8, 1975, 261–8.
3 Goffman, E., *Asylums*, Harmondsworth, Penguin Books, 1961.
4 Kurasik, S., 'The need for recreation in hospitals, nursing homes and homes for the aged,' *Journal of the American Geriatric Society*, 13, 1965, 556–60.
5 Wells, T. J., *Problems in geriatric nursing care*, Edinburgh, Churchill Livingstone, 1980.
6 Cumming, E. and Henry, W. E., *Growing old. The process of Disengagement*, New York, Basic Books, 1961.
7 Sommer, R. and Ross, H., 'Social interaction on a geriatric ward', *International Journal of Social Psychiatry*, 4, 1958, 128–33.
8 Holden, U. P. and Woods, R. T., *Reality Orientation*, London, Churchill Livingstone, 1982.
9 Hoyer, W. J., 'Applications of operant techniques to the modification of elderly behaviour,' *Gerontologist*, 14, 1973, 149–52.
10 Blackman, D. K., Howe, M. and Pinkston, E. M., 'Increasing participation in social intereaction of the institutionalized elderly,' *Gerontologist*, 16, (1), 1976, 69–76.
11 Jenkins, J., Felce, D., Lunt, B. and Powell, E., 'Increasing engagement in activity of residents in old people's homes by providing recreational materials,' *Behaviour Research and Therapy*, 15, 1977, 429–34.
12 Gray, P. and Stevenson, J. S., 'Changes in verbal interaction among members of resocialisation groups,' *Journal of Gerontological Nursing*, 6, 1980, 86–90.
13 Kiernat, J. M., 'The need for recreation in hospitals, nursing homes

and homes for the aged,' *Journal of the American Geriatric Society*, 13, 1965, 556–60.
14 Butler, R. N., 'The life review: an interpretation of reminiscence in the aged,' *Psychiatry*, 26, 1963, 65–76.
15 Erikson, E. H., *Childhood and Society*, New York, W. W. Norton, 1950.
16 Havighurst, R. J. and Glasser, R., 'An experimental study of reminiscence,' *Journal of Gerontology*, 27, 1972, 245–53.
17 McMahon, A. W. and Rhudick, P. J., 'Reminiscing: adaptional significance in the aged,' *Archives of General Psychiatry*, 10, (3), 1964, 292–8.
18 Lewis, C. N., 'Reminiscing and self concept in old age,' *Journal of Gerontology*, 26, (2), 1971, 240–3.
19 Lo Gerfo, M., 'Three ways of reminiscence in theory and practice,' *International Journal of Ageing and Human Development*, 12, (1), 1980, 39–48.
20 Fallot, J. C., 'The impact on mood of verbal reminiscing in later adulthood,' *International Journal of Ageing and Human Development*, 10 (4), 1980, 384–400.
21 Norris, A. D., *Reminiscing as Reality Orientation*, Unpublished paper presented at the Annual Conference of the British Association of Behavioural Psychotherapy, University of Bristol, 1981a.
22 Norris, A. D., *Reminiscence – a new therapy for old therapists?*, Unpublished paper presented at the Annual Conference of the British Society of Gerontology, 1981b.
23 Norris, A. D. and Abu El Eileh, M.T.R., 'Reminiscence Groups,' *Nursing Times*, 78, 1982, 1368–9.
24 Norris, A. D., *The role of reminiscence in improving quality of life in extended care wards*, Unpublished paper, private communication to the author, 1984.
25 Langley, G. E. and Corder, J. M., *The contribution of reminiscence theatre to reminiscence therapy with the elderly*, Report on conference at Exe Vale Hospital, Exeter, 1978, Quoted in Holden and Woods, *op. cit.*
26 *Recall – A Handbook*, London, Help the Aged Education Department, 1981.
27 Harvey, T. and Kinsman, R., *Reminiscence*, submitted for publication, 1981, quoted in Holden and Woods, *op. cit.*
28 Brown, E. F., *Bibliotherapy and its widening applications*, Metuchen, New Jersey, Scarecrow Press, 1975.
29 Kilko, D. J. and Milan, M. A., 'Misconception correction through reading in the treatment of self injection phobia,' *Journal of Behaviour Therapy and Experimental Psychiatry*, 11, (4), 1980, 273–6.
30 Nimmo, J. M. and Koch, H., 'A methodology for self help booklets,' *Clinical Psychology Forum*, 1, (4), 1986, 16–19.
31 Morgan, S. R., 'Bibliotherapy: a broader concept,' *Journal of Clinical Child Psychology*, 5 (2), 1976, 39–42.
32 Rubin, R. J., *Bibliotherapy Sourcebook*, London, Oryx Press, 1978a.

33 Rubin, R. J., *Bibliotherapy: A guide to theory and practice*, London, Oryx Press, 1978b.
34 Pomeroy, E., *Book therapy in veterans' hospitals*, U.S. Government Publication, 1927, Reprinted in Rubin, 1978a, *op. cit*.
35 Coomaraswamy, S. D., 'Therapeutic aspects of a library service to hospital patients,' *Health and Welfare Libraries Quarterly*, 2, 1975, 29–32.
36 Coomaraswamy, S. D., *Reading as a means of communication with psychiatric and psychogeriatric patients*, Unpublished paper presented at the Library Association Medical, Health and Welfare Libraries Group on Bibliotherapy, 1983.
37 Sweeney, D., *Bibliotherapy and the elderly*, from Rubin, 1978a, *op. cit*.
38 Marr, J., 'The capacity for joy,' *Nursing Times*, 80, 1983, 58–61.
39 Hoy, S., *The promotion of books and reading with elderly people*, unpublished paper presented at the Library Association Medical, Health and Welfare Libraries Group on Bibliotherapy, 1983.
40 Lesser, W., Lazarus, L. W., Frankel, R. and Havasy, S., 'Reminiscence group therapy with psychotic geriatric patients,' *Gerontologist*, 21, (3), 1981, 291–6.
41 Alexander, R. H. and Buggie, S. E., 'Bibliotherapy with chronic schizophrenics,' *Journal of Rehabilitation*, 55, 1967, 26–7.
42 *op. cit*., 8.
43 Moos, R. H., *Ward Atmosphere Scale Manual*, California, Consulting Psychology Press, 1974.
44 Cameron, J., *Memory Lane. A Photographic Album of Daily Life in Britain 1930–1953*, London, Dent, 1980.
45 Donaldson, F., *Those Were the Days – A Photographic Album of Daily Life in Britain 1919–1939*, London, Dent, 1983.
46 MacCrae, I., 'Growth and development for elders: reminiscence, an underused nursing resource,' *Nursing Papers*, 14, (1), 1982, 48–56.
47 Butler, R. N., 'Intensive psychotherapy for the hospitalised aged,' *Geriatrics*, 15, 1970, 644–53
48 Ebersole, P., 'Reminiscing and group psychotherapy with the aged', 1976, from Burnside, I. M., (ed.) *Psychosocial nursing care of the aged*, 2nd ed., New York, McGraw-Hill, 1980.
49 Perrotta, P. and Meacham, J. A., 'Can reminiscing alter depression and self esteem?', *International Journal of Ageing and Human Development*, 14, (1), 1981, 23–30.

Bibliography

Allison, R., *The Country Life book of Britain in the Seventies*, London, Country Life Books, 1980.

Bailey, D. M., *Children of the green*, London, Stepney Books, 1981.

Bates, H. E., *The triple echo*, Harmondsworth, Penguin Books, 1972.

Battle, L., *War brides*, London, W. H. Allen, 1983.

Bleasdale, A., and Miles, K., *Boys from the Blackstuff*, London, Granada, 1983.

Blythe, R., *Akenfield*, Harmondsworth, Penguin Books, 1969.

Blythe, R., *The view in winter – reflections on old age*, Harmondsworth, Penguin Books, 1979.

Braine, J., *Room at the top*, Harmondsworth, Penguin Books, 1959.

Bricketwood Society, *A souvenir of Bricketwood*, 1982 (locally published booklet).

Brittain, V., *Chronicle of youth: Vera Brittain's war diary 1913–1917*, London, Victor Gollancz Limited, 1981.

Brittain, V., *England's hour. An autobiography 1939–41*, London, Futura, 1981.

Burnett, J., *Useful toil*, Harmondsworth, Penguin Books, 1977.

Cameron, J., *Memory lane. A photographic album of daily life in Britain 1930–1953*, London, Dent, 1980.

Comyns, B., *Our spoons came from Woolworth*, Bath, Cedric Chivers Portway, 1950.

Donaldson, F., *Those were the days. A photographic album of daily life in Britain 1919–1939*, London, Dent, 1983.

Eliot, G., *The mill on the Floss*, Harmondsworth, Penguin Books, 1973.

Foley, W., *No pipe dreams for father*, London, Macdonald, 1978.

French, M., *A Victorian village. A record of the parish of Quethiok in Cornwall*, Falmouth, Glasney Press, 1977.

Graves, R., *Goodbye to all that*, Harmondsworth, Penguin Books, 1960.

Hackney Workers' Education Association, *A Hackney camera 1883–1918* (locally published booklet, no publication date).

Hall, C., *The twenties in Vogue*, London, Octopus, 1983.

Harrison, R., *Rose: My life in service*, London, Futura, 1975.

Holden, A., *Great royal front pages*, London, Collins, 1983.

Holtby, W., *The land of green ginger*, London, Virago, 1983.

Hooton, T., *Spitfire special*, London, Ian Allen, 1972.

Hudd, R., *Music hall*, London, Eyre Methuen, 1976.

Hudson, W. H., *Nature in downland*, London, Macdonald Futura, 1981.

James, C., *Unreliable memoirs*, London, Picador, 1981.

Jenkins, A., *The twenties*, London, William Heinemann, 1974.

Kelsall, F., *How we used to live 1936–1953*, London, Macdonald, 1981.

Kent, J., *Binder twine and rabbit stew*, Folkestone, Bailey Bothers and Swinfen, 1978.
Kent, J., *Wood smoke and pigeon pie*, London, Coronet Books, 1977.
Klein, D., *All colour book of art deco*, London, Octopus, 1974.
Lee, L., *As I walked out one midsummer morning*, Harmondsworth, Penguin Books, 1971.
Lee, L., *Cider with Rosie*, London, Hogarth Press, 1973.
Lloyd, A., *Movies of the thirties*, London, Orbis Press, 1983.
Lloyd, A., *Movies of the sixties*, London, Orbis Press, 1983.
Lunn, J. E., and Vaughan Williams, U., *Ralph Vaughan Williams. A pictorial biography*, London, Oxford University Press, 1971.
Mannin, E., *Young in the twenties*, London, Hutchinson, 1971.
Metcalfe, J., *Sunnyland: A 1920's childhood remembered*, London, Michael Joseph, 1980.
Millar, A., *British buses of the 1930's*, Cambridge, Patrick Stephens, 1982.
Minns, R., *Bombers and mash: The domestic front 1939–45*, London, Virago, 1980.
Newman, A., *Alexa*, Harmondsworth, Penguin Books, 1976.
Noble, I., *Emmeline and her daughters: The Pankhurst suffragettes*, Folkestone, Bailey Brothers and Swinfen Limited, 1974.
Owen, W., *War poems and others*, London, Chatto and Windus, 1973.
Palmer, T., *All you need is love: The story of popular music*, London, Weidenfeld and Nicolson and Chappell, 1976.
Pember Reeves, M., *Round about a pound a week*, London, Virago, 1979.
Powell, M. with Mackenzie, L., *Beryl's lot book 2*, London, Sphere Books, 1976.
Powell, M. with Mackenzie, L., *Beryl's lot book 3*, London, Sphere Books, 1977.
Roberts, P., *Veteran and vintage cars*, London, Octopus, 1974.
Silver Jubilee Book, *The story of twenty five years in pictures 1910–1935*, London, Odhams Press.
Storey, D., *The prodigal child*, London, Jonathan Cape, 1982.
Struther, J., *Mrs Miniver*, London, Futura, 1980.
Thompson, F., *Lark Rise to Candleford*, Harmondsworth, Penguin Books, 1973.
Thompson, P. and Harkell, G., *The Edwardians in photographs*, London, Batsford, 1979.
Toms, E., *St Albans as it was*, Nelson, Hendon Publishing Co., 1973.

Wayne, J., *Brown bread and butter in the basement. A twenties childhood*, London, Victor Gollancz, 1973.

Whitmore, R., *Victorian and Edwardian Hertfordshire from old photographs*, London, Batsford, 1978.

11 Ageing and the interests of the elderly, with special reference to reading

Martin Skelton-Robinson

Who are the elderly?

From the day we are born we are growing older. But ageing is not simply the passage of time. It may be possible to define the different stages of our life by using a calendar, but this is at best a rough guide to human development. Moreover, the older we grow the more difficult it becomes to distinguish between the stages of our life. Infancy, childhood and adolescence are relatively easy episodes to identify: but how can we tell when a person has become middle-aged, or old?

For the psychologist there are two ways of answering this question: one hard and one easy; one that is genuinely psychological and one that begs the question. The hard approach tries to define ageing developmentally. It asks: what characteristic changes do our thought processes, our emotions, our personalities pass through in the course of a lifetime? It tries to define what is characteristic of each stage of development. Once this has been done it is possible to say which stage of their life a person has reached independent of how old they are.

This was the approach of the first developmental psychologist to study old age. In his book entitled *Senescence*, G. Stanley Hall prefaced one of his chapters with the following provocative idea:

> Perhaps no one but a genetic psychologist can realize how very widely the successive stages of life in man differ from each other. Underneath the tenuous memory continuum that is the chief basis of all feeling of identity between our present and former selves, deeper even than every unity of life plan and persistence of disposition, are the great changes the years bring. These are, indeed, so great that although they very commonly modulate, each into the next stage of the series by almost imperceptible gradations, we all really live not one but a succession of lives.[1]

Two themes picked out for discussion by Stanley Hall are still central in developmental studies of old age: life review and preparation for death.

This developmental approach to ageing is not only stimulating as an outlook, but in my own opinion the right method of study to adopt. However for many reasons, not least of all the difficulty of securing agreed conclusions, it has rarely been practised by psychologists. Stanley Hall's book was published in 1922 and there has been nothing written quite like it since. The elderly are still awaiting their Piaget to make a developmental psychology of old age academically respectable.

The other approach to defining age is to use time alone as an indicator of a person's development. This is not a psychological approach (it is not even a biological approach because different organisms in the same species and different cells in the same organism 'age' at different rates), but it is an approach that permits precise definitions of who we are going to study, and easy comparisons between age groups and cultures.

As far as old age is concerned legislators have come to the aid of sociologists and defined the elderly population for them. By fixing an age at which citizens are eligible for a state pension governments have effectively fixed the retirement age for the bulk of the population; in Britain women at 60 and men at 65.

Social scientists, preferring not to discriminate between the sexes, have adopted 65 as the threshold of old age. This is a convention more arbitrary than most. The age of retirement, for men in particular, is falling and under great pressure to fall further. Meanwhile there is a gradual but remorseless increase in the average life expectancy for those of us living in the industrialized countries of the world. If we continue to define old age as beginning with retirement we shall soon be obliged to recognize that old age will be the longest phase of most people's lives, exceeding by a large margin the time we pass being young adults or middle-aged.

All the studies I am about to review try to define the mental changes that accompany ageing by using a chronological definition of age. They study some feature of the mind, memory for example and compare how people in different decades of life perform on a standard memory test. From the results of such a study it is possible to conclude that on average this memory test is harder or easier as people age (there may of course be no difference). Let us suppose that people over 65 tend to do less well overall than any other age group (e.g. 25–35 or 45–55). It might be concluded that the memories of people aged over 65 are usually less retentive than when they were younger. But because the study is not developmental the question was never asked as to whether the test of memory used (e.g. learning a list of words) is equally appropriate for young and old. Or put another way: does the role of memory change as life advances? Because such developmental questions are not often asked when we study the effects of ageing on the mind the conclusions psychologists have to offer leave a great deal to be desired.

Normal ageing

What happens to the mind as we grow older? Psychologists seem to be almost unanimous in their reply to this question. Speaking generally people's reactions grow slower as they age; their reasoning ability and the retentiveness of their memory declines; they become more cautious when facing decisions and once they have decided on a course of action they find it harder to change their minds (rigidity). These changes do not all begin at the same time; for example speed of reaction begins to slow in the 30s but memory doesn't start to decline until the 50s. Some abilities decline faster than others, and some people seem to enjoy a relative immunity to change, whilst others are surprisingly badly affected.

Reaction time

The most striking change of all to some psychologists is the dramatic decline in human productivity beginning around the mid-thirties. By productivity I mean how fast we work, and how quickly we can react to events.

Naturally the rate at which we can do a task (press a switch when a signal shows, count out change at a supermarket till) depends on more than one factor. The senses are required to detect information, decisions are made about how to react, the reaction itself must be initiated and then scrutinized to check its effect. Which of these various parts of making a response is affected by ageing?

There is no doubt that our senses grow weaker with age. The chapters in a standard psychology text on ageing devoted to the special senses make gloomy reading.[2] Sensitivity for hearing begins to decline from about age 50, and sight, smell and taste begin to decline about age 60. Only some parts of touch sensitivity seem to preserve their acuity into old and very old age.

However it is not weakness of our senses that makes our reactions slower as we age. We can equate the strength of the stimulus we use to test young and old by allowing for the decline in sensory acuity. This makes no difference to how quickly they react to a signal.

Another proof that the senses are not the important factor is what happens if we make a task more complex. Let us suppose that instead of saying 'when you see the light press the button' we say 'press the red button for the left-hand light and press the green button for the right-hand light'. As people age they seem to find the complicated instruction harder to act on, and it slows them up more than it does the young.

This draws our attention to the fact that it is deciding and making the reaction that becomes slower with age. There is also evidence that as we grow older we take less notice of the effects of our actions, and so are less ready to correct what we are doing.

Studies of the types of manual work people do as they grow older are thought to confirm these laboratory findings. Older people 'tend not to be found in jobs which demand rapid decisions or continuous activity paced by the machinery used'.[3] Further 'the types of industrial and road traffic accidents and road traffic violations which increase with age can be attributed mainly to slowness in making decisions rather than to any sensory or motor impairment'.[4]

The conclusion is drawn that whilst our senses grow weaker with age this is a less disabling handicap than the difficulty the elderly have with central processes; the slowness of their decision-making. But slow decision-making is not always a disadvantage. Experiments have shown that if the task allows the elderly to perform at their own pace then they make fewer errors than the younger groups, who are all working more quickly.[5] Also the type of error made by the elderly is of interest. When asked, for example, to press a button to show they have noticed a signal they mainly make errors of omission (not reacting to a signal) rather than errors of commission (reacting when there is no signal). With younger ages the second kind of error is more common. This change in style is thought by some to be linked to a supposed increase in 'cautiousness' of people's behaviour as they age.[6]

Memory

One feature of ageing that today everybody is aware of is the gradual decline in memory it commonly brings. This is one of the few areas of psychological experiment where the results of studies have passed into common language and it is not uncommon to hear people complain they have a bad 'short-term memory'.

It is often the case that when technical terms are adopted in everyday language they are misapplied and in fact short-term memory (the amount you can hold in mind at any one time) is little affected by ageing. It is long-term memory that is vulnerable as a large body of research over many decades shows. The confusion of terms seems to have arisen because people as they grow older find it harder to remember recent events, whilst still able to recall without difficulty remote memories. As far as psychologists are concerned remembering both recent and remote events is a test of long-term memory.

The question we have to ask is: why is long-term memory affected as we grow older? There seem to be two answers. The first is that the elderly are less good at learning (getting things from the short to the long-term memory), and this is quite possibly related to the fact that they do not classify or analyse (technical term: encode) what they want to learn as well as younger people.[7] We could imagine memory as a filing store. For the elderly things are put into it rather haphazardly.

This brings us to the second explanation: retrieval. If things are not systematically stored they are hard to recover. We can prove that the elderly learn more than they can demonstrate when just asked to recall something by testing their recognition. For example, if instead of saying 'which words do you remember from the list you read?' we ask 'was word X or Y on the list you read?' elderly subjects are able to remember more of what they studied, and their performance is much closer to that of younger subjects.[8]

There is a useful distinction to be made between two sorts of memory store. On the one hand there is episodic memory or memory for things that are personal and part of a series of events (e.g., I last visited the hairdresser a week ago); on the other hand there is semantic memory or memory for things that are impersonal and not time marked (e.g., a square has four sides). There is evidence that it is the first of these memory stores that is the most susceptible to the effects of ageing, and also that if we are unfortunate enough to begin to forget what we once learnt it is the personal store that is the more perishable.

Intelligence

These findings (slowing of performance, difficulty with new learning) are in large part the explanation of why as we age our performance on intelligence tests declines. Consider for example the most widely used of these tests; the Wechsler Adult Intelligence Scale. There are eleven different subtests that make up this scale. Six of them are tests of verbal intelligence, and five of them tests of perceptual-integrative intelligence.

As far as tests that measure semantic memory, or acquired knowledge are concerned these stand up to ageing well. Information, Vocabulary and Comprehension show little decline until persons are into their 70s.[9]

In contrast such tests as Picture Arrangement, Block Design and Digit Symbol which are all timed tests and require decisions about how to do an unfamiliar task begin to show appreciable age related changes as early as age 35 years.[10]

However the intelligence test that is regarded as the purest measure available of reasoning ability, Raven's Matrices, shows an age related decline in scores beginning after age 25. This test is untimed and does not rely on memory. There must therefore be some important aspect of intelligence different from those already mentioned that begins to wane early in adult life. The special adaptability of our reasoning powers that psychologists have called problem-solving may well be the ability in question.

Language

When we come to the abilities most relevant to this chapter, those connected with language, there are very few studies that have investigated the effects of ageing, except in respect of the most elementary functions of speech. As already stated we know that the ability to define the meaning of words is hardly affected by age at all. On the other hand finding a word when we need it grows more difficult with age. This is proved by tests of verbal fluency (finding words as quickly as one can that belong to a definite category, e.g., names of animals) and tests of naming to confrontation (when an object is presented and the name must be found). Both procedures show an age related decrement.[11, 12]

Conclusions relating to the complex aspects of language have to be tentative because typically there is only one study published on a topic, and the number of subjects investigated so far very small (twenty or less). Two of these preliminary studies seem worth referring to. One is a comparison of language patterning in the elderly (over 75) and pre-middle-aged (30–45). This study concludes that results from three different tests requiring comprehension of spoken complex syntax show 'a *direct* relationship between age and deficit in syntatic processing'. Pronouns, prepositions, irregular verbs and verb tenses were frequently misconstrued by the elderly.[13]

The second study suggests that the elderly are more prolix when describing an event, but without conveying more information. An elderly group (60–69) used more words for each theme they identified in a picture than a younger group (50–59) and their sentences were more complicated with a higher ratio of prepositions and conjunctions to each noun and verb.[14]

As far as the psychology of reading is concerned I can find no studies of the effects of age. However we might feel entitled to put forward some obvious suppositions, so long as we recognize they could be mistaken.

Written language seems to have two advantages over spoken language for the elderly where the communication of precise meaning is involved. Firstly the message can be received at a speed determined by the reader. Secondly there is a permanent trace available to consult if there is any suspicion of misunderstanding. Had the experiment mentioned above on the comprehension of syntax by the elderly used written instead of spoken messages the degree of understanding might well have been greater.

Next we know that memory for events is less reliable in old age than memory for information. This might affect the choice of reading matter made by the elderly. History and fiction would perhaps grow less popular except when the events are either simple or familiar. Factual books on the other hand dealing with such subjects as art, natural history, gardening etc., might become more popular.

Finally we know that word comprehension is not affected by ageing and this is one good reason we might expect reading to remain a viable and popular activity amongst the elderly, other factors such as eyesight, education and access to books, permitting.

The gifted elderly

So far we have discussed what happens on average as people age. But what is average is only a part of the whole picture. Ageing, in the sense of time passing, involves a constant widening of the limits between the least able and the most able people, so that what is average becomes less and less representative of the group as a whole. It is of great practical interest to ask: how do the most gifted elderly compare with their younger counterparts?

The classic study in this field is the work by Lehman entitled *Age and Achievement*.[15] He compared the scientific and artistic productivity of young and old over the centuries, where possible comparing the record of the same individuals over their entire life span. He found that there were different peaks of achievement in each area of endeavour. For example the peak for chemical science came at age 25–30, for physics 30–35, and for many subjects (biology, medicine, mathematics) 35–40.

In the arts there was a similar distribution with productivity reaching a peak in most forms of poetry age 25–30, in painting age 30–35, and in music and most forms of prose literature age 35–40 or even a little later. Of great interest is the fact that in many of the humanities productivity and quality of achievement decline far less slowly from their peak than they do in the sciences.

Reviewing these facts has prompted one commentator to reflect:

> compared with other fields, a surprisingly high level of literary productivity is maintained after the age sixty-five – and even after eighty. Poetry, for example, may decline only by about 50 per cent in productivity between the age of peak, around thirty, and later life. Granted good health and opportunity, vocabulary continues to expand throughout the life span. Thus the literary worker continually has more experience and skill available for his productions. If one were going to select a career for late life, a literary career would seem to be an ideal choice.[16]

A more recent study, looking at more modest gifts, recruited 50 people over 70 all in good health who held bachelors degrees from American universities and had worked all their lives in professional jobs.[17] Tests of memory and intelligence showed that compared with the younger gifted these people were disadvantaged, though they were at least as able in most respects as persons 50 years younger of only average ability.

An interesting aspect of this study was that each person's degree of contact with the environment was measured using such indices as numbers of meetings with friends and young people, membership and attendance at clubs and churches, amount of time spent in leisure activities. For a majority of the elderly persons these social activities had decreased since retirement, but for a small minority there had been a definite increase.

Those whose social activities had increased seemed to be the ones whose intelligence was best preserved. But whether the active pursuit of social contact and recreation helped to preserve intelligence, or a better preserved intelligence favoured sociability and recreation is something not answered by this study.

A glance at the gifted elderly shows that age may restrain but does not prevent productivity in the sciences, and the arts. It does however seem to affect memory and intelligence without exception as measured by psychological tests. But the question remains: are the tests we use suitable for detecting abilities that might increase with ageing? The poet Chaucer tells us: 'The old may be out-run but not out-reasoned.' The sort of prudence and wisdom traditionally attributed to the elderly is not something that would be evident on any of the tests psychologists have so far devised. By assuming that intelligence and memory remain the same qualities throughout the life-cycle psychologists perhaps participate in the general prejudice that prevails throughout our society towards ageing.

Interests in later life

A major life event for many people is their own or their spouse's retirement from paid employment. One result of retirement is a large increase in time available for leisure activities. There are some studies of how this time is used.[18, 19, 20] Recently retired and more elderly respondents may be asked to name their hobbies and interests. Sometimes they are provided with a checklist and asked to indicate what activities they were engaged in 'yesterday'. They may even be asked to assess the amount of time spent on each activity.

This kind of information does not tell us anything about ageing. In order to introduce a developmental perspective we need to know how people's leisure activities have changed as they grow older.

Retirement is of course a social event, and as such has an ill-determined relation to ageing. Like unemployment it creates a great deal of leisure time whilst reducing the person's income and social standing. Reaction to being redundant or retiring is for all we know the same at any age. But as most people retire around the age of 60 this will compound changes consequent with ageing with those resulting from retirement. I have not found any studies that acknowledge this conceptual problem. At the very least a comparison between retired elderly people and a much younger group of long-term unemployed might help decide how much 'enforced leisure' is a problem that both groups try to solve in similar ways.

Psychological studies of the leisure interests of the elderly are few and far between. Moreover their results usually relate to highly unrepresentative groups, most often the gifted elderly. For example Hall in preparation for writing his study of old age circulated a questionnaire to 'a few score names of mostly eminent and some very distinguished old people, both acquaintances and strangers'. Those who replied were all 'cultivated Americans and thus they represent a single class'.[21]

One question Hall asked was: 'In what do you take your greatest pleasure?' He presents the answers he received as generalizations. Most respondents had discovered new sources of satisfaction in old age and the one most often specified was reading. The other most common development was finding pleasure in nature 'for example, walks in the open, gardening, birds, stars, celestial phenomena'.

Trying to compare the various changes described by respondents Hall concluded: 'Of the three muses, solitude, society and nature, while all have a new if not stronger attraction it is the first that, from our returns, would seem to increase most with age.'

A much more extensive psychological study was made by Strong.[22] He surveyed about 1900 men aged 20–49, and 400 aged 50–60. As well as excluding women no manual workers were included amongst the eight occupations surveyed and this casts doubt on the representativeness of his conclusions. All subjects completed the Strong Vocational Interest Blank which requires the respondent to indicate whether he likes, dislikes or is indifferent to each of 420 occupations and pastimes. No person could have experience of each item and therefore many replies must have been suppositional. Also the Blank makes no provision for measuring the degree of a person's liking or disliking. Hence changes found with age cannot be evaluated in terms of strength and weakness of someone's feelings.

Given these limitations let us look at Strong's conclusions. Amongst the most interesting from our point of view is the following observation:

> Many amusements are liked by large percentages at all ages. But there is a distinct tendency for all of them to decline except those that may be characterized as cultural. These increase in liking. Older men also prefer, more than younger men do, those amusements pursued largely alone in contrast to ones involving others.

It is worth adding in this connection that the activities for which liking increased with advancing age were gardening, bird watching and visiting museums.

A further conclusion of interest is that: 'Linguistic activities of an oral and written nature decline in interest, but those involving reading increase in liking with age.'

In respect of reading Strong showed that most of the change measured in expressed preference came in the age range 25–45. This finding has two cautionary implications. First, when a comparison is made between old and young any differences found may not be attributable to the elderly as a group but have eventuated earlier in life. Second, we must recognize that when the elderly make retrospective statements about themselves there may easily attribute change to the recent past which in fact transpired far earlier in their lives.

A final point on the way our preferences alter with age: 'In general, the things we like most at 25 years of age are liked better and better with increasing age, and the things we like least at 25 are liked less and less.'

When Birren reviewed this and similar studies he noted three general findings:[23] with increasing age there is a tendency to lose interest in strenuous physical activity and participation in sport; an increasing interest in relatively solitary activities; an increased interest in 'cultural' reading and decreased interest in being amused. But Birren qualified the last of these observations by saying: 'It has been pointed out that there are social class differences in leisure-time interests. Taken in perspective, the values of leisure-time activity seem to be more related to social class and personal adjustment than to age and sex.'

This means that we can predict more about a person's leisure interests by knowing their social class than their age; ageing has only a minor influence on already established habits.

I will finish this section by reviewing a new psychological approach to the interests of the elderly. Two recently published studies have tried to identify the different types of leisure satisfaction that exist and the psychological benefits associated with them.[24,25] By means of a statistical technique called cluster analysis a group of six benefits were identified: companionship, compensation, temporary disengagement, comfortable solitude, expressive solitude, expressive service. Some 1600 people over 55 filled in a standard interview about their interests (Paragraphs About Leisure Questionnaire) and leisure activities were grouped according to the benefits derived. Reading proved to be associated with three other activities: raising house plants, collecting photographs, collecting antiques. The type of psychological benefit derived in common from these joint interests was said to be 'comfortable solitude'.

The shortcoming of this approach is that we have no idea as to whether the benefits of participation reported by elderly people are any different from the benefits younger people derive from the same leisure activities. Until some comparative work has been done these studies cannot be said to show anything specifically related to age.

Reading and the elderly

Reading to an elementary standard is, one imagines, an almost universal accomplishment in our society. It is also a necessary skill in various aspects of daily life. Like speaking, reading is an act that can fulfil many purposes and it seems useful to give a moment's thought to how acts of reading might be classified.

First there is the matter of occasion. Much reading is incidental, and required by some other goal we are pursuing. Street names, price tags, timetables, recipe books are all consulted in the process of achieving a definite end for which reading need not be necessary.

This type of reading cannot always be distinguished from the next class, which is purposive. Purposive reading is studying a subject by reading about it. Printed material is consulted deliberately and the act of reading is sustained over a period of time. Here reading is not an end in itself but usually the sole or main means of achieving some other end.

Finally we have reading that serves mainly an aesthetic purpose. This category is intended to refer to all forms of reading intended as amusement or recreation. The type of material involved is as diverse as comic strips and epic poetry.

When we look at studies of reading done by social scientists we find they do not pay any attention to this question of purpose. Often in a survey a person is simply asked 'do you like reading?' as if the question had only one meaning. If the investigation is more detailed reading material is distinguished either by subject matter, or by type of commercial product (newspaper, magazine, book). Hence such studies do not show us why people spend time reading, nor what types of reading they are referring to when they say they enjoy it. The general implication seems to be however, that reading with an aesthetic purpose (reading for pleasure) is the sort of reading inquired about.

The most reliable information available on the reading habits of the elderly in Britain is contained in a survey carried out by Audrey Hunt in 1975 for the Department of Health and Social Security.[26] The reason the results of this survey are particularly reliable is that it was conducted using a very large number of people (more than 2,500 aged over 65) and that respectable sampling methods were used to ensure that all classes in the population were represented and that a sufficient number of very elderly (84+) were included (over 200) for generalizations about this group to be meaningful. The chapter in this survey we are interested in is called: 'Interests and hobbies of the elderly and their attitudes to life'. Results are presented so that they can be related to a variety of factors: sex, increasing old age (65–74, 75–84, 84+), whether a person has any form of employment, marital status, and living circumstances. Questions about interests were asked in several different ways, and this has the advantage of giving a degree of perspective to the results obtained.

People were first asked: 'Have you any hobbies or interests?' If they replied 'yes' they were asked to name them. Next people were prompted with a list of hobbies and interests to see what they had failed to mention spontaneously.

In reply to the first question reading was mentioned by some 20 per cent of men and some 30 per cent of women. After prompting the figures were 65 per cent and 50 per cent respectively.

Even the prompt, however, failed to identify how many people actually spent some of their time reading. A subsequent question showed that some 80 per cent of men and 70 per cent of women said they usually read a newspaper, and only 17 per cent of men and 18 per cent of women said they never did any reading at all.

As well as being asked about their interests people were asked to name things they 'particularly enjoyed' doing. Reading was mentioned by seven per cent of the sample, rather more often by women than men.

With increasing age there was an interesting tendency for behaviour to become more pronounced. Thus amongst the very elderly (84+) an increasing proportion either specially enjoyed reading (15 per cent of men, 10 per cent of women) or did not read at all (25 per cent of men, 30 per cent of women).

From the tables provided it is possible to deduce a profile of the person who 'particularly enjoys' reading. They are more likely to be female than male, single or widowed rather than married or divorced, and live alone or with an elderly sibling rather than with a spouse or younger relatives.

These replies bear out the earlier observation that reading cannot be treated as if it had always the same purpose. The great majority of the elderly do some reading, but not many of them regard reading as an interest, and very few derive special pleasure from it.

It would be interesting to know something about the preferences of the elderly in terms of reading matter, how much time they actually spend in reading, and how these change with advancing age. I have not been able to find any authoritative information about these subjects. However a small but suggestive survey has been carried out with a sample of 35 elderly housebound persons who used a mobile library service, recording their borrowing preferences. Fiction proved more popular than non-fiction (96 and 79 books borrowed respectively in the course of the survey). However if these two categories are broken down by subject matter then biography (a class of non-fiction) proved to be the most popular type of book accounting for almost 30 per cent of all books borrowed. Especially interesting was the fact that the type of enjoyment readers most commonly took in these books was the opportunity to reminisce. Biographies proved especially stimulating in this respect.[27] Nothing general can be deduced from so small and select a study, but it underlines the value to librarians and publishers of knowing in more detail about the reading interests of the elderly.

Given the very large number of elderly persons in the population and the fact that a substantial proportion of them are interested in reading we might expect the public library service to see the elderly as an important client group with distinctive needs.[28] In so far as this happens it is 'access to books' that is made easier rather than special thought being given to how some elderly people might use the service differently to others.

There have however been ideas canvassed and some practical work done in encouraging groups of elderly persons to make special use of printed and related book materials. This small movement fits loosely under the general heading of bibliotherapy, a term that is intended to suggest the part that books can play in sustaining and enhancing mental health.[29, 30]

There are three ways, I think, in which the use bf the book in bibliotherapy differs from our normal reading practices. Firstly there is sustained guidance and encouragement in the use of materials. Secondly the book is used in conjunction with other forms of information (e.g. photographs, films, actual objects), and perhaps read aloud or replaced by someone's own composition. Thirdly, bibliotherapy is carried out in a group setting.

Some of this may sound similar to conventional educational practices, especially with young children learning to read. This analogy is a useful one because it emphasizes the importance bibliotherapy places on participation. The difference lies in the fact that for the child participation helps with learning, whereas for the elderly the bibliotherapist may see learning as a way of encouraging participation.

The potential applications of this approach with the elderly are considerable. First there are matters of practical interest and importance which some people would want to learn about, for example preparation for retirement, guidance on state benefits and social service provision and health care. There is good reason to think that formal lectures and impersonal leaflets on these topics are not well received. It remains to be seen whether a group approach with someone facilitating study by providing the 'books' would work better.

Next there are those leisure interests we have identified that become more popular as we age. Gardening, nature study, local history are obvious examples of subjects where one could usefully marry the resources of a library with a group of people not wanting instruction but mutual encouragement.

In this conversation it is perhaps worth saying that, apart from the books it contains, a public library would have special advantages as a meeting place for a group of elderly people. It is a place without stigma for the elderly, and without threat.

Books also have a part to play in the lives of some of those elderly people who are specially disadvantaged by ill health, physical and mental. Many of these frail elderly are long-term residents in hospitals, old people's homes, or attend some kind of day centre.

Often the frail elderly are demoralized by their infirmities and their dependency, and their social relations may become tediously repetitive. An approach to encouraging more social participation, and enhancing self-respect that is increasingly used in residential settings for the elderly is called 'Reminiscence Therapy' (see Chapter 10 by Heather George).

A group of residents are chosen who are broadly compatible and an hour set aside for them to share their reminiscences. The conversation is prompted and guided to a degree, and for groups where the participants have appreciable memory loss it is important to use materials that readily prompt reminiscing, such as slides depicting representative scenes and events from the past, or pictures showing famous people and familiar household objects.

Libraries would seem to be able to play a valuable part in assisting reminiscence work. Books and photographs about local history, books about film stars, royalty and other celebrities, old newspapers and magazines, and collections of oral history would assist in, and increase the range of work that can be done.

Librarians must have an almost unique opportunity to

identify and collect such resources. Perhaps some libraries could have a special section devoted to this purpose, and a librarian could be identified who would take special responsibility for developing such a collection and cooperating with staff in the health service, local authority and private residential homes to ensure the resources were in regular use.

Encouraging the various forms of bibliotherapy and assisting in the development of reminiscence work are two ways in which the public libraries could enlarge the services they offer to the elderly.

What we should like to know, of course, is whether any of the recreations we pursue in life, and in particular reading and related activities have any part to play in arresting or slowing down the gradual decline in faculties that psychologists have described as the typical effect of ageing on our minds. There is absolutely no way of answering this question at present. But one thing that does seem probable is that if there are any benefits of this sort then the reading habit must be established early in life because those who reach middle-age indifferent to books are unlikely to be attracted to regular reading in later life.

In this connection one might take notice of certain cultural influences. Those who are elderly today were brought up at a time when there was no television and when education and literacy were held in higher esteem. Over the next fifty years we shall see a remarkable change in these factors. Respect for books is ever decreasing in our society as other forms of disseminating information have become universally accessible. For a generation who have been brought up as television watchers, both for recreation and education, it is far from clear that reading will be for many more than a necessary survival skill. Aesthetic readers are perhaps an endangered species.

References

1 Hall, G. S., *Senescence*, New York, Appleton Century Crofts, 1922.
2 Birren, J. E., and Schaie, K. W., (eds.), *Handbook of the Psychology of Aging*, New York, Van Nostrand Reinhold, 1977.
3 Welford, A. T., 'Motor performance', Chapter 19 in *Handbook of the Psychology of Aging op. cit.*
4 *Ibid.*
5 *Ibid.*
6 Botwinick, J., *Aging and behaviour*, New York, Springer, 1978.
7 Craik, F. I. M., 'Age differences in human memory', Chapter 17 in *Handbook of the Psychology of Aging, op. cit.* 2.

8 *Ibid*.
9 *Op. cit.*, 6.
10 *Op. cit.*, 6.
11 Schaie, K. W., 'Cognitive development in aging', Chapter 1 in *Language and Communication in the elderly*, Obler, L. K., and Albert, M. L., (eds) Lexington, Lexington Books, 1980.
12 Goodglass, H., 'Naming disorders in aphasia and aging', Chapter 3 in *Language and Communication in the Elderly*, *op. cit.*, 11.
13 Emery, O. B., 'Language and aging', *Experimental Aging Research*, 11, (1), 1985, 3–61.
14 Obler, L. K., 'Narrative discourse style in the elderly', Chapter 6 in *Language and communication in the elderly*, *op. cit.*, 11.
15 Lenhman, H. C., *Age and Achievement*, Princeton, Princeton University Press, 1953.
16 Birren, J. E., *The Psychology of aging*, Englewood Cliffs, Prentice-Hall, 1964.
17 Schaie, K. W., and Strother, C. R., 'Cognitive and personality variables in college graduates of advanced age', in *Human aging and behaviour*, ed. Talland, G.A., New York, Academic Press, 1968.
18 Dobbin, I., *Retirement and leisure a preliminary research report*, Manchester, Centre for Leisure Studies, 1980.
19 Hunt, A., *The Elderly at home*, London, HMSO, 1978.
20 Kleemeier, R. W., (ed.), *Ageing and Leisure*, London, Oxford University Press, 1961.
21 *Op. cit.*, 1.
22 Strong, E. K., *Changes of interest with age*, Stanford, Stanford University Press, 1931.
23 *Op. cit.*, 16.
24 Tinsley, H. E. A., and Kass, R. A., 'The latent structure of the need satisfying properties of leisure activities', *Journal of Leisure Research*, 11, 1979, 278–91.
25 Tinsley, H. E. A., Teaff, J. D., Colbs, S. L., and Kaufman, N., 'A system of classifying leisure activities in terms of the psychological benefits of participation reported by older persons', *Journal of Gerontology*, 40, 1985, 172–8.
26 *Op. cit.*, 19.
27 Wigmore, H., *Housebound Readers: a study of the housebound reader service in Harrow*, Cranfield Institute of Technology, MSc Thesis, 1985.
28 Dee, M., 'Bringing to book – a service for those who enjoy reading in their later years', *Municipal Journal*, 92 (41), 1984, 1593–4.
29 Howie, M., 'Bibliotherapy in social work', *British Journal of Social Work*, 13, (3), 1983, 287–309.
30 Marr, J., 'The capacity for joy', *Nursing Times*, 79, (38), 1983, 58–61.

12 Bibliotherapy – its value in occupational therapy

Jan Wanless

Since traditionally occupational therapists tend to be seen working in domestic rehabilitation units, light and heavy workshops, art rooms and 'the occupational therapy department' you may wonder what place bibliotherapy has in the realm of his/her work. In addition to the traditional role, occupational therapists now do a considerable amount of group work of various kinds – drama, discussion, communication. Many extend their training to include psychotherapy. There has been considerable expansion in recent years in the use of creative therapy – whereby exploration, expression, fantasy and communication takes place through creative media such as drama, art, music etc. More recently I was introduced to bibliotherapy, which I feel now has a place in the creative therapies.

In thinking about the possibility of reading and writing as therapy, what came to mind was the great pleasure that can come from being engrossed in an exciting book, or the escapism that one can enjoy from reading books based on a different time, lifestyle or planet. Extending this to poetry there is the soothing effect of the language and rhythm of emotions, feelings, ideas and beauty portrayed in the written form. Also I thought of how helpful it can be to write a letter to a friend when one is feeling troubled by a problem, annoyed by a series of events or bursting with good news. Yes, I did think bibliotherapy could be a worthwhile therapy for a lot of patients.

The idea of forming a reading therapy group was first introduced to me by our hospital librarian and as we discussed its possibilities it did seem to have potential. I also read accounts of bibliotherapy being used in America and Finland which further endorsed its benefits.

We ran the first groups together therefore being able to utilize our different skills – her knowledge of literature and my experience in working with groups. Initially we found it was received quite readily without the frequent objections of, 'I'm no good with my hands', 'can't paint' or 'would feel daft doing that'. It had adult appeal.

Organization of groups

For the first group the selection criteria was very informal and in fact has never become so specific as say criteria for a social skills group. Myself and co-therapist hospital librarian discussed which patients we felt would be interested in joining such a group. We did not restrict ourselves to particular wards but considered both long- and short-term patients. The hospital was a psychiatric hospital with about 400 beds and run on traditional lines. We felt it preferable to have both male and female, some short- and some long-stay. We set the number at about eight but I have since gone on to run much larger groups that have been successful. I have found that mixing abilities is helpful – to have too many withdrawn patients does not work as it becomes too therapist dominated but one needs to be very aware that they should not be left out but gently encouraged to contribute. If patients are not active verbally, I have often found that they would contribute by writing something which indicated to me that they had gained quite a lot from the session even though they may have appeared to be withdrawn. There have been times when psychotic patients have been disruptive by shouting, or constantly pacing the room and it has been necessary to suggest they come back another time if they cannot behave appropriately. However, frequently I have found psychotic patients appear to be uninvolved and out of touch and then come up with a very relevant observation or contribution. I have also mixed in-patients with out-patients and found this often broadens horizons and challenges in-patients to think beyond the confines of hospital. These groups were all run on an open and informal basis taking place once a week.

Whilst it is workable to have mixed sex and ages (25 – 65) it would not be suitable for individuals with serious hearing and sight defects. Some sight problems can be overcome by providing magnifying glasses and reminding people to bring their glasses. One would need to be particularly aware of these problems when working with a geriatric group and may need to use the large print section available in most libraries.

I have mentioned the possibility of working in a mixed-ability group but reading therapy can also be valuable for work with specific groups where patients have a common problem – for example agoraphobics, anxiety states, alcoholics etc. It can be used as a media for sharing problems, expressing difficulties and also used educationally to deal with ways of overcoming problems. To write about a problem, in poetry, prose or story form can help a patient to feel better in a similar way to that of a counselling or psychotherapy session. The expression of troubled emotions, the recognition and exploration of them is working towards rehabilitation.

On the staff side, ideally two therapists are needed to run these groups. The reading can stimulate lots of discussion and issues whereby the balance of a therapist and co-therapist is needed. It also helps after each session to evaluate what has taken place and where the group should move on to.

The seeking out of suitable material is very time-consuming but once done can be used again with different groups. For one of the therapists to be a librarian is an asset as they have an extensive knowledge of literature and poetry. This, combined with a therapist's knowledge of skills for running a group is an ideal mix. As a therapist it is important to be aware of one's listening skills – to have the ability to remain silent appropriately and to demonstrate empathy. Patients are quick to recognize insincerity. Having a co-therapist from a different discipline also means you have contact with a wider range of patients. They may not, therefore attend occupational therapy but may still benefit from reading therapy. (Contact would have to be made with the patient's consultant to ensure he agrees with the patient attending.)

Finding an appropriate location for the group is important. I feel it should be a warm comfortable environment and not a clinical one. A room that is not too large, is decorated in pleasant light colours, has curtains and comfortable chairs and maybe a central low coffee table on which to place books, paper etc. If the room can be 'yours' then all the better as it can be used to display work (if the patient agrees), posters, poems and stories that have been read or written by the group.

I'd like now to move on to the practical details of selection of material and how the groups run. The first part – selection of material – as mentioned earlier is very time-consuming. It becomes a habit in fact as every time you pick up a magazine, journal or newspaper you're thinking, 'is there anything in here that would be appropriate for my group next week?'

When choosing material it is important to be in touch with patients' feelings and the emotional climate of the group. It would be incongruous to select happy stories or poems if the group was feeling 'down'. Since not everyone is likely to be feeling the same, skill is needed to ensure it is suitable for everyone. It may be necessary to look for hope in the most sad of stories or poems. If the climate of the group is a happy one then choose material that goes with those feelings.

I first started with a selection of short stories taken from the *Evening Standard*. The local library kept a year's store and it was a question of spending many enjoyable hours reading all the stories. We then duplicated them so that everyone in the group had their own copy. We looked for stories with 'human interest appeal'. (We found they had to be not too long, otherwise interest would be lost.) Stories that dealt with life situations e.g. a husband going off with another woman and his later disillusionment, someone starting off their day which seemed to hold for them a great emptiness, stories with character studies, were all useful. Adventure stories were always popular especially with men. They would often evoke memories of events in the war or stimulate the imagination. One very popular story was about a man shipwrecked on an island who was tricked by another so he missed being rescued. We went on to discuss the characters in the story, how they may have felt and how the story made us feel. We developed it further by writing a different ending.

We had a story called 'The Widow' which gave rise to discussion about the loss of a partner and then more broadly to loss resulting from illness. Many had lost partners and friends through their psychiatric illness and separation resulting from hospitalization.

Once the group became established we asked patients to bring in stories they would like to read.

To read the story we would sit in a circle and take a turn at reading part of it. No one was ever forced to read if they did not want to. There is often reluctance at first until confidence increases. I found this a valuable exercise to help improve confidence and clarity of speech. It also introduces an element of social skills training of which verbal communication is a part. An important factor about bringing in material is that it encourages the patients to continue to think about reading between sessions (hopefully) and the session then becomes more theirs rather than the institutionalized tendency to present information which is passively accepted. It also ensures that they are reading stories they like rather than what I think they ought to like.

I have later carried this a stage further by having the sessions arranged in a more open, club form. The group was much larger, up to about twenty and a mixture of in- and out-patients but most of whom had been attending hospital for a long time. It was called 'reading and expression' and I also introduced music. Music was played at the beginning to set a relaxed atmosphere and encourage general chat about its appreciation. On a central table I set out books, articles, poems and journals for patients to browse through and select extracts to read and discuss.

Our occupational therapy department was once given a large box of back-dated *Reader's Digest* magazines. They proved an invaluable source of literature containing adventure stories, humour stories and articles of human interest.

I felt this group to be a lively one but quite a lot of supervision was necessary to ensure less abled patients could participate. My role was very much that of a facilitator taking as low a profile as possible and putting as much responsibility for what happened during the sessions on to the patients. Which authors, what type of poems or stories did they like, and encouraging them to bring in material. My role was also to direct discussion to maximum benefit of all, building on contributions, relating where relevant to their own experiences and feelings, and to bring in more withdrawn members.

I mentioned that the group was called 'reading and expression' – the expression part being both verbal and written. Verbal by reading or recounting articles, poems etc. The written side some people found a little daunting – 'I've never written a poem in my life' or 'I wasn't any good at school'. One way of getting people launched was to ask them to write an alternative end to something they have just read or write something along similar lines. When confidence increased people found they could write more easily.

The following are two poems written by patients who thought they wouldn't be able to write anything:

I dreamed I did a dancing go
And the music was simply grand
But that was long ago, not now
I have to sit listening to the band.

****

I walked through a leafy lane on a summer's day
The birds were singing happily as I went along my way
The scent of roses filled the air and I didn't have a care.
It's different when I'm shopping and I am in a hurry,
I feel so hot and tired and in a dreadful scurry.
My bags are very heavy, and I'm not fancy free,
I long to hurry home again and have a cup of tea.

****

Returning to a more structured group, I would choose

material based on a theme. At first I chose the themes and then asked for suggestions from the group. The themes ranged from simple ones like the seasons to more complex ones like emotions, or reminiscences.

Themes

emotions – joy, happiness, envy, hate, unhappiness, contentment etc.
seasons – autumn, winter, spring and summer

Christmas	money
war	marriage
peace	friendship
time (passing/free)	things we like
age – young to old	illness
things that matter	animals
the community	countryside – local area
the immigrant	(being an outsider)

I would choose a selection of material and we would read and discuss and usually write something ourselves. Patients tended to prefer to write in poetry form – or sometimes just statements. I was working with varied ability and for some a statement was a major achievement since they find expression of any kind difficult:

Love of you, love of you
Will bring happiness
Happiness will bring you

The following are some examples of patients' work written on some of the above themes:

I walk alone in the park
Why should we live in buildings apart
Share your colour and happy things and have a heart
Love makes the world go round
What a happy place this would be if we loved each other
So cold and bleak on this dismal street
A street that cries unwanted. (community)

The author of this poem was expressing how alone he felt in his community, in fact from discussion it emerged that he felt alone even in the group. He had a low self-esteem and did not feel anyone would want to know him. He was pleasantly surprised by the group's reaction as it emerged he was quite well-liked. It also was thought he did not do anything to make contact with others in his street and some discussion followed as to how he could overcome this.

A negro child came over here
With not a house in sight
He had to join the waiting list
And face the cold black night
His parents came and joined him
And brought their money too
It wasn't long before they had
A mortgage on one soon. (the immigrant)

The sky is light
With stars so bright
Should I wish that I was white
I feel alone but will walk on to find a friend
Friends, there must be some . . . .

It was nice to have been at home
How sad I was to leave my friends and roam
It was so warm where I did live
No high storey buildings
With no one to give.

My God its cold
I'm all alone
I can't understand a word they say
The food is so strange
I'm feeling sick
I'd better get the plane home quick! (the immigrant)

It's fine this day
The sun and its ray
Shines down
The trees shimmer
With light and glimmer
Leaves aglow
The sky is blue
What to do
This fine day. (countryside)

It's a hot August day
The sun shines on its way
Underneath the tree which is shady
There sits a lady.
She dozes in the shade
Thinking of what made her come to this beautiful spot
On this August day that's so hot. (summer)

Love and marriage initially was responded to by cliches and gradually developed into more realistic writing and discussion. The introduction of romantic stories helps patients to overcome inhibitions about talking about relationships. Particularly with long-stay patients where romance is often a taboo subject for them. I remember a 30-year-old long-stay (so we thought) female patient who would giggle and behave in a very immature way when sex or love was mentioned – even the odd reference in a story. With more exposure, however, she became less embarrassed and became able to talk about such subjects reasonably sensibly. She has now, by the way, been resettled in the community under a foster parent scheme with day care support. I still see her occasionally and she greets me with open arms telling me of all the romance stories she has read.

A different way of using a theme was to conclude with a group poem. Each member would write a line of poetry which we would join together to form one poem. The results were surprisingly good and everyone enjoyed doing it:

The World's End

There was a world of peace
God made a perfect world
It was once beautiful with green pastures
Then nation fought against nation
Then a bolt of fire came from outer space
Darkness looms
There is destruction, dust and decay
What is there to build upon
For another day.

Shades of Autumn

The summer's gone but not forgot
The autumn is here but all beauty is not lost
Gold, brown, green, the leaves fall from the trees
blow in the wind
See the trees how they are golden brown
How quietly slips the night away
And soon smiles tomorrow's day
Spring is past and leaves are falling
The woods are full of gold and green
A beautiful woodland scene.

D-Day

War is declared
All lights go out in the shops
In war time we forgot our troubles
Singing and working in groups
A new beginning
A bitter end for many
From such awful times

Can come good
Feelings of unity
Shared grief
Shared hardship
We had to have sad memories
But also happy ones
War really ends
Men are at peace
Banners fly
At last a new lease
We are all happy and gay
On victory in Europe day!

I would display group poems and individual work provided patients were agreeable. It helped to spread interest about the group and reinforced the idea that they had something worthwhile to say.

A further expansion on themes is to follow the lives and work of different authors and poets. This proved to be very enjoyable and stimulated a lot of interest.

Students

As with the majority of departments we usually had several nursing and occupational therapy students for which we had to provide a comprehensive timetable to ensure they gained experience that would be of value to them. Sometimes it can be difficult to find activities that will achieve this and will accommodate a person outside the group. Students who participated in reading and expression groups did say it had been of considerable value to them and they found it quite easy to be able to contribute in a positive way.

I would discuss with the student beforehand how the group was run and what I felt their role should be. After the session we would have time for feedback, questions and discussion. Students generally thought it was a good situation for observing patients' behaviour and for getting to know and understand them better. They were frequently surprised at the level of participation of some in comparison with behaviour on say, the ward.

I would usually set an exercise for the student before the session to be completed afterwards. Such tasks as observation of a particular patient, what they thought the aims of the group were, evaluation of reading therapy.

If a student is scheduled to be with the group for a number of sessions it is possible to upgrade the level of responsibility taken whereby the student looks for appropriate material for use in the group and introduces it, increasing until she/he takes on the role of co-therapist. As to what level she goes does of course depend on the stage of training. A finalist would be expected to achieve the latter but a first-year student may not go beyond observation and participation as a group member.

On the whole students bring fresh ideas to the group, make positive and lively contributions that benefit everyone.

Community

The recent development for psychiatric occupational therapists to now be community based has necessitated the evaluation of our roles. We continue to work in a similar way to that of being hospital based but we now have to work without the facilities and equipment available to us in hospitals and day centres. There is also more work done with clients on a one to one basis than in groups (for the time being anyway). The need to work with creative therapy still exists whether we work with individuals, groups, in or out of hospital but of course the scope is more limited when working with individuals. Bibliotherapy is one media that is ideal for work with individual clients at home, and I put it into practice when I became community based.

One lady I worked with was being treated for depression and was quite difficult to work with as she always said she felt fine and nothing was wrong. After chatting with her it emerged that she enjoyed painting, reading and said she 'occasionally wrote a little herself'. I suggested that as she seemed to find difficulty in talking about how she felt would she like to write something down when she felt in the mood. On my next visit she presented me with the following:

> Diabolical, devastating, damnable depression
> Leaving you void of all expression
> Creeping up stealthily like a snake
> Leaving no feelings, just a dull ache
> Where does it come from I don't know
> But I wish the flaming thing would go
> Bringing things to mind you know not existed
> Terrifying thoughts mangled and twisted.
> Hold on to all you loved and fought for
> It's the only way out
> But it must be sought for
> No wallowing in self pity wondering why
> We're only here once
> So never say die.

We discussed how she felt and that her anxiety had worsened by the fact that she thought she had a serious illness when in fact they were classic symptoms of depression and anxiety. Her anxiety was lessened by this knowledge and we also arranged for her to have a medical check-up. I was also able to counsel her and help her recognize the emergence of depression with events in her life – loss of job, family leaving home. She was gradually able to take more positive steps to put some purpose in her life which she ultimately felt she lacked.

Another client was being treated for obsessional neurosis that was related to housework. I had a varied rehabilitation programme for her which was based on behaviour and cognitive therapy. When I suggested to her that she might find it helpful to write about how she feels she said she was no poet but started to keep a diary. In it she would describe her feelings, e.g. panic and anxiety when dusting. She was also able to record how she dealt with them and this provided her with a record of progress. It also showed her the pattern of 'bad days' and that she would come out of these. We also read stories and articles about housework looking at it historically about the time of her childhood to the present day when much less needs to be done. This helped her to evaluate the amount of work she felt compelled to do.

Therapeutic evaluation

In the early stages of setting up the group I did formalize my aims. These are:

1) To encourage greater autonomy
2) To facilitate greater expression of individuals' emotions
3) To give greater understanding of emotions
4) To encourage individuals to take responsibility for themselves and what happens in the group
5) To increase levels of self-confidence
6) To increase levels of concentration
7) To stimulate imagination
8) To foster interest in books and encourage further reading
9) To promote enjoyment and a sense of fun
10) To encourage communication
11) To rehabilitate

If I now look at the alteration of behaviour of individuals within the groups I would say that in varying degrees, the aims are achieved. Initially patients tend to be inhibited and often lack the ability to express their ideas, opinions or feelings about the topics. Within the group, however, confidence increases and expression becomes easier. Confidence also improves in being able to read aloud and contribute verbally in the sessions. Through discussion and exchange of experiences, reading of poetry and stories understanding can grow. Often patients are not required to concentrate for very long and are not sufficiently interested in anything to bother. I have noticed that the attention span does increase provided interest is held.

We are working more towards encouraging patients to have greater autonomy through creative therapy, bibliotherapy being one of these. Often patients will say they feel a sense of relief or relaxation and this in itself is therapy. Frequently patients – particularly those who spend a lot of time in hospital become very bored and lack motivation towards anything as the boredom is so chronic. I have found informal 'club' type groups do stimulate interest and lessen boredom to a degree. It can also involve visits to the theatre and other places of interest in the community that are connected with what is being read e.g. authors, home towns, bookshops, libraries, museums. Sometimes the element of having fun and enjoying what one is doing is overlooked in rehabilitation and this is something that can be gained from bibliotherapy from the pleasure of the reading material to humorous stories.

All these factors combine in the united aim of various hospital and community staff – that of rehabilitating the patient.

Some Useful Books

Ayres, P., Various volumes of poetry, London, Severn House.
Berry, J. (ed.), *News from Babylon: book of West Indian British poetry*, London, Chatto and Windus, 1984.
England in cameracolour. Series published by Town and Country Books, Newton Abbot.
Herriot, J., *James Herriot's Yorkshire*, London, M. Joseph, 1979.
Herriot, J., *Vets might fly* and other titles, London, Pan Books.
Porter, P., (ed.), *The Faber book of modern verse*, London, Faber.
Wilson, M. (ed.), *My favourite poems*, London, Corgi, 1985.

Readers Digests.

13 Poetry Therapy

Gerard Benson

My work in hospitals has for the most part been with psychiatric patients and it is of this work that I intend mainly to treat in this chapter. Much of what I shall say will apply equally to different kinds of patients – and indeed to people who are not ill. I have used many of the same ideas when working with teachers, writers, librarians and members of the general public.

It is important, perhaps, to emphasize that I am not medically trained, and that I am not (although I have sometimes been described as such) in the usual sense of the word, a therapist. I am a poet/performer who, under the aegis of Shape has done a good deal of work in hospitals. My work is informed by a strongly held conviction that practice of and participation in the arts have a powerful therapeutic function – but that this is 'natural' therapy. Through our attempts to organize materials (line and colour, clay, carved wood or words), through our attempts to structure these and similar elements in a coherent and satisfying way and through our apprehension of other people's attempts to do these things, we arrive, it seems to me, at an understanding of our lives, our environments, our feelings, our thoughts, our relationships of a different and more profound kind than can be achieved through logical processes. We are able vicariously to solve conflicts. We are able safely to discuss the dangerous and the forbidden. We are able to place before ourselves and the world at large an expression of our state of mind, our emotions, our spirituality, in coded form. We are able to recognize in the work of others some of our own dilemmas. And perhaps most simply of all, in yielding to beauty (a Keats ode, a Mozart sonata, *Les Sylphides*) we are made happy and we are made whole for a while.

The art I work with in hospital workshops is literature, and in particular poetry. Poetry has certain advantages as a creative form. At its most elevated levels, in the creations of such geniuses as Shakespeare, Milton and Browning, poetry can be a vehicle for the expression of the most complex and controversial of human experiences in a manner which in the truest sense sublimates them, that is, makes them sublime; and at these high levels there is no doubt that particularly gifted individuals have applied technique and imagination to skills to which they have dedicated much of their time and attention; and no doubt also, this recourse is not available to most people. However, just as many of us, without being draughtsmen of the order of Dürer or Hockney, can record our impressions through drawing, so some degree of achievement in verse-writing is possible and most people improve with practice and growing confidence. At the workshop level with careful and sensitive leadership, poetry can be made quite 'easy' to write. Certain of the inhibiting restraints which make written expression forbidding to some individuals, especially those with unsuccessful school careers, can be lifted: a poet may if he/she wishes, ignore the rules of conventional grammar, may invent language, may use familiar words in unfamiliar ways. Also, poetry does not have to be long. Anyone might cringe at setting out to write a 5,000 word short story – but four lines of poetry might seem a realistic target – and in four lines much may happen:

Vain the ambition of kings
Who seek by trophies and dead things,
To leave a living name behind,
And weave but webs to catch the wind.

John Webster

A succinct and satisfying piece. The poet's analysis of royal pretension extends, it seems to me, beyond its original subject matter to embrace all human ambition. The final image is very powerful. The last line almost seems to escape through our fingers. And the second couplet is indeed poignant, to be the creation of a man named Webster. The piece is very skilfully made, with much interplay of sound quite apart from the obvious rhymes (leave/living; leave/weave; *w*eave/*w*ebs/*w*ind; see*k*/*k*ings/*c*atch), and is, of course, the work of an accomplished poet of the Jacobean age.

Consider the following poem, written by a patient at a London hospital during the 1980s.

Nasturtium

You smell sweet and strange
Like the taste of fruit
You taste bitter and hot
The leaves in salads.

M.C.

This seems to me a very successful quatrain, with subtle

rhythmic balance, a cunning evocation of the senses, with sharp alliteration in the first line picked up in the last word, and a neat little semi-rhyme in the two middle lines. It also seems to me to transcend its surface subject matter. It is perhaps subjective that I find a certain rather elusive eroticism in this piece, but as the reader I have that right. The right I do not have, as the leader of a Poetry Workshop, is to push my interpretation at the author. I must accept the poem at the level offered: it is a poem about a nasturtium. If the poet herself, or other members of the group discuss other resonances, that is a different matter.

It is perhaps a commonplace that many adolescents have a phase when they express some of their feelings in poetry. For some of us this phase does not stop. It seems to me undeniable that in poetry it is possible to undertake some discussion of powerful subjects such as love, sex, death, birth, mankind's relation to the universe, neurosis, family relationships, the nature of God even – the list is truly infinite. The following poem is by an elderly man who spoke but rarely:

The Death of My Father

I don't think I'll be long
  he says
They're getting ready for me up there
  he says
I won't be long
  he says

Don't talk like that
  I says

I'm going now
  he says
I won't be long
  he says
Get my sister
  he says

And I stayed with him
While they went up in the car
And got his sister

I'm going
  he says
I'm going

I was with him at the end.

H.J.

A moving evocation of a terrible episode in H.J.'s life. He

was not able to write – but the words – and the very individual rhythm are entirely his own. I wrote it down at his dictation; the lay-out is mine – my attempt to present his phrasing in visual form. H.J. was very pleased with his poem – and I am of the opinion that it had more value for him than just the pride in creation.

Reading and writing, like listening and talking, are interconnected skills. So now I would like to discuss the reading for a while. Again, it is mostly poetry that I use in my workshops. Two main things happen. One is that I read poetry to the patients; the other, that they read poetry to each other and to me. (I have never used recorded poetry; the experience seems too remote, but this is certainly a possible strategy and one which has been used successfully by others.) The choice of text is important but so many factors come into it that it will not be possible to give more than a brief outline of my practice. When I first conducted poetry sessions with psychiatric patients I used to try and find poems that I judged to be 'relevant' to the group: poems for instance in which guilt, despair, disorientation are explored. Vernon Scannell's *A Case of Murder* was one such. This is a poem in which very terrible aspects of guilt and concealment are dealt with in powerful but simple language. One morning after I had read it to a group, a woman rounded on me, asking why I should bring such depressing material. And she had a valid point, which caused me seriously to reconsider my methods, and although I still do include poetry which deals with serious contemporary problems, I try not to overload my sessions with them.

There are also 'favourite poems', usually clearly rhymed and with a strong, recognizable rhythm. I could not guess how many times I have been asked for Wordsworth's *Daffodils* or Kipling's *If*, which runs it a close second. Third perhaps is Max Ehrmann's *Desiderata*, written during the 1920s but popularly believed to have come from a seventeenth-century American graveyard. It begins 'Go placidly amid the noise and the haste', and for many people has an almost talismanic power (and it proves my rule by neither rhyming nor scanning.) These 'favourites' have several advantages. They are very often rather good. They often clearly articulate fairly simple ideas and emotions. For a group and for many individuals they provide the comfort of the known and repeated. It seems certain that repetition, that continued contact with a familiar set of words, has values for all people. We greet each other with formulated phrases: 'Good morning. Nice day. How are you?' We sprinkle our conversations with them: 'Know what I mean? As I always say. Give my respects to matron.' And we note our partings with their use: 'Cheerio then. Don't do anything I wouldn't do. Safe home to you all.' Anyone who has brought up children will know how children will return again and again to a favourite story and how they will brook no deviation from the known version. And, for many people, prayer relies partly on a strict form and sequence of words. I ask any reader who prays, to imagine a prayer that he or she habitually says after it has been paraphrased; I don't mean ridiculously – I just mean changed formally. I suggest it will immediately reduce its seeming power. I offer an example. 'Give me peace of mind, Lord, to bow to the inevitable', may seem to be a perfectly good start to a prayer, but to anybody accustomed to saying 'God grant me the serenity to accept the things I cannot change', it is simply not the same prayer.

These well-known and often repeated poems can be used to introduce an element of ritual, which helps to establish a sense of safety in the group. For these reasons, it seems to me that a repertoire of 'standard' pieces is a valuable thing for any group to have. It is a good idea to carry some anthologies which contain a number of such poems.

Particular groups also sometimes adopt particular poems or poets. The poetry of Anna Wickham, with its rebellion against 'ordinariness' appealed very strongly for a few months to a group I was working with. At absolutely every session one or more of her poems was read and discussed. Many of the patients, mostly women, achieved a great deal of personal identification with her poetry. As a twentieth-century woman who discussed problems similar to their own in terms they understood, she communicated strongly to them, far more than Elizabeth Barrett Browning or Christina Rossetti, who, although admired seemed remote, or than some more modern overtly feminist writers, whose writing the patients found too complicated or too hectoring in tone. These remarks are not meant as a criticism of either the Victorian or the current women writers, merely a record of the attitude of a particular group for a period of a few months. A great deal of mileage was gained from Ms Wickham's work for quite a while. People were able to discuss their own feelings, misgivings about society and so on, in terms of comments on the poems. Then one week a patient said, 'I'd rather not hear one of Anna's today' (by this time we were on first name terms) and, as far as I recall, she was never mentioned again.

Other 'adopted' poets have been Robert Graves, Robert Burns, Christina Rossetti and John Masefield.

Choosing the poems to read to the patients is done in several ways. Sometimes we have a theme that we are pursuing (animals, cities, love) – and in these circumstances I usually take along one or two subject anthologies – or choose a few poems from general anthologies which I take in. Sometimes the poems are read without comment. More usually comment is invited. Quite often not much is forthcoming. Depressed or medicated patients can be quite apathetic. In this case I choose whether to pursue it or leave it. If the latter, we move on to something else. But if it seems a good idea to pursue it, I try to do so by means of specific questions to particular individuals. The questions might relate to the poem directly: 'What do you think he means, Alice, by "fearful symmetry"?' or 'What do you see this poem as being about, John?' Sometimes, however, the questions relate some of the subject matter of the poem to the individual. 'Do you like autumn, Laura?' 'Do you like the town or would you rather live in the country?' Sometimes genuine discussion emerges from this, sometimes not.

At other times the poetry is chosen as a preparation for the written work we mean to do. This might be done in terms of subject (four or five poems about food and drink to introduce writing about the same), alternatively it might be done in terms of style, form or similar considerations, not that we go deeply into the technical side of things, but it sometimes comes up. For instance some *haikus* would introduce an attempt to write some ourselves.

Yet again, in spite of what I have written above, in collaboration with the occupational therapist or nursing staff, I will sometimes choose poems relating to particular problems (for instance alcoholism, childhood trauma, mourning, anger). The best way to find such pieces is by wide personal reading, I am afraid, but Peter Marcan's *Poetry Themes* (pub. Clive Bingley, 1977) – an index (with helpful descriptive commentary) of almost 2,000 subject anthologies, although in need of updating, is extremely helpful. So also is *Granger's Index to Poetry*.

Currently with one of my groups I am working on the months of the year. Of the written side of this, I shall have more to say further on. From the point of view of the reading it is yet again a question of personal research and the use of subject anthologies. I try to spend some time during one of the sessions each month reading some poetry written about that month. Some are easier to find than others. It will come as no surprise to learn that April and December offer more material than for instance February. This reading is partly in support of the written project, but another motive here is to try and articulate our experience of the year and see if it accords with that of our chosen poets. In a rainy June we get small association with the flaming ecstasy of some of our poets – on the other hand, was any November ever quite as bleak as Thomas Hood's? Or as funny?

Yet another method of selection is to hand round books, and let the patients choose poems to read or have read for them. In this way we often come upon all kinds of odd treasures and insights. And of course there is the matter of requests. A patient remembers a poem from school days, 'It was about going to Kew Gardens, not far from London. Can't remember who wrote it', or 'It was by Keats, called "Autumn" '. It is always a pleasure to find (by the next session if possible) a text of these remembered poems and bring them to read. Here a good dictionary of quotations is very useful – and the Arts Council Poetry Library does a very good service in tracing poems and quotations – by phone even, if you are in a hurry.

A word about physical arrangements for workshops. These will obviously depend a lot on what is available. However, taking into account the various types of room, building, ward, (corner even) that we are asked to work in, it is my view that the more informally the space is set up, the better. A carpeted room with armchairs for all, set in a rough circle, and with books, papers and so forth in the middle is what I try for. If refreshment can be provided, so much the better. However, many other arrangements are possible. At one hospital we sat at a big round oak table and sometimes it is possible to conduct sessions out of doors. The guiding principle it seems to me is that the space used should be as un-school-like as possible. If the room is a lecture theatre or the like, try to subvert the implications of the spacing and furniture arrangement. Put patients on the platform, break up the arrangement of chairs, go for curves rather than straight lines.

I also like all the people present to participate in the workshop – and I always do so myself. If the poetry groups are perceived as something which the nursing staff, therapists, etc. provide but do not take part in, they are devalued in the eyes of the patients. I insist that any helper or visitors take part and several startled overseas experts on this or that have found themselves discussing and writing poetry. Why should the patients tackle tasks we are not prepared to try ourselves?

The reading and discussion of poetry and its themes form the first part of most of my sessions but it is in the creation of poetry that the kernel lies. I have several techniques and a number of exercises of varying complexity which I use. And I am constantly devising more. Here, for use and development by anybody interested, is a dozen outlines of exercises to stimulate the writing of poetry. Rather like party games, they are much better in practice than they look described in brief on the page. They have different functions: some will work with almost any group. With others, some practice, self-confidence, acquired skill are needed.

1 Very simple. We choose a subject (say *Birds*, or *Evening* or *A Childhood Memory*) and allow ourselves a period of time (say fifteen minutes) to write a poem. Alternatively, with more advanced students, a form or schematic idea might be set (e.g. an eight-lined rhymed poem, a limerick, an alliterative poem). Keats's *The Grasshopper and the Cricket* and Shelley's *Ozymandias* were written as a result of 'games' of this sort. They allowed themselves twenty minutes to write a sonnet on a set subject. It is worth pointing out and continuing to point out that if somebody is involved in what he/she is doing it is not compulsory to stop at the end of the allowed time.

2 This one is very good with new groups – and as well as producing poems, it is very effective as a way of introducing people to each other. It is rather elaborate to describe but it always works well. I have never known it to fail. It goes through four stages.

a) Ask each person to write five true statements about him/herself. Ask for simplicity (I live in Bedford, I am a mother, I have blue eyes, I often wear jeans etc.). Read back, round the group.
b) Ask each person to write five untrue statements about themselves (e.g. I am fond of rock music, I have fifty pairs of shoes, etc.). Again read and discuss a little.
c) Ask each person to write five *impossible* statements about themselves (e.g. I was awarded the Military Cross by Florence Nightingale next Wednesday; I eat London buses; I grow yellow fur on the soles of my feet; I breathe solid rock; I travelled in from Aldebaran this morning). Ask for extravagance. Again, read round and discuss.
d) Use one or more of these final statements as the starting

point of a brief poem, adding two, three or four more non-rhyming lines and developing the logic of the opening e.g.

I am the ace-spot on a dice
'Six! six!' the children shout,
As I fall
Flat on my face.
G.B.

3 Play music (tapes or records) and ask the patients to write an impression of it in poetry, or a response to it.

4 Introduce by use of examples the idea of 'kenning'. This is a technique much used in old Norse poetry, whereby a person, animal or object is 'named' not by the use of a simple noun but by a short descriptive expression. For instance a vocabulary is a word-hoard, and to speak is to 'unlock your word-hoard'. An owl might be a 'night-bird' – (in colloquial New York speech a Black Maria is a Paddy-wagon). An accumulation of kennings can build up quite a strong picture. A subject could be set – or individuals could choose their own – a pet, a friend, a season, a garden (flowery-acre, back-breaker). The list could go on. Here is part of a poem of kennings by a member of one of my workshops.

Beer-giver, fun-chatter
Bright-dresser, hair-changer,
Big-bum, nail colourer,
Time-caller, tonic-drinker,
Firm on the optic,
Slapper down of change;
I dream about you. . . .

You are never
Short-changer, chucker-outer,
Nose-picker, armpit-stinker,
Straggle-hair, lean shank,
Draggle-tights, gin-guzzler,
Foul-breath, mean-speaker,
Pourer of tiny measures,
Like some I have known. . . . .
C.J.D.Doyle

5. *Riddles* Not the verbal sleight of hand which is current, but, related to the above, cryptic description of an object, person or animal, such as was very popular in Anglo-Saxon times. Here is a riddle of my own.

I am taken from earth and wrung from rock.
Rounds are locked together.
Stiff-hard I am, yet I twine and twist.

Heavy I am for the moonstricken and the wrongdoer,
Yet I am light for the lovely lady
Who treasures me and places me close to her breast.
By me are kingdoms ruled. By me are wooden towns
Held on the water's surface.
I am known by both dog and bear.
I am no stronger than my frailest part. Name my name.
G.B.

(In case you are interested in solving it, I will delay the answer until later in the chapter).

6 *Seasonal work* As I mentioned above, I am currently working on a calendar poem – related to the months of the year. This is a long-term project. Each month one of the sessions is given to the month – and I set a simple writing exercise, to write about the month, either from imagination and memory, or by direct observation of what is there before us (for instance new leaf, ice patterns, thundery cloud). These poems are filed and it is our intention after a year (the project began in September) to collate a calendar poem from the various contributions and to reproduce it in the form either of a short pamphlet, or perhaps of a calendar.

7 *Aleatoric verse* This is a method of establishing a form for writing. By use of cards, dice and the like it is possible to establish a set of rules for writing. For instance, by these means a group I worked with produced the 'Dianic' (named after one of the group) – a five-lined stanza with three words (or syllables) in the first line, four each in the second and third, six in the fourth and only one in the final line. The first and last lines rhyme. Thus:

Dear Mother Earth,
We love you dearly,
We are your children,
You gave us our first gift,
Birth.
Anne Rodgers

Each of these forms has its own quality: in this case the sharp finish which rhymes gives it very much a character of its own. Above all, the writer works without 'ancestors'; nobody has written such verses before. There are no comparisons to be made with great dianics by Chaucer and Wordsworth.

8 This can be combined with the above. Having chosen a

myth or story (for instance the *Genesis* Adam and Eve story) allocate different parts of it to different individuals to write – perhaps assigning a particular form to the poem. When all the parts have been made, they can be assembled into a narrative poem. It is always possible to extend such a story if you have a large group. Suppose that the essential elements of the story are: *God creates Adam, God creates Eve, issues His instructions, the Serpent overhears, the Serpent tempts Eve, Eve eats, Adam eats, they make clothes, God discovers them, they are driven from the garden,* and that you have more than ten people in your group. Then is the time to elaborate: Adam and Eve could garden, they could converse, Adam and Eve could be described, they could name creation, the garden could be described, the tree could be described, an angel with a fiery sword could be introduced – the possibilities proliferate. The story of course could be something less intense (like *Cinderella*), or indeed it could be invented by the group. Here again is a possible 'book' for in-house publication.

9 *Personification* I am indebted to the poet Kit Wright for this: a group poem in which some element of nature is described as if it were a person. The leader does the work of the scribe and asks pertinent questions when necessary, such as: 'What sex?' 'How old?' 'What does she wear?' 'What does she eat?' 'Has she any children?'. The leader will also choose amongst what he/she is offered, and press for more interesting vocabulary and more precise ideas and imagery. It is essential, if this exercise is to work properly that the subject should be sufficiently grand to merit such treatment: the sea, the forest, the wind.

The following is the work of a group of psychiatric patients. They not only got immense pleasure from producing this piece, but it formed the basis of some magnificent artwork (a large Chagall-like painting in blues and silvers), and also some drama. The following week they wrote a companion piece about the Sun (a 'fierce prince' with 'blazing amber eyes').

The Moon

The moon is a young woman
Made by the old man, God,
His beautiful daughter.
She has silver hair
And wears a silver dress.
Long and flowing.

She lives in a cave
At the top of a blue mountain,
Sleeping all day
In a bed of white feathers
And thistledown

At night
She glides across the sky
Eating only air,
And watching the world
Her unattainable lover,
With whom she circles
In an everlasting dance.

She polishes the stars
With the lullabies she sings.
She guides and torments people
And trees,
They think they catch her
But she always escapes from their branches.

The sea she picks up and throws down
Playing a game like a child with a toy.

She is immortal
She will never die.

(North Middlesex Poetry Group)

10 The patients can be asked to concentrate on an object, something familiar perhaps or perhaps something brought in – an antique, or an ornate seashell. They look at the object for a length of time and write, pushing beyond the barrier when it seems that there is no more to say. This can produce very interesting results. A fair amount of time may be allowed for this.

11 Akin to the above. Objects are produced which the writers are shown for a short length of time (say 90 seconds). The writers look and write as fast as possible whatever words come into their heads, trying not to block. If they block, they should re-write the word they just wrote. If they block at first, they should name the object. After discussion of the lists, challenge them to form the words into a short poem. With sophisticated groups I ask the writers to put the words into alphabetical order and then by the use of spacing, punctuation etc., to try and write a poem. Although it does not always work, it is surprising how often it does. It is a good idea to have the objects prepared beforehand. I like to establish clear differences

between them, making one metallic (a pair of steel-rimmed glasses), one fabric (a woolly sweater) and one organic (a fruit or vegetable – or even an animal if there is one available).

12 *Haikus* Although at the highest level these are difficult to write, even a beginner can write quite an effective *haiku*. This is a brief poem of seventeen syllables. It has three lines and ideally each line presents an image, which when juxtaposed with the other two creates a whole. The form is Japanese, and Japanese poetry is syllabic. There is no rhyme. The first line has five syllables, the second has seven, and the third has again five. Ideally it should be spoken in one breath.

Two men climb the hill
A rabbit sits bolt upright
Clouds darken the grass.
A.E.L.

The above list is far from comprehensive, and individuals will be able to devise many more. For instance, just as *haikus* can be used, so also can any other known form, from limericks to sonnets. It is in the reading of poetry that the easiest source of new exercises is to be found. You observe that Blake in his poem *The Tyger* asks a number of questions of the animal; you base an exercise on this, asking questions of a squirrel, a snake, an oak tree, a primrose, a mountain, a star, a bar of soap. You notice that William Morris closes every single stanza of a poem 'Two red roses across the moon', and you do the same, inventing a refrain and putting it to good use. The balance to be kept in mind is that between subject matter and form. It is essential that the one should serve the other although the emphasis might fall now on one side, now on the other.

The riddle? Well, you probably guessed. I saw a beautiful girl in a tube train with a light gold chain round her neck on the same day that I was reading a book about eighteenth-century asylums.

It seems to me almost axiomatic, a point not in need of arguing, that it is through the expression of our creativity that we get well and stay well. I also believe that all people are creative and should have creative outlets.

For the past five years I have worked at the North Middlesex Hospital in partnership with the occupational therapist, Kathryn Hudson. Although she has no training in literature she joined in the sessions enthusiastically and was, indeed, very important in their success. A totally unexpected by-product was the remarkable improvement in her own poetry. Through working a week at a time at a variety of tasks she has built and established a voice and method of her own. The following poem, based on the Moors Murders, is just one of many good poems she has written.

The murder of four children

Shudder
To birth
Scratched to light
Their fragments the bleached bones
Of a dove
Whose shadow strokes the contour
Of a barren land.

Fly towards the city
And
Kiss the hard wood of your mother's door.

Eyes scan the letters
Watch her follow through a fire.

Lips move . . . .
Come back to me
Curl deep into the moss softness of my womb.

Kathryn Hudson

I have emphasized before, the importance of participation by all people present. For Kathryn Hudson this has had personal rewards – but the woman doctor at St. Clement's Hospital who passed by my group, stopped to talk to us and made a small contribution to the poem in progress has probably forgotten the event. But the effect her effort had on the whole occasion was enormous.

Here then is a description of my practice. The examples have come from patients, from members of outside poetry workshops, from myself and from a therapist. It is my method to work by means of acceptance and encouragement. There are individuals who can produce very little, or who are so tentative that they do produce very little. I had a patient who wrote every week: 'I had my hair done.' The group and I accepted this. And then one week she wrote: 'I had my hair done. And it looks nice.' This was a woman in her fifties who rarely stirred out of her chair. It is impossible to describe how pleased she and the group were with this small achievement.

I hope some of these ideas are of use. They are none of them copyright and they are all extendable.

I would like also to say that the production of a book is always a great boost to the morale. This can be done simply by the use of an electric typewriter and a good photocopier. The whole can be included in a card cover and stapled or sewn. The precise technology will vary but the fact of having a book of 'our' work is very valuable.

As to ordering books for use with such groups, the advice is to be eclectic and wide-ranging as possible. An anthology of well-known 'standards' (of which there are many) is essential. A few specialist anthologies on subjects of interest to the particular group (animals, say, or feminism or sport or gardens) will help. At least one book of nature poetry and one of urban will swell the collection. But the best advice is to listen to the patients. Find out what they like and then do the necessary research to provide it.

I would like to close this chapter by relating an experience of mine from when I first began to work in hospitals. I had a large group (about 30–40 people) in a large sitting room. The chairs, as in a station waiting room, were all back by the walls. Some of the patients were quite noticeably ill. Some were twitching, restless. I had read, with reasonable success in terms of response and attentiveness, a number of short modern poems. A young man asked if I had anything by Keats. I looked among my books. The only Keats poem I had was the *Ode to a Nightingale*. My heart sank. It is highly wrought, long, full of classical references and incomprehensible phraseology ('blushful Hippocrene') and among all poems of its period, one of the most high-flown. It is also very beautiful and is one of my favourite poems. Common sense said, 'Don't'. But I had been asked. So I began:

'My heart aches, and a drowsy numbness pains
My sense . . .

The poem's interplay of vowels and consonants is very musical and the rhythm is smooth and powerful – great, rippling ten-line stanzas. Gradually, as I read on, all activity in the room stopped – the twitching, the fidgeting, the hyperactivity. All became very calm, very peaceful, serene, as if a spell had been cast. It is hardly possible that most of those present could have *understood* the poem. And yet it worked a strange magic in the room.

'Fled is that music. Do I wake or sleep?'

The poem finished and there was a deep silence. Discussing the occasion later with a friend, Don Chapman, a poet, I ventured some half-baked pseudo-scientific theory about brain electricity: alpha waves, gamma waves. His reply was astonishing in its simplicity. 'The poet's wing brushed the room.'

Index